Aging and Life Course Transitions: An Interdisciplinary Perspective

Aging and Life Course Transitions: An Interdisciplinary Perspective

EDITED BY
Tamara K. Hareven
CLARK UNIVERSITY AND HARVARD UNIVERSITY
AND
Kathleen J. Adams
WHEATON COLLEGE

Foreword by Mortimer Herbert Appley

The Guilford Press
NEW YORK   LONDON

© 1982 The Guilford Press
A Division of Guilford Publications, Inc.
200 Park Avenue South, New York, N.Y. 10003

Printed in the United States of America

LIBRARY OF CONGRESS CATALOGING IN PUBLICATION DATA
Main entry under title:

Aging and life course transitions.

(Adult development and aging)
Based on papers presented at the Conference on Aging and the Life Course in Interdisciplinary and Cross-Cultural Perspective, held in Walferdange, Luxembourg, in June 1979 and sponsored jointly by Clark University and the Government of Luxembourg.
Includes index.
Contents: The life course and aging in historical perspective/Tamara K. Hareven—Biography and identity/Leopold Rosenmayr—Discontinuities in the study of aging/Leonard I. Pearlin—[etc.]
1. Aging—Congresses. 2. Life cycle, Human—Congresses.
I. Hareven, Tamara K. II. Adams, Kathleen J.
III. Conference on Aging and the Life Course in Interdisciplinary and Cross-Cultural Perspective (1979: Walferdange, Luxembourg)
IV. Clark University (Worcester, Mass.) V. Series.
HQ1061.A456   305.2   82-989
ISBN 0-89862-125-9   AACR2

Contributors

KATHLEEN J. ADAMS is an anthropologist who teaches at Wheaton College, Norton, Massachusetts. She has written several papers focusing on self-narration and life course studies.

DANIEL BERTAUX was trained in mathematics and physics at the Ecole Polytechnique in Paris and at the University of California at Berkeley. He worked for several years with computers before moving to sociological research, his long-lasting vocation, in 1967. He has published about 15 papers on social mobility and epistemology and a book, *Destins Personnels et Structure de Classe*, Presses Universitaires de France, 1977. Currently Chargé de Recherche (full-time research worker) at the National Center for Scientific Research, he works at the Center for the Study of Social Movements in Paris.

GLEN H. ELDER, JR., is Professor of Sociology and Human Development at Cornell University and Codirector of the SSRC Committee on the Life Course. He is currently involved in a long-term study of social change in the family and the life course that draws upon longitudinal data from the well-known archives of the Institute of Human Development, Berkeley, California. His most recent books, authored and edited, are *Children of the Great Depression*, University of Chicago Press, 1974; *Adolescence in the Life Cycle*, coeditor with S. Dragastin, Hemisphere Press, 1975; and *Family Structure and Socialization*, Arno Press, 1980.

DAVID EVERSLEY is Senior Research Fellow at the Policy Studies Institute, London. He formerly taught at Birmingham and Sussex Universities and at University College, London, and was Chief Strategic Planner at the Greater London Council from 1969 to 1972. His principal publication is *The Planner in Society*, Faber, 1973. He has edited and contributed to *The Inner City: Industry and Employment*, with A. W. Evans, 1980, and *Population Change and Social Planning*, with W. Koellmann, 1981, and has also published numerous smaller monographs.

ANNE-MARIE GUILLEMARD is Associate Professor of Sociology at the University of Paris VII and Research Fellow at the Center for the Study of Social Movements in Paris. She has published a number of works on the sociology of aging and the sociology of governmental policies on old age. She is author of *La Retraite: Une Mort Sociale* (*Retirement as a Social Death*), Mouton, 1972, and *La Vieillesse et l'Etat* (*Old Age and the State*), Presses Universitaires de France, 1980.

TAMARA K. HAREVEN is Professor of History at Clark University, Research Associate at the Center for Population Studies of Harvard University, and Editor of the *Journal of Family History*. She is the author and editor of a number of books on the history of the family and the life course. Her most recent books are *Amoskeag: Life and Work in a Factory City*, with R. Langenbach, Pantheon Books, 1978; *Transitions: The Family and the Life Course in Historical Perspective*, editor, Academic Press, 1978; and *Family Time and Industrial Time*, Cambridge University Press, 1982. She is currently a fellow at the Center for Advanced Study in the Behavioral Sciences.

GISELA LABOUVIE-VIEF is with the Department of Psychology at Wayne State University. She has written numerous articles and book chapters dealing with cognitive changes in adulthood. Her effort to reinterpret prevalent deficit views of such changes within a comprehensive theory of developmental processes in adulthood is currently supported by a Research Career Development Award from the National Institute of Aging.

LEONARD I. PEARLIN is a Research Sociologist in the Laboratory of Socio-environmental Studies of the National Institute of Mental Health. His research in recent years has been concerned with the social origins of stress and depression over the life course and with the use of coping repertoires and support systems in dealing with life strains. He is the author of *Family Relations and Class Context: A Cross-National Study*, Little, Brown and Company, 1971, and of a number of articles seeking to identify various social structural links to psychological functioning.

DAVID W. PLATH is Professor of Anthropology and Asian Studies at the University of Illinois at Urbana–Champaign. He has written and edited a number of books on modern Japanese society and culture, the most recent of these being *Adult Episodes in Japan*, editor, E. J. Brill, 1975, and *Long Engagements: Maturity in Modern Japan*, Stanford University Press, 1980.

LEOPOLD ROSENMAYR is Professor of Sociology at Vienna University and Director of the newly founded Ludwig Boltzmann Institute for Social Gerontology and Life Span Research, Vienna, Austria. He is author and editor of many books on adolescent youth, family relations, various problems of aging, and issues of the theory of science, particularly those concerning the practical applicability of social-scientific knowledge. He has worked in applied research and acted as author of government reports and as a consultant to such international organizations as OECD, WHO, and UNESCO. His most recent books are *Die Menschlichen Lebensalter: Kontinuität und Krisen*, editor, Piper 1978; *Der alte Mensch in der Gesellschaft*, editor with H. Rosenmayr, Rowohlt, 1978; and *Youth and Society*, with K. Allerbeck, Sage Publications, 1979.

LARS TORNSTAM is Assistant Professor of Sociology at the University of Uppsala, Sweden, and Director of Studies for the academic course on gerontology given at that university. He is also the project leader of a nation-wide research project entitled "Elderly Persons in Society: Yesterday, Today, and Tomorrow." He has published numerous articles and some monographs in Swedish, among them *The Social Psychology of Aging.* For the international public he has also published articles in the journal *Gerontologist.*

Acknowledgments

The majority of the chapters in this volume were written for the Conference on Aging and the Life Course in Interdisciplinary and Cross-Cultural Perspective, which was held in Luxembourg in June 1979, and directed by Tamara K. Hareven. Sponsored as part of a series initiated by Clark University faculty and the Institut Péda-gogique in Luxembourg, the conference was hosted by the Institut and financed by a grant from Mr. and Mrs. Henry J. Leir to Clark University specifically for the development of research conferences and for continued collaboration between the University's programs and the Institut Pédagogique.

Tamara K. Hareven is indebted to President Mortimer Appley for his support of this conference in his capacity as president and for his active participation and stimulating discussions as a psychologist in the deliberations at the conference. She is extremely grateful to Gaston Schaber for his active support of the entire program, for the special care he invested in every aspect of this conference, and for the fine setting that he provided in the Conference Center in Luxembourg. She is personally indebted to him and to his family for their hospitality and friendship, and is also grateful to Walter Schatzherg at Clark University, who has encouraged the formulation of the plans for this conference and who has greatly contributed to keeping the Luxem-bourg connection alive.

The conference participants brought with them not only their original papers and stimulating contributions to the discussions but also the spirit of friendship that made the four-day conference an intellectually as well as a humanly rewarding experience. We are grateful to Glen Elder and Anne-Marie Guillemard, who contributed their papers even though their schedules did not permit participation in the conference. Our gratitude also goes to Joyce Ingham and Kathy Larson, who helped in the administration of the conference; to James

Allen, for editorial help; and to Shirley Riopel, who has handled the final typing of this book.

Tamara K. Hareven is indebted to the National Institute of Aging for its support in the form of a Research Career Development Grant, and both editors are grateful to the staff of the Center for Population Studies of Harvard University for assistance in numerous ways in the editing process.

T.K.H.
K.J.A.

Foreword

This book is based on a Clark–Luxembourg International Seminar, held in the conference facilities of the Institut Pédagogique in Walferdange, Luxembourg, in June 1979 and sponsored jointly by Clark University and the Government of Luxembourg. This international conference series, begun in 1977, has been made possible through grants from Mr. and Mrs. Henry J. Leir of Luxembourg and New York to Clark University, and we are grateful to them for their continued interest in and support of this valuable effort.

It was my privilege to be a participant–observer at the life course conference, organized and led by Professor Tamara Hareven, which resulted in this book. I am confident that you will share my enthusiasm for the quality and seminal value of the chapters that appear in this volume, preliminary versions of which were discussed in Luxembourg. The chapters reflect the cross-disciplinary exchanges and are the richer for having been so extensively discussed before being published. But this printed outcome is only one of the values of the Clark–Luxembourg meetings. The opportunity for the participants, drawn from several nations and disciplines, to interact intensely and the resultant correspondence network that was begun as a result of this interaction are outcomes that make the effort and cost of such meetings worthwhile.

It is interesting to note that in her chapter, Professor Hareven refers to G. Stanley Hall and his pioneering work in developmental psychology (particularly of older persons) as an early precursor of the life course concept. Reading through the successive chapters, written from the perspective of the varied disciplines involved, you see the recurrent references to ideas similar to those introduced by Hall early in this century.

But this was not the only way that Hall contributed to this volume. Those familiar with Hall's extraordinary career will know that he was not only an original and prolific scholar in his own field, but he also served as founding president of both Clark University

(1889–1920) and of the American Psychological Association (in 1892 and again in 1924). As the first president of Clark, Hall brought together a distinguished faculty to establish the first graduate institution in New England. Despite inordinate difficulties in obtaining funding, Clark, under Hall, developed as an unusually creative center of advanced learning.

It was at Clark that organizing meetings were held for the American Physical Society as well as for the American Psychological Association. And, in response in Hall's personal initiative, Sigmund Freud came to Clark in 1909 to participate in an international psychology conference and gave the lectures that finally established the field of psychoanalysis.

As a result of the climate Hall created at Clark, innovation in an atmosphere of "elbow teaching" became the hallmark of the small, selective institution that Clark remains today, nearly 100 years since its founding.

In his role as educator, then, as well as scientist, Hall began traditions at Clark that continue to survive and flourish. This particular book, and the conference that led to it, owe debts to Hall for both form and content. The chapters live up to the very high standards of the Hall and Clark traditions and will present, for scholars in the many disciplines involved in life course study, a set of provocative ideas and useful insights to further their own work in this innovative field of investigation.

MORTIMER HERBERT APPLEY
Clark University

Preface

The chapters in this book present different approaches to the study of the life course and aging in different societies. They are by no means intended to be exhaustive or representative. Rather, each individual chapter offers a specific approach that could be applied to other substantive topics and societies that are not covered in this volume.

Diverse as they may be, however, the chapters converge around a common approach: Whether they examine transitions in the work life, the status of the elderly, intellectual development, or generational relations, they share in common the life course approach, which views life transitions and changes in work status and family relations as a life process, rather than as an isolated state or segment of human experience. Even when they examine individual acts, they take into account the merging of individual pathways into collective configurations—be they families, age groups, or occupational groups. In doing so, each of these chapters is also concerned with the interaction of individuals and social groups studied within the social structure. In this respect, the time perspective is crucial for all of them. By following a life course approach, they view development over individual, social, and historical time.

The life course approach provides a way of examining individual as well as collective development under changing historical conditions. It shifts the focus of study of human development from stages and ages to transitions and the timing of life events. Rather than focusing on stages of the life cycle, a life course approach is concerned with how individuals and families made their transitions into those different stages. Rather than viewing any one stage of life, such as childhood, youth, and old age, or any age group in isolation, it is concerned with an understanding of the place of that stage in an entire life continuum.

Thus, the study of aging would not be limited to old age alone but would include an attempt to understand old age in the context of earlier life experiences and the social conditions affecting them. A life course approach is concerned with the timing of life events in relation to the social structures and historical changes affecting them. It thus takes into account the synchronization of individual life transitions with collective family configurations under changing social conditions.

Within this larger framework the chapters fall into several groups: The essays by Rosenmayr and Bertaux examine the intellectual roots of the study of lives and of the life course approach. While Rosenmayr's exploration of the philosophical and epistemological roots of the life course approach illuminates its emergence within traditional sociology and psychology, Bertaux rejects traditional sociology as well as Marxist and structuralist approaches to the study of lives. Describing his own intellectual migration through these different approaches, he uses the example of the study of work careers and marriage patterns of bakers in France to suggest an alternative approach. Bertaux's method examines the process by which individuals time their life transitions into occupational advancement and marriage from their own perspectives in the context of the strategies dictated by their occupations.

From a phenomenological point of view, both Bertaux and Plath interpret the timing of life transitions as perceived by the individuals undergoing them within the structural constraints and cultural dictates of the society within which they are undergoing those transitions. Both Bertaux's French bakers and Plath's middle-aged Japanese townsmen pursue their life goals and attempt to come to terms with the transitions that they experience within the constraints of the societies and the time periods in which they live. In each instance, these individuals undergo important life transitions while plotting strategies to reconcile their personal preferences with the cultural prescriptions of their respective societies. Even though both the bakers and the Japanese face these transitions at specific ages, the status associated with age at different points in the life course, rather than age itself, are the determinant factors. In these two instances, as under many other similar conditions, the life course approach suggests that chronological age is a less significant variable than the status within which individuals or groups find themselves at a particular point in time. This is a recurring theme in most of the chapters in this volume: Labouvie-Vief provides an important revision for prevailing theories that intelligence declines in old age. Intellectual capabilities, she points out, are not determined by old age alone. "Intellectual aging" is a social phenomenon as much as a physiological one.

Similarly, when approaching the timing of life transitions from a psychological perspective, Pearlin not only rejects the traditional definition of life stages as age graded, he also questions whether life transitions (except for widowhood) are necessarily stressful. While Pearlin examines life transitions in contemporary society, Elder explores the impact of loss during the Great Depression on the subsequent lives of women as they were reaching old age. Elder, who in his many writings has given intellectual coherence to the life course approach, documents one of the most salient features of the life course—the impact of historical events experienced earlier in one's life on one's later life. The most important conclusion from Elder's essay is that neither age nor the events of the Great Depression affected all members of a cohort encountering these events uniformly. Rather, he demonstrates that differences within a cohort were significant in shaping the adaptation of different members of that cohort to the impact of the Great Depression. Most significant in their adaptation was the historical and cultural equipment that people had when the Depression occurred.

The importance of the location of different cohorts in historical time is recognized as a crucial aspect of the life course approach. It is particularly significant for understanding adaptation to "old age," a recurring theme in several essays. In their respective discussions of policy measures for the elderly, Guillemard, Eversley, and Tornstam emphasize the differences in experiences and problems encountered by different cohorts as well as within cohorts. Although each chapter concerns a different nation, in all of them there is the recurring theme that one needs to understand the demographic, familial, and structural constraints that shaped the earlier life experiences of the cohorts currently reaching old age. In her critique of contemporary retirement policies, Guillemard stresses the need to differentiate a variety of retirement models among different cohorts and to treat these in relation to the retirees' earlier life experiences. Like the other chapters, these also question whether age is indeed a meaningful category, and they carry this debate into the realm of policy.

All of these authors see the solutions to the problems that older people are facing in contemporary societies as a shift from a pathological, remedial policy approach to a constructive view of aging as a

positive life course development and to the use of constructive resources in facilitating individuals' adaptation to old age. Tornstam
proposes the "liberation of bound resources" in order for people to
control their own lives in relation to society and nature. Eversley
recommends a return to the family as the major source of support for
older people as an alternative to public welfare. Hareven points out,
however, that even in earlier periods older people could hardly depend on family members for consistent support. Whenever such
assistance was forthcoming, it was accomplished at a high price of
individual sacrifice. In the United States, at least, it would be highly
unrealistic to turn the clock back and to return the major responsibilities of old-age support to the family, unless the family was accorded
the necessary public supports to enable it to shoulder such responsibilities.

TAMARA K. HAREVEN

Contents

Aging and Life Course Transitions: An Interdisciplinary Perspective

1 The Life Course and Aging in Historical Perspective[1]

TAMARA K. HAREVEN

Introduction

The emergence of "old age" as a social, cultural, and biological phenomenon can be best understood in the context of the entire life
course and of the historical changes affecting it. The social conditions
of children and adolescents in a given society are related to the way
adulthood and old age are perceived in that society; and, conversely,
the role and position of adults and older people are affected by the
treatment and roles of those in earlier stages of life. A full understanding of the current trend toward the isolation and segregation of
older people in contemporary American society would especially depend on a knowledge of the larger process of age segregation that has
affected different age groups.

Underlying a life course approach is the assumption that the
family status and position that people experience in later years of life
is molded by their cumulative life history and by the specific historical conditions affecting their lives at earlier times. For that very
reason, the differences in the experiences of various cohorts that
result from their location in historical time is critical to our under-

1. This chapter was written while I was a recipient of a Research Career Development
Grant from the National Institute of Aging. I am grateful to the NIA for its support.
This chapter benefited from the comments of Raymond Smith and Maris Vinovskis
and from discussion at the workshop on Aging and the Family held by the National
Research Council in Annapolis, Maryland.

Some portions of this chapter were also presented at a 1979 symposium held by
the American Association for the Advancement of Science in Houston and were
published in K. Back (Ed.), *Life Course: Integrative Theories and Exemplary Populations*, Boulder,
Colorado: Westview Press, 1980.

standing of their respective adaptations to old age (Riley, Johnson, & Foner, 1972).

The adaptation of individuals and their families to the social and economic conditions they face when they reach old age is contingent on the paths by which they reach old age. The differences in their respective backgrounds, particularly the ways in which their earlier life experiences and their cultural heritages have shaped their views of family relations, their expectations of support from kin, and their ability to interact with public agencies and bureaucratic institutions are crucial to determining their ability to adapt to conditions they encounter in old age.

The life course framework offers a comprehensive, integrative approach, which allows us to interpret individual and family transitions as part of a continuous, interactive process of historical change. It helps us to view an individual life transition (such as leaving home or marriage) as part of a cluster of concurrent transitions and a sequence of transitions that affect each other. It views a cohort not only as belonging to its specific time period but also as located in earlier times, its experience shaped, therefore, by different historical forces.

From such a perspective, older people are not viewed simply as a homogeneous group, but rather as age cohorts moving through history, each with his or her distinct life experiences, influenced by the historical circumstances encountered earlier in life. The life course approach links individuals' biographies with their collective behavior as part of an ongoing continuum of historical change.

This chapter examines, first, the basic concepts of the life course framework as they illuminate changing historical conditions affecting aging and the family. It next discusses the historical developments in the timing of life transitions as they affect the family status of older people. Finally, it presents a detailed discussion of patterns of timing and generational relations among American families in the late 19th and early 20th centuries and implications of those patterns for generational relations in old age.

The Contribution of Existing Historical Research

The state of historical knowledge on aging and family status of older people is still in its formative stages and cannot provide, therefore, a comprehensive picture of change over time. It has provided, however, valuable insights that help revise preconceived notions about the past and, by implication, about current conditions.

First, an historical life course approach warns us against what Riley calls "the reification of age" (Riley, 1978). Historically, age in itself has not been as significant a factor in the timing of life transitions and in the definitions of old age. More important than age was family status, work status, and one's relationship to the community.

Second, the historical evidence regarding family relations of older people dispels the myth about a golden age in the family relations of older people in the past. In the colonial period older people were as insecure as they are today, even though they were revered and accorded higher status (Demos, 1978). The very fact that aging parents had to enter into agreements with inheriting sons to secure old-age supports in exchange for land suggests the potential for tension and the insecurity in such arrangements (Greven, 1970; Smith, 1973).

Nor did older people experience security and guaranteed support from their children in urban industrial society. While the evidence presented here suggests a strong interdependence among generations, we must not lose sight of the fact that familial supports for older people were strictly voluntary and were carried out at a high price. For that very reason they were precarious and not always continuous.

Historical research has laid to rest the assumption that the isolation older people are facing now is the result of the breakdown of the three-generational extended family under the impact of industrialization. The prevailing pattern over the past three centuries in American Society and in western Europe has been one of continuity in nuclear household arrangements. The residential arrangement preferred by older people seemed to have been those that Rosenmayr defined as "intimacy from a distance." The commitment to independent residence on the part of older people has been a continuous theme in American society. The historical difference lies, however, in the ways in which such autonomy was achieved or sustained. Historically, the independence and self-sufficiency of older people was conditioned on assistance from relatives, especially from their own adult children. Currently, the double bind in which generations were caught has been alleviated to some extent by the welfare state, but the need for kin assistance persists. But the historical ambivalence and the potential conflict underlying kin support and sociality for older people have survived in the United States even after many of these functions were taken over by the welfare state.

This historical shift in the responsibility for the care of older people has generated considerable ambiguity in American society, particularly in the expectations for support and assistance for aging relatives from their own kin. On the one hand, it is assumed that the welfare state has relieved children from the obligation of supporting their parents in old age; at the same time, these public measures are not sufficient in the economic area nor do they provide the kind of support and sociability in areas traditionally provided by the family. It is precisely this ambiguity and the failure of American society to consummate the historical process of the transfer of functions from the family to the public sector that is one of the major sources of problems currently confronting old age.

The Life Course as an Interdisciplinary and Historical Concept

The interaction between individual development and collective family development in the context of changing historical conditions has only recently begun to attract scholars' attention. While the study of the individual life span has for some time commanded the attention of psychologists and while family development has been the domain of sociologists, it is only recently that an effort to examine these processes from a historical perspective has begun to mature.

The application of developmental concepts to the past brought home the important realization that many aspects of human behavior, which social scientists had previously considered constant over time, have actually been subject to major historical changes. In this respect, historical research in recent years has had a similar impact on the study of human development as anthropological research; while anthropological research has shown that human development is relative to different cultures, historical research has demonstrated that it is time bound.

As a result, the very focus of historical study has shifted. For historians, human development has ceased to be merely an explanatory framework for behavior in the past. Instead, the process of development itself has become a subject of historical investigation in its own right. Since it became clear that childhood, adolescence, youth, adulthood, middle age, and old age were not constant over time, the process of change in their respective definitions and experiences under different historical conditions has become an important research subject in itself.

The historical study of aging from a life course perspective is currently very much on the frontier of research. In their application of the life course to past populations, historians have greatly benefitted from the conceptual and methodological contributions of sociology, psychology, and economics. In their turn, historians can make certain contributions to other social sciences, which result from a historical, contextual view.

The life course approach is interdisciplinary by its very nature: Its heritage combines several psychological, sociological, and demographic traditions. It draws on life history analysis, on life span psychology, on the sociology of age differentiation, and on the concept of cohorts as developed by demographers. It focuses on the interaction among individuals and collective timing of family transition as they are shaped by different historical conditions. It examines the synchronization of individual behavior with the collective behavior of the family unit as they change over time and in their relation to external historical conditions (Elder, 1978).

The life course approach is also historical by its very nature: Its essence is the interaction between "individual time," "family time," and "historical time."[2] It attempts to follow the movement of individuals through different family configurations and roles and is concerned with the determinants of timing patterns that affect these transitions (Hareven, 1977). As Elder defines it, the life course encompasses "pathways" by which individuals move throughout their lives, fulfilling different roles sequentially or simultaneously (Elder,

2. Glen Elder has provided conceptual and methodological coherence to the life course approach and has formulated it in a way that made it applicable to historical data (Elder, 1978). The applicability of the life course approach to historical data was explored in a series of interdisciplinary workshops sponsored by the Mathematics Social Science Board of the National Science Foundation, which I directed. The workshops produced resulted in a volume that examined the timing of life transitions in the historical context of Essex County, Massachusetts, in the late 19th century (Hareven, 1978b).

Initially, the family cycle approach as developed by Hill (1964) was valuable to historians because it provided a developmental approach to cross-sectional data (Hareven, 1974). A more careful examination has shown, however, that the a priori stage did not always fit historical populations. The life course approach takes a broader point of view—rather than focusing on stages, it examines the process of individual transitions as they relate to the family as a collective unit (Elder, 1978; Hareven, 1978b).

1978). In following such movements of individuals and families from one role or status to the next or the simultaneous balancing of roles, the life course concerns itself with the process of such transitions under different historical conditions.

Three essential features of life course analysis are particularly significant to an understanding of historical changes in the family: first, timing, which entails the synchronization of different individual roles over a person's career; second, interaction, which involves the relationship between individual life course transitions and changing historical conditions; and third, integration, which represents the cumulative impact of earlier life course transitions on subsequent ones.

TIMING

The life course concerns itself with two essential kinds of timing: first, the timing of transitions over an individual's career, particularly the balancing of entry into and exit from different roles; second, the synchronization of seemingly individual transitions with collective family behavior. These aspects of timing cannot be understood out of context of their interaction with external historical forces. For that reason, the use of the term "timing" in an historical population requires a specific definition that takes into account the historical context since in the past, age in itself was not the most critical aspect of the timing of life transitions.

On the individual level, the crucial question is how people plan and organize their roles over their life course and how they time their life transitions both on the nonfamilial and familial levels in such areas as entry into and exit from school or the labor force, migration, leaving home or returning home, marriage, and setting up an independent household. Most important for an understanding of transitions into old age are the ways in which earlier life transitions are linked to later ones—the fact that the timing of marriage, for example, depended on the needs of aging parents.

The metaphor that best captures the interrelationship of individual transitions and changing family configurations is the movement of schools of fish. As people move over their life course in family units, they group and regroup themselves. The functions that they adopt in these different clusters also vary significantly over their life course. Most individuals are involved simultaneously in several family configurations, fulfilling different functions in each. A married person, for example, is part of both a family of origin and a family of procreation (occupying a different position and fulfilling a different role in each); in addition, such an individual also figures in his or her spouse's family of orientation and in the spouse's kin network. When a son leaves home, his departure changes the configuration of his family unit. Depending on the status he held, his family might find itself either less one bread winner or less one dependent. When he marries and forms a new family unit, his roles and obligations differ from the ones he had in his parents' family. This seemingly individual move affects the collective conditions of at least three family units—his family of origin, his newly founded family, and his wife's family of origin. In situations where remarriage follows death of a spouse or divorce, the new spouse's family enters the orbit of relationships, while the former spouse's family does not necessarily disappear completely. In case of divorce, especially, a woman would stop relating to her former husband's mother as her mother-in-law but may continue to relate to her as her child's grandmother. Thus, the multiplicity of familial relationships in which individuals are engaged changes over the life course, and along with these changes an individual's transitions into various roles are also timed differently. In this respect age, although an important variable defining life transitions, is not the only variable. Changes in family status and in accompanying roles are often as important as age, if not more significant.

HISTORICAL TIMING

The second important feature of life course analysis is the impact of historical processes on the timing of individual or family transitions. The timing of life course transitions is influenced by the interaction of demographic, social, and economic factors as well as by one's cultural background. Fertility can abstractly account for the number of children born and the proportion of the life course spent on childbearing, but the commencement of childbearing and the spacing of children are determined (within biological limits) by personal decisions that are often governed by social and cultural values or prescriptions. Age at leaving home and age at marriage are similarly subject to complex interactions.

Social change has an important impact on timing in several areas. Demographic changes in mortality, fertility, and nuptiality affect the age configurations within the family and the number of years of overlap among family members. Cultural changes in norms of timing and economic changes in the opportunity structure affect entry into the labor force, job availability, and, ultimately, retirement. Institutional and legislative changes, such as compulsory school attendance, child labor laws, and mandatory retirement, affect the transitions of different age groups into and out of the labor force.

In any examination of the timing of life transitions the very question of cohort historical or social changes in the life course requires more elaborate definitions. "Historical change" is usually defined by nonhistorians as characterized by macrodevelopments, often represented by one specific major event, such as the Great Depression or a world war. But actually, the important contribution that historical research makes is in specifying and examining diachronic changes, which often have a more direct impact on the life course than macrosocial changes. Most importantly, historians can identify the convergence of socioeconomic and cultural forces, which are characteristic of a specific time period and which more directly influence the timing of life transitions than more large-scale or long-term linear developments. For example, migration and changing local employment opportunities within a community can affect changes in the timing of life transitions more directly and dramatically than such grand external events as World War II.

Ryder has suggested that social change occurs when there is a distinct discontinuity between the experiences of one cohort and those of its predecessors (Ryder, 1965). From an historical perspective we would want to modify Ryder's assertion to argue that important historical discontinuities could also occur within the same cohort. For example, the cohort that reached adulthood during the Great Depression experienced major discontinuities in family and work lives that were not only part of an overall process of social change but which, in turn, may have catalyzed further social change. Or, consider the cohort that reached age 65 around 1910 and was faced with compulsory retirement. This cohort would have found mandatory retirement at a set age in the work life far more traumatic than did the cohort following, which had come of age early in the 20th century, when entry into and exit from the labor force were already becoming age defined and legislated.

At the same time, however, differences within cohorts are also of great significance. Variations in exposure to historical events by class and community background within each cohort would affect important differences among members of the same cohort. For example, within the same cohort, ethnic differences, or differences in income, and especially historical differences affecting members earlier in their lives would cause differences in their respective responses to historical conditions when they reach old age.

CUMULATIVE IMPACT OF LIFE TRANSITIONS

The previous discussions lead us to the third feature of life course analysis—the cumulative impact of earlier transitions on subsequent ones. Rather than following a static view of life experiences, a life course approach views a cohort as an age group moving through history whose social experience is influenced not only by contemporary conditions but also by experiences of earlier life course transitions. These transitions are affected in turn by a set of historical circumstances specific to their own time. This complex pattern of cumulative life course effects can be grasped on two levels: First, the direct consequences of earlier life course experiences on subsequent development must be taken into account.

Elder's *Children of the Great Depression*, one of the outstanding studies addressing these questions, documents the impact of Depression experiences in childhood and early adulthood on subsequent adult experiences (Elder, 1974). Within the same cohort of unemployed adults caught in the Great Depression, coping with unemployment differed not only in terms of the availability of other resources, personality, and family backgrounds, but also in terms of earlier transitions experienced—how long the individual had been working and whether his or her career had been continuous and stable or had already been disrupted.

Second, historical conditions that individuals encountered throughout their lives shaped their earlier life history and, therefore, also indirectly affected their transitions into the later years of life. This means that the social experiences of cohorts are influenced not only by the external conditions at the particular point in time when they reach old age but also by their earlier life experiences as they were shaped by historical conditions earlier in time.

Historical Changes in the Timing of Life Transitions

The contours of the emergence of old age as a distinct stage of life were shaped by a larger historical process, involving the segmentation of life course, into specific developmental stages (Fischer, 1977;

Hareven, 1976; Keniston, 1971; Kett, 1977; Neugarten, 1968). New stages of life were only gradually recognized historically. Their characteristics were first experienced in the lives of individuals. They were subsequently recognized in the culture and were finally institutionalized and given public affirmation. This public recognition occurred through the passing of legislation and the establishment of agencies for the realization of the potential of people at a specific stage of life and for their protection during those stages. This is not to say that in earlier time periods there was no awareness of an individual's movement through a variety of age-related roles through life, merely that this awareness was not institutionalized.

The historical difference lies in the recognition of distinct age-related stages of life, with their specific needs and societally recognized functions. To the extent to which it is possible to generalize about the historical emergence of stages of life, it appears that the "discovery" of such a stage is itself a complex process since it involves the convergence of institutional and cultural factors in their formulation and acceptance. First, individuals become aware of the specific characteristics of such a stage in their private experiences. The articulation of its unique conditions are then formulated by the professionals and are eventually defined and followed in the popular culture. Finally, if the conditions peculiar to the stage seem to be associated with a major social problem, the stage attracts the attention of public agencies, and its needs and problems are dealt with in legislation and in the establishment of institutions aimed directly to meet its needs. Those public activities in turn affect the experience of individuals going through such a stage and clearly influence the timing of transitions in and out of such a stage by providing public supports and at times constraints that affect timing.

In American society childhood first emerged as a distinct stage in the private lives of middle-class urban families in the early part of the 19th century. The redefinition of the meaning of childhood and of the role of children was related to the retreat of the family into domesticity, to the segregation of the work place from the home, to the redefinition of the mother's role as the major custodian of the domestic sphere, and to the emphasis on sentimental as opposed to instrumental relations at the very base of familial relationships. Philippe Ariès explained that the new child centeredness of urban domestic families in western Europe in the late 18th and early 19th centuries was also a response to two major demographic changes: the decline in infant and child mortality and the increase in the conscious practice of family limitation (Ariès, 1960). Having emerged first in the life of middle-class families and having become an integral part of their life style, childhood as a distinct stage of development became the subject of the voluminous body of literature on child rearing and family advice. This literature popularized the concept of childhood and the needs of children, prescribed the means to allow them to develop as children, and called for the regulation of child labor.

The discovery of adolescence as a stage in the later part of the 19th century followed a similar pattern to that of the emergence of childhood as a stage. While puberty in itself is a universal, biological process, the psychosocial phenomena of adolescence were only gradually identified and defined, most notably by G. Stanley Hall, in the later part of the 19th century. There is evidence that the experience of adolescence, particularly some of the problems and tensions associated with it, was noticed in the private lives of individuals reaching puberty during the second half of the 19th century (Demos & Demos, 1969). The congregation of young people in peer groups and styles of behavior that might be characterized as a "culture of adolescence" were also observed by educators and urban reformers from the middle of the 19th century on. Anxiety over such conduct increased, particularly when it was connected with the presence of large numbers of immigrants in American cities because of the fear that reformers had over the formation of gangs and unruly groups. Adolescence as a new stage of life was articulated in the work of psychologists, particularly by Hall and his circle, and was also widely popularized in the literature. The extension of school age through high school in the second part of the 19th century, the further extension of the age limits for child labor, and the establishment of juvenile reformatories and vocational schools, were all part of the public recognition of the needs and problems of adolescence (Bremner, Barnard, & Hareven, 1969–1972).

The boundaries between childhood and adolescence on the one hand and between adolescence and adulthood on the other became more clearly demarcated in the 20th century. The experience of childhood and adolescence became more pervasive among larger groups of the American population as immigrant families adopted American life styles and as working-class families made their entry into the middle class. As Keniston has suggested, the extension of a moratorium from adult responsibilities beyond adolescence has resulted in the emergence of yet another stage—that of youth. Despite the growing awareness of these preadult stages, however, no clear boundaries for adulthood in America emerged until much later, when "old age" became prominent as a new stage of life and with it the need to differentiate the social and psychological problems of middle from those of old age.

There are many indications that a new consciousness of old age along with institutional definitions and societal recognition emerged in the late part of the 19th and early part of the 20th centuries. The convergence of a growing body of gerontological literature, the proliferation of negative stereotypes about old age, and the institution of mandatory retirement represented the first moves in the direction of a public and institutional formulation of old age as a distinct stage of life[3] (Achenbaum, 1978).

In the late 19th century, American society changed from accepting aging as a natural process to viewing it as a distinct period of life characterized by decline, weakness, and obsolescence. Advanced old age, which had earlier been regarded as a manifestation of the survival of the fittest, was now denigrated as a condition of dependency and deterioration. Writers began to identify advancing years with physical decline and mental deterioration (Achenbaum, 1974).

In the beginning of the 20th century, public concern for and interest in old age converged from various directions. In addition to physicians, psychologists, and popular writers, efficiency experts and social reformers were especially instrumental in attracting public attention to old age as a social problem. A variety of medical and psychological studies by industrial efficiency experts focused on the physical and mental limitations of old age. At the same time, social reformers began to expose the poverty and dependency suffered by many old people as part of a general investigation of how the other half lives, and to agitate for social security and social insurance (Hareven, 1976).

Government recognition of old age evolved more gradually and began on the state level. By 1920 only 10 states had instituted some form of old-age legislation; all programs were limited in scope, and most of them were declared unconstitutional by the Supreme Court. Nevertheless, agitation for old-age security continued and finally

3. On the periodization of old age in American history, Fischer (1977) has argued that changing perceptions toward old age had actually emerged in the late 18th and early 19th centuries.

culminated in the Social Security Act of 1935. It was not until the 1940s, however, that gerontology was recognized as a new medical field, and it was even more recently that social scientists identified old age as constituting a new and pressing problem for society. Social definitions of age limits and public treatment through institutional reform, retirement legislation, and welfare measures represent the most recent societal recognition of this stage of life.

The historical developments of the past half century have since contributed to the sharpening of the boundaries between old age and middle age. But the boundaries of adulthood in itself are not yet clearly defined, and the transitions into middle age are still fuzzy. Old age is now recognized as a specific period of adulthood with its intrinsic problems, needs, and opportunities.

More recently, rather than being viewed as a homogeneous stage, the concept of old age itself has been refined and subdivided into the "young old" and the "old old" in an effort to reflect developmental characteristics within the "elderly." Increasing consciousness of problems and crises related to middle adulthood, particularly as reflected in problems of parenting, has also resulted in the recognition of "middle age" as a distinct stage. On the public level it has a formal beginning—age 65, at least where an individual's working life is concerned—and it is institutionalized by a rite of passage—retirement and eligibility for Social Security (Hareven, 1976).

The conscious segmentation of the life course into publicly recognized stages and the preoccupation with their meaning has had significant implications for the relationships among age groups in American society, for patterns of age segregation within the family, and for the timing of life transitions.

The important connection between historical development and the emergence of such new stages has not yet been fully documented. The general contours of the pattern are beginning to emerge, however, with some clarity. Whether childhood, adolescence, youth, middle, and old age were first experienced on the private, individual level or acknowledged on the public, collective level, their very appearance and increasing societal recognition have affected the timing of individual and family transitions in the past.

Not only has the experience of these stages of life changed over time, but the timing of people's entry into and exit from such stages and the accompanying roles involved in such timing have changed as well. The existential as well as the institutional changes that have buttressed the extension of a moratorium from adult responsibilities have also affected the timing of both individual and familial transitions and have resulted in new pressures on individuals and families undergoing them.

Transitions at different points in the life course were interlocked and interdependent. Timing on one end of the life course affected timing on the other end and vice versa. The postponement of the assumption of adult responsibilities has meant longer residence of children in the household without contributing to the family's economic effort and a resulting increase in the state of "dependency" or "semidependency" as a typical experience of adolescence. On the other end, the recognition of old age as a distinct stage, and especially its imposition of discontinuity in the form of mandatory retirement, has had a serious impact on the timing of transitions in the family status of older people leading to the emergence of dependency or semidependency in old age and the imposition of tensions and demands on family obligations.

These large-scale societal developments as expressed in the discovery of new stages of life are reflected in changes in the timing of life transitions on the microlevel. Demographic changes in American society since the late 19th century have significantly affected the timing of life transitions and the age configuration within the family over the life of its members (Uhlenberg, 1974, 1978; Hareven, 1977). Important changes have also occurred in the synchronization of individual time schedules with the collective time tables of the family.

Demographic, economic, and cultural factors have combined to account for differences in the timing of such transitions as leaving home, entry into and exit from the labor force, marriage, parenthood, the "empty nest," and widowhood, resulting in different pacing of these transitions inside and outside the family. Uhlenberg (1978) suggests, over the past century, demographic developments have tended to effect greater uniformity in the life course of American families and have considerably increased the opportunities for intact survival of the family unit over the lifetime of its members. As a result of the decline in mortality since the late 19th century, the chances for children to survive into adulthood and to grow up with their siblings and both parents alive have increased considerably. Similarly, the chances for women to survive until adulthood and to marry, raise children jointly with a husband, and survive with husband through the launching stage (Uhlenberg, 1974) have increased steadily between the 19th and early 20th centuries. For women, these changes, combined with earlier marriages and earlier completion of maternal roles, have meant a more extended period of life without children in their middle years. At the same time, women's tendency to live longer than men has resulted in a protracted period of widowhood in later years of life. Men, on the other hand, because of lower life expectancy and a greater tendency to remarry in old age, normally remain married until death (Glick, 1977).

A comparison of different cohorts of white American women from 1870 to 1930 has shown that an increasing proportion of the population has entered prescribed family roles and, except for divorce, has lived out its life in family units (Uhlenberg, 1974). Contrary to conventional assumptions, the American population has experienced an increasing uniformity in the timing of life course transitions into family roles and survival through the entire family cycle.

The very demographic factors that are responsible for these continuities have also generated major discontinuities in the timing of life course transitions over the past century. Such discontinuities are expressed in the timing of transitions into and out of family roles and work roles and are closely related to the gradual segmentation of the life course into societally acknowledged stages as discussed above (childhood, youth, adolescence, adulthood, middle age, and old age).

The most significant expression of such discontinuities is most clearly evident in the timing of transitions to adulthood, especially in leaving home, marriage, family formation, and parenthood. As Modell, Furstenberg, and Hershberg have shown (1976), over the past century age uniformity in the timing of life course transitions has been increasingly more marked. Transitions have become more rapidly timed and abrupt. In contrast to our times, 19th-century transitions from the parental home to marriage, to household headship, and to parenthood occurred more gradually and were timed less rigidly. In the late 19th century the time range necessary for a cohort to accomplish such transitions was wider, and the sequence in which transitions followed one another was not rapidly established. In the 20th century, on the other hand, transitions to adulthood have become more uniform for the age cohort undergoing them, more orderly in sequence, and more definitive. The very notion of embarking on a new stage of the life course and the implications of movement from one stage to the next have become more firmly established. Most importantly, the timing of life transitions has become more regulated according to specific age norms rather than in relation to collective needs of the family.

In the late 19th century, later life transitions, for example, transitions into the empty nest, into widowhood, and out of household headship among urban populations, followed no ordered sequence, were not closely synchronized, and extended over a relatively long period of time. For most men surviving to old age, labor force participation and family status generally resembled those of their earlier adult years. Only at very advanced ages, when their capabilities were probably impaired by infirmity, did a substantial number experience definite changes in their household status. These men, however, represented a fraction of their age peers. On the other hand, because widowhood was such a common experience, older women experienced more marked transitions than did older men, although the continuing presence of adult children in the household meant that widowhood did not necessarily mark a dramatic transition into the empty nest (Chudacoff & Hareven, 1979; Hareven, 1982; Smith, 1979).

In summary, the 19th-century pattern of transitions allowed for a wider age spread within the family and for greater opportunity for interaction among parents, adult children, and other kin. Demographic changes, combined with the increasing rapidity in the timing of transitions, the increasing separation between an individual's family of orientation and family of procreation, and the introduction of publicly imposed transitions have converged to isolate and segregate age groups in the larger society and, at the same time, have generated new stresses on familial needs and obligations.

The most important marked discontinuity has occurred in the middle and later years of life, namely, the emergence of the empty nest in a couple's middle age. The combination of earlier marriage and fewer children with childbearing occurring in the early stages of the family cycle and children's leaving home earlier in their parents lives has resulted in a more widespread emergence of the empty nest as a characteristic of middle and old age (Glick, 1977).

In contemporary society, the empty nest period comprises one-third or more of the married adult life span. Glick concludes that the duration of this period has increased over the past 80 years by 11 years (from 1.6 years to 12.3 years). "The couple now entering marriage has the prospect of living together 13 years (without chil-

dren) or more than one-third of the 44 years of married life that lay
ahead of them at the time of marriage" (Glick, 1977, p. 9). Growing
sex differentials in mortality above age 50 have dramatically increased the ratio of females to males and have made widowhood a
more important feature in a woman's life. In this respect, Uhlenberg
(1978) has noted that the major change since the late 19th century
has not been so much the emergence of an empty nest but rather the
proportion of a woman's lifetime that this period encompasses. Earlier marriage and earlier completion of childbearing and childrearing,
on the one hand, and greater survival into older age, on the other,
have resulted in a higher proportion of a woman's life spent, first,
with a husband but without children and, then, alone without either
husband or children.

By contrast, in the 19th century, later age at marriage, higher
fertility, and shorter life expectancy rendered different family configurations from those characterizing contemporary society. Thus,
for large families, the parental stage with children remaining in the
household extended over a longer period of time, sometimes over the
parents' entire life. Since children were spread along a broad spectrum in families, younger children could observe their older siblings
and near relatives moving through adolescence and into adulthood.
Older siblings in turn trained for adult roles by acting as surrogate
parents for younger siblings (Hareven, 1977). Most importantly, the
nest was rarely empty as usually one adult child remained at home
while the parents were aging.

Family Timing and Transitions into Old Age

Demographic factors only in part explain the presence or absence of
an empty nest. As shown by the correlation of children's ages with
that of the heads of household, the reason children were not present
in the households of their aging parents was not only because they
were too young to move out. Even in situations where sons and
daughters were in their late teens and early twenties, and therefore
old enough to leave their parents' households, at least one child
stayed because it was customary for an adult child to remain at home
to care for aging parents if there was no other source of assistance
available. Autonomy in old age, in part expressed in household headship, hinged on some form of support from one or more working

children in the household or on the presence of boarders. The transition into the later years of life was thus marked by the continued effort of aging parents to maintain the integrity of their family through the continued residence of at least one child at home.

Recent historical analyses of late 19th-century American communities suggest that older couples and, especially, aging widows who had children were more likely to reside with their children than with other kin or strangers.[4] Childless couples or those whose children had left home took in boarders and lodgers as surrogate kin. Widows or women who had never married and who were unable to maintain independent households moved in with their relatives or boarded in other people's homes (Chudacoff & Hareven, 1979; Hareven, 1982). Solitary residence, a pattern that is becoming increasingly prominent among older people today was rarely experienced in the 19th century (Kobrin, 1976).

Older people struggled to retain the headship of their own households rather than move in with their relatives and strangers. Nuclear household arrangements were often broken or stretched, however, during parent's dependency in old age or during apparent housing shortages that made it more difficult for newlyweds to afford separate housing. Thus, under certain circumstances some children returned home with their spouses to live with their aging parents, and other children, most commonly the youngest daughter remaining at home, postponed marriage in order to continue supporting older parents. Commitment to autonomy was so pervasive that the commonly followed pattern was that of adult children stay-

4. The patterns of timing and household arrangements of older people reported here are based on the analysis of family and household patterns in select communities of Essex County, Massachusetts, in 1880 (Chudacoff & Hareven, 1978), a population sample for Providence, Rhode Island, from the 1860, 1870, and 1880 censuses (Chudacoff & Hareven, 1979), and a sample from the 1900 census for Manchester, New Hampshire (Hareven, 1982). The patterns found in these local analyses are consistent with the national picture emerging from the analysis of a cross section of the older population in the United States from the 1900 census, a study carried out by Smith (1979). Any generalizations on this subject are necessarily limited by the cross-sectional nature of the data on which these studies are based. On the other hand, the application of life course questions to cross-sectional data has allowed us to infer longitudinal patterns if only to a limited extent. Nor do census data provide insight into the quality of relationships. On the other hand, oral history interviewing for my study of Manchester, New Hampshire, has provided insight into familial norms and into the sense of familial obligations in generational relations. Most importantly, it has helped identify the areas of strain and conflicts in generational relations as parents were aging (Hareven, 1978a, 1982).

ing in their parents' household rather than that of parents moving in with their children. Even older widows, who were generally the most vulnerable, continued to hold on to the headship of their household as long as they could. If there were no children available or able to help, they took in boarders and lodgers. Once they were unable to continue to maintain independent households, they, more than widowed men, eventually had to move into the households of relatives or strangers (Chudacoff & Hareven, 1978, 1979; Hareven, 1982).

The nature of interdependence in a familial setting imposed demands as well as constraints on the timing of life transitions that involved balancing and juggling of a number of roles. A potential source of conflict lay in the fact that older children had already left home and younger ones were entering adulthood while their parents approached old age.

Such strain was intensified by the conflict between two sets of norms in American culture that often placed generations in a double bind: One was the prevailing expectation that the integrity of the family of orientation be preserved. The other was the presumption that young adults would achieve autonomy as soon as possible and carve out their own places in the world. How could young men and women fulfill those apparently conflicting sets of requirements? How could they become independent adults who headed their households and care for their own children and, at the same time, continue to support their aging parents?

The basic commitment in American culture to residence in a nuclear household rendered such choices even more difficult. As in our time, nuclear household structure seems to have been the norm throughout the 19th century and was the predominant residential form for the majority of the population. While the majority of households did not include extended kin, a considerable portion of households included strangers who were residing as boarders and lodgers. Boarding and lodging to some extent alleviated this generational strain by providing surrogate family arrangements: young people, who had left their own parent's household boarded with older people, whose own children had left home (Modell & Hareven, 1973). This practice thus enabled older people to continue to head their own households, even after their own children had left. Only in cases where older people were too weak to continue heading their own households or to live alone was the function reversed; aging widows in particular went to board in other people's households.

The rather powerful commitment to the continued autonomy of the household and to the nuclearity of the family was clearly in conflict with the needs of people as they were aging. In the absence of adequate public and institutional means of support, older people were caught in a conflict where, on the one hand, they had to rely on the continued support from their children, and, on the other hand, they were committed to living in nuclear households.

In the late 19th-century setting, the norms of familial assistance and autonomy seemed to prevail over age norms of timing. This is precisely an area where the historical difference with our time is drastic. Life course transitions in contemporary society have become more strictly age related and more rigidly governed by age norms. Neugarten's definition of being "late" or "on time" in one's fulfillment of certain age-related roles reflects the standards of a society bound to age norms, while in earlier time periods, economic needs and familial obligations prevailed over age norms (Neugarten, 1968). Thus, the current trend toward specific age-related transitions is closely related to the decline in instrumental relations among kin over the past century and their replacement by an individualized and sentimental orientation toward family relations. This trend has led to the isolation of the elderly and to increasing age segregation in American society.

Historically, the family was the central arena in which many of the life transitions were converging. Many of the transitions that we could consider today as *individual* were actually collective and familial. They were either shared by a number of family members or, even if they involved strictly individual activity such as the work life, they still affected the entire family as a unit or at least several members within the family. Marriage, for example, was not merely subject to individual or couple decisions, but rather its timing hinged on the need of each partner's family of origin, particularly on the status of parents if they were aging.

The family also played a major role as the locus for most important economic and welfare functions. This central role of the family persisted even after the work place had been removed from the home, following the initial phase of industrialization, and after many of the family's earlier educational, welfare, and social control functions had been transferred to other institutions, under the impact of industrialization. Despite the growing tendency of middle-class urban families to serve as a retreat from the outside world and to concentrate on domesticity and child nurture as the family's exclusive role, the majority of families in the larger society continued to function as economic units, indeed, often as work units. Families and individuals therefore had to rely heavily on kin relations as their very essential social base. Timing was a critical factor in the family's efforts to maintain control over its resources, especially by balancing the contribution of different members to the family economy. Thus, under the historical conditions where familial assistance was the almost exclusive source of security, especially during critical life situations, the multiplicity of obligations for assistance and support to other family members that individuals incurred over their life course was more complex than in the present setting of the welfare state, where such responsibilities are primarily the domain of public agencies. (This is not to say that present kin do not continue to fulfill such obligations, but major welfare functions that were earlier carried out by kin have been transferred to the public sector.)

Nineteenth-century family economy was out of necessity flexible because individual resources were precarious and institutional buttressing slim or nonexistent. Family adaptation was crucial, therefore, in coping with critical life situations or even with regular life course transitions. The family was the most critical agent, both in initiating as well as in absorbing the consequences of transitions among individual members. Clearly, when viewed from this perspective, the essential aspect of the *timing* of a transition was not the *age* at which a person left home, married, or became a parent, but rather how this transition was related to those that other family members were undergoing and especially to the needs of parents as they were aging.

Under the economic conditions of the late 19th century, pressing economic needs and familial obligations took precedence over established norms of timing. The timing of early life transitions was bound up with later ones in a continuum of familial needs and obligations. More significant than age was the *sequence* or *coincidence* in which transitions were expected to occur. Modell *et al.* (1976) have also shown that even though 19th-century transitions to adulthood were more flexibly timed than today, they nevertheless followed a certain set seqeuence: Marriage was conditioned on the establishment of a separate household and of means of self-support. The timing of life transitions was not so much governed by age norms as by family economic strategies and interdependence. It was also influenced by the economic opportunity structure in the community and was limited by institutional constraints such as compulsory school attendance or child labor legislation. The absence of institutional supports such as welfare agencies, unemployment compensation, and social security added to the pressures imposed on family members.

The timing of transitions along the life course converged around interdependence and mutual obligations among different family members. Individual life transitions were not always self-timed. In modern society we are accustomed to thinking of most family roles and work careers as individual. Historically, each apparently individual transition was treated as a family move and had to be synchronized with family needs. In addition to the ties retained with their family of origin, individuals took on obligations toward their families of procreation and toward their spouses' families. The complexity of obligations cast family members in various overlapping and at times conflicting functions over the course of their lives. One role might gradually come to dominate while another receded in importance, but the alteration was not always a smooth one.

The major historical change was not the decline of co-residence, but rather the decline in the interdependence of kin. The increasing separation between the family of origin and the family of procreation over the past century combined with a growing privatization of the family and the discontinuities along the life course discussed above all occurred in the context of changes in the quality of kin relations. In the 19th and early 20th centuries, family relationships were characterized by a higher degree of kin integration. Relatives served as the most essential resource for economic assistance and security and carried the major burden of welfare functions, many of which fall now within the purview of the public sector. Exchange relationships among parents and children and other kin thus provided the major, and sometimes the only, base for security (Anderson, 1971; Hareven, 1978a).

The gradual erosion of instrumental kin relationships has tended to increase insecurity and isolation as people age, especially in areas of need that are not met by public programs. In examining this particular aspect of historical change, it is important to distinguish between the availability of kin and the nature of kin interaction and support systems. Recent historical studies have documented the multiplicity of functions of kin in the 19th century, especially their critical role in migration, job placement, and housing (Hareven, 1978a,

1982) and in assistance in critical life situations (Anderson, 1971). Contrary to prevailing theories, urbanization and industrialization did not break down traditional kinship patterns. There are thus many parallels between the role that kin fulfilled in the 19th and early 20th centuries and patterns of kin assistance found by sociologists in modern American society (Sussman, 1959; Litwak, 1965; Shanas, 1979). Their studies, particularly that by Shanas, have emphasized the frequency of interaction among older parents and adult children and the flow of assistance to older people from their relatives. The difference lies, however, in the degree of integration with kin and the dependence on mutual assistance. While more intensive patterns of kin interaction have survived among first-generation immigrant, black, and working-class families, there has been an overall erosion of instrumental ties among relatives, especially in the almost exclusive dependence on kin for consistent support over the life course.

Contemporary studies insisting on the prevalence of kin assistance among older people have not documented the intensity, quality, and consistency of kin support that older people are receiving from their relatives. Until we have more systematic evidence in this area, it would be a mistake to assume that kin are carrying or should be expected to carry the major responsibility for assistance to older people. The current involvement of the elderly with kin, as Shanas (1979) and others have found, represents a cohort phenomenon rather than a continuing historical pattern. The elderly cohort of the present has carried over into old age the historical attitudes and traditions that were prevalent when he or she was growing up earlier in this century, especially a strong reliance on relatives. The cohort also has kin available because of the larger family size of earlier cohorts. Future cohorts, as they reach old age, might not have the same strong sense of integration with kin nor might there be sufficient numbers of available kin on whom to rely. It would be a mistake, therefore, to leave kin to take care of their own at a time when the chances to do so are considerably diminishing. Nor should the historical evidence about the continuity in kin relations be misused in support of proposals to return welfare responsibilities from the public sector to the family without basic additional supports. An examination of the historical patterns reveals the high price that kin have had to pay in order to assist each other in the absence of other forms of societal support. The historical precedent thus offers a warning against romanticizing kin relations, particularly against the attempt to transfer responsibility for children and the elderly back to the family without adequate governmental assistance.

REFERENCES

Achenbaum, A. W. The obsolescence of old age in America, 1865–1914. *Journal of Social History*, 1974, **8**, 48–62.

Achenbaum, A. W. *Old age in the new land*. Baltimore: Johns Hopkins University Press, 1978.

Anderson, M. S. *Family structure in nineteenth-century Lancashire*. Cambridge, England: Cambridge University Press, 1971.

Anonymous. Apology from age to youth. *Living Age*, 1893, **193 (14) January**, 170.

Ariès, P. *L'enfant et la vie familiale sous l'ance régime*. Paris, 1960. (Translated by R. Baldick, *Centuries of childhood*. New York: Knopf, 1962.)

Bremner, R. J., Barnard, J., & Hareven, T. K. *Children and youth in America* (Vols. I–III). Cambridge, Mass.: Harvard University Press, 1969–1972.

Chudacoff, H., & Hareven, T. K. Family transitions to old age. In T. K. Hareven (Ed.), *Transitions: The family and the life course in historical perspective*. New York: Academic Press, 1978.

Chudacoff, H., & Hareven, T. K. From the empty nest to family dissolution. *Journal of Family History*, 1979, **Spring**, 69–83.

Demos, J. Old age in early New England. In J. Demos & S. Boocock (Eds.), *Turning points*. *American Journal of Sociology*, 1978, **84**, Supplement, 284–287.

Demos, J., & Demos, V. Adolescence in historical perspective. *Journal of Marriage and the Family*, 1969, **31**, 632–638.

Elder, G. *Children of the Great Depression*. Chicago: University of Chicago Press, 1974.

Elder, G. Family history and the life course. In T. K. Hareven (Ed.), *Transitions: The family and the life course in historical perspective*. New York: Academic Press, 1978.

Fischer, D. H. *Growing old in America*. New York: Oxford University Press, 1977.

Glick, P. C. Updating the life cycle of the family. *Journal of Marriage and the Family*, 1977, **39 (February)**, 5–13.

Greven, P. *Four generations: Population, land and family in colonial Andover, Massachusetts*. Ithaca, N.Y.: Cornell University Press, 1970.

Hareven, T. K. The family as process: The historical study of the family cycle. *Journal of Social History*, 1974, **7**, 322–329.

Hareven, T. K. The last stage: Historical adulthood and old age. *Daedalus*, 1976, **Fall**, 13–27.

Hareven, T. K. Family time and historical time. *Daedalus*, 1977, **Spring**, 57–70.

Hareven, T. K. The dynamics of kin in an industrial community. In J. Demos & S. Boocock (Eds.), *Turning points. American Journal of Sociology*, 1978, **84**, Supplement, 151–182. (a)

Hareven, T. K. (Ed.). *Transitions: The family and the life course in historical perspective*. New York: Academic Press, 1978. (b)

Hareven, T. K. Historical changes in the life course and the family. In J. M. Yinger & S. J. Cutler (Eds.), *Major social issues: A multidisciplinary view*. New York: The Free Press, 1978. (c)

Hareven, T. K. Cycles, courses, and cohorts: Reflections on theoretical and methodological approaches to the historical study of family development. *Journal of Social History*, 1978, **12**, 97-110. (d)

Hareven, T. K. *Family time and industrial time.* Cambridge, England: Cambridge University Press, 1982.

Hareven, T. K., & Langenbach, R. *Amoskeag: Life and work in an American factory city.* New York: Pantheon, 1978.

Hill, R. Methodological issues in family development research. *Family Process*, 1964, **3(March)**, 186-206.

Hill, R. *Family development in three generations.* Cambridge, Mass.: Schenkman, 1970.

Keniston, K. Psychological development and historical change. *Journal of Interdisciplinary History*, 1971, **21 (Fall)**, 329-345.

Kett, J. *Rites of passage: Adolescence in America, 1790 to the present.* New York: Basic Books, 1977.

Kobrin, F. E. The fall of household size and the rise of the primary individual. *Demography*, 1976, **February**, 127-138.

Laslett, P., & Wall, R. (Eds.). *Household and family in past time.* Cambridge, England: Cambridge University Press, 1972.

Litwak, E. Extended kin relations in an industrial democratic society. In E. Shanas & G. F. Streib (Eds.), *Social structure and the family: Generational relations.* Englewood Cliffs, N.J.: Prentice-Hall, 1965.

Modell, J., & Hareven, T. K. Urbanization and the malleable household: Boarding and lodging in American families. *Journal of Marriage and the Family*, 1973, **35**, 467-479.

Modell, J., Furstenberg, F., & Hershberg, T. Social change and transitions to adulthood in historical perspective. *Journal of Family History*, 1976, **1**, 7-32.

Neugarten, B. L. (Ed.). *Middle age and aging: A reader in social psychology.* Chicago: University of Chicago Press, 1968.

Neugarten, B., & Daton, N. Sociological perspectives on the life cycle. In P. Baltes & K. W. Schaie (Eds.), *Life span development psychology: Personality and socialization.* New York: Academic Press, 1973.

Neugarten, B., & Hagestad, G. O. Age and the life course. In R. H. Binstock & E. Shanas (Eds.), *Handbook of aging and the social sciences.* New York: Van Nostrand Reinhold, 1976.

Riley, M. W. Aging, social change and the power of ideas. *Daedalus: Generations*, 1978, **107 (Fall)**, 39-52.

Riley, M. W., Johnson, M. E., & Foner, A. (Eds.). *Aging and society: A sociology of age stratification.* New York: Russell Sage Foundation, 1972.

Ryder, N. The cohort as a concept in the study of social change. *American Sociological Review*, 1965, **30 (December)**, 843-861.

Shanas, E. Social myth as hypothesis: The case of the family relations of old people. *Gerontologist*, 1979, **19**, 3-9.

Smith, D. S. Parental power and marriage patterns: An analysis of historical trends in Hingham, Massachusetts. *Journal of Marriage and the Family*, 1973, **35(August)**.

Smith, D. S. Life course, norms, and the family system of older Americans in 1900. *Journal of Family History*, 1979, **4(Fall)**, 285-299.

Sussman, M. B. The isolated nuclear family: Fact or fiction? *Social Problems*, 1959, **6 (Spring)**, 333-347.

Taeuber, I. B. Continuity, change and transition in populations and family: Interrelations and priorities in research. In *The family in transition* (Fogarty International Center Proceedings, No. 3). Washington, D.C.: U.S. Government Printing Office, 1969.

Uhlenberg, P. Cohort variations in family life cycle experiences of U.S. females. *Journal of Marriage and the Family*, 1974, **34**, 284–292.

Uhlenberg, P. Changing configurations of the life course. In T. K. Hareven (Ed.), *Transitions: The family and the life course in historical perspective*. New York: Academic Press, 1978.

Vinovskis, M. A. From household size to the life course: Some observations on recent trends in family history. *American Behavioral Scientist*, 1977, **21**, 263–287.

2 Biography and Identity[1,2]

LEOPOLD ROSENMAYR

The Growing Interest of the Social Sciences in the Life Course

The study of the life course and the significance of phases and periods of time in life have begun to play a greater role not only in modern sociology but also in the interdisciplinary interests of the social sciences, even in medicine. Several concurrent tendencies have stimulated the present focusing on the life course, which might be summarized as follows.

The impact of historical thought through the widespread introduction (or reintroduction) of Marxism in the social sciences has philosophically enlivened academic sociology. Historical thinking was reintroduced into the social sciences in Europe as a result of the renewed interest in social change and democratic action in the 1960s. On the other hand, the growing application of demographic and sociological methods and concepts in historiography contributed to

1. Background research for this chapter was carried out with the help of the Ludwig Boltzmann Institute for Social Gerontology and Life Span Research, Vienna, Austria.

2. This chapter is a revised version of a paper entitled "Age, Life Span, and Biography," given at the Luxembourg Conference on Aging and the Life Course in Interdisciplinary and Cross-Cultural Perspective, June 18–20, 1979. The revision, however, is a technical one only. Recent literature could not be integrated. As important contributions I should like to mention the following: J. Olney (Ed.), *Autobiography: Essays Theoretical and Critical*, Princeton, New Jersey: Princeton University Press, 1980; and a brief historical sketch of the biographical method in sociology, *Wie es zur "biographischen Methode" kam und was daraus geworden ist. Ein Kapitel aus der Geschichte der Sozialforschung*, a paper by M. Kohli presented at the meetings of the German Sociological Association, Bremen, September 1980.

progress in multidisciplinary research; it furthered a general rap-
prochement of traditional disciplines.

Moreover, a great need for a better understanding of the creative
possibilities of individuals has emerged. While Marxism underlined
the dependence of consciousness on social structure and process,
other historical approaches contributed to the rediscovery of subjectivity of life experiences and the individual's interpretation thereof.
The acceptance of pluralism in values in postindustrial society and
the insecurity of otherwise powerful institutions do not seem to
meet most of the individual's needs for assistance in interpreting a
meaningful life. The less individuals can affect and shape their world,
the more important their needs become to find a "meaning" for their
lives. Such quests lead to some sort of a life course perspective.
"Meaning" can only be found and tested over time.

The world of production, with its rapidly changing requirements
and techniques, demands constant training and retraining. The process of "unlearning" deepens the impression that survival techniques
and coping styles that were useful to the individual 30 years ago have
to be revised. Even existential orientations and the value system
acquired in childhood are no longer reliable; they cannot cope adequately with newly arisen value conflict. A longitudinal view of life
seems to be an appropriate method for establishing the prerequisites
of retraining, of adjustment in later phases of life, preparation for
retirement, and so on. For many practical purposes, the longitudinal
view is also more useful than an approach to problems only at one
point in time.

Many findings of learning theory and of psychoanalysis have
already been utilized by developmental psychology. Freud, in his
"Perpetual Analysis," saw that as a consequence of therapy, a continuously analytical relationship to oneself ought to be developed
(Freud, 1950). The aim is now to relate these thoughts to a larger
social-scientific context and to transform such ideas into sociological
concepts or at least to integrate them into a multidisciplinary approach.

Interactionism, by renewing G. H. Mead's original theories,
relates processes of self-discovery and self-representation to the
creation and recreation of relationships to relevant partners and to
significant others. This interdependence between self and other is
now being viewed in a life course perspective, often in the context of

intergenerational relationships as well as in love and friendship relationships. This explains the otherwise not so obvious theoretical and methodological coalition between life course theorists and the followers of the school of symbolic interactionism.

The interpretation of important social movements and political events, such as the student revolt in the late 1960s, made it necessary to seek the connection between some phases of the life course, on the one hand, and historical conditions on a social macrolevel, on the other. This led to an increasing empirical utilization and theoretical elaboration of the concepts of "cohort" and "generation," from which such a connection between individual and social levels was expected. Currently, this is being developed further. For example, the Italian sociologist Franco Ferrarotti has suggested that individual life courses should not be studied but rather "bunches" of individuals in primary groups since the individual can only be understood in terms of adjustment through group processes (Ferrarotti, 1978). Such concepts of "bunches" also appear in literature and literary historiography. Yuri Trifonov's book *Fires' Reflection* (1966/1979) provides the life courses of his father and uncle, their friends and comrades from the 1905 uprising in Rostow to the October Revolution in 1917 and the fight with the White Russians in the 1920s. Trifonov combines the diaries, telegrams, announcements, and minutes preserved by his father with other archival data. Historical processes become visible through the description of individual life spans and their coordination with personal initiatives and actions in "bunches" of revolutionary careers.

As a result of this example, we may note a more personal understanding and interpretation of the October Revolution processes. There emerges a more correct and individually proven evaluation of the adjacent spheres and subcultures that had been the basis for the world historical process of the revolution: A "preparation" of the chain of events through the learning and the suffering of prerevolutionary groups in Czarist prisons, forced labor camps, and Siberian exile takes on profile.

Explanation of societal movements and upheavals from the historical "rapids" demands documentation from several domains, including the comprehensive structural conditions and the derived milieu affecting disadvantaged individuals and outsiders. The "subjective" reconstruction of the life spans of individuals within these fringe groups (in which motivations are fostered) must be used for understanding what is called social or political change. An inclusive historicosociological explanation brings together the macrosocial structures and the microsocial ensemble of individual developments.

There the mediating notions of cohort and generation no doubt play an important role. Recent studies show, however, that the cohort is a less strictly definable unit than was originally expected and hoped for. Impacts on identical cohorts do not create equal or even similar effects on all members of the cohort (Rosow, 1978). The separation of aging and cohort effects is theoretically necessary and methodologically desirable. The interplay between the dynamics of cohorts and age standards, however, interferes with identifying aging processes. New cohorts tend to change age standards (Rosenmayr, 1980). In addition, it appears to be theoretically more adequate to distinguish not only between (individual) aging, on the one hand, and cohort change, on the other, but to introduce the "period effect" as a third analytical category (Rosenmayr & Allerbeck 1979; Rosenmayr & Rosenmayr, 1978).

Similarly, the concept of generation, the forerunner of the notion of cohort, needs revision. This notion, developed by Wilhelm Dilthey in the 1870s, was changed in meaning and elaborated by Karl Mannheim in the 1920s. It saw a renaissance and has been rediscussed for the last decade after having been neglected for nearly 50 years (Rosenmayr, 1976b). Some 60 years ago Siegfried Bernfeld with a psychoanalytic maturation concept had already emphasized the life phase character of youth: In the period after childhood there is a special plasticity and receptivity to values. In adolescence, according to Bernfeld a phase of value plasticity, basic attitudes are formed that remain for life (Rosenmayr, 1976b). Without referring to the value-plasticity hypothesis, Mannheim advocated the idea that for each new generation there is a new and historically unique approach to culture. The actually existing elements of a culture at any specific time will be taken up, enforced, and internalized by youth. These values then survive over one's entire life. Mannheim in this respect tacitly agreed with the psychoanalytic internalization theory of Bernfeld. Mannheim's view had a major influence on various developmental sociological inquiries during a decade in which simple and sometimes crude empiricism was overcome because of conceptual clarification and empirical contributions by Riley, Foner, and Johnson (Riley & Foner, 1968; Riley, Johnson, & Foner, 1972). Today we have reasons to doubt that values once taken over in youth remain integrated for life to the extent Mannheim expected. Social and cultural change affect life styles and values, and important changes in midlife, like revision and reintegration of values, can no longer be ignored under conditions of social and political pluralism. This necessarily entails the differentiation of the traditional concept of cohort and generation. On the basis of Glen Elder's investigation of historical cohorts during the Great Depression, it is demonstrable that there is no homogeneity in the realization of value legacies. For example, deprivation during the depression years influenced the careers of the 1950s cohort in very different ways, depending on the individual's earlier life histories and environments (Elder, 1974; Elder & Rockwell, 1978).

The search for a sociological personality theory is growing. In France, sociologists referring to the Marxist Lucien Sève have attempted to develop a personality theory based on certain Marxist preconceptions, on the one hand, and on life span research, on the other. Through a sociologically founded conception of personality, institutional identity of individuals and their loyalties might be re-examined. Empirical data from life course research can be used to complete or criticize developmental theory based on Jean Piaget, Lawrence Kohlberg, and Erik Erikson. Important insights into a dynamic personality model may certainly be gained through developmental psychology. The resulting view of invariance in the sequence of the life course, however, is doubtful. Sociological research has attempted to elaborate a variety of types of life phases and life spans, developmental psychology has not (sufficiently) accounted for such variation.

Moral autonomy, the development of self-reliance, and inner security, the capacity for cognitive differentiation, correspond to advantaged developments. Stagnation, "other dependency," and topical "poverty" (economic deprivation, lack of stimulation for intellectual curiosity, unidimensionality of explicatory modes of every day life, and a reductionist, often self-accusing interpretation of basic life events) are typical for disadvantaged development. This can be shown for several life phases. I have addressed this issue with empirical studies of youth, early adulthood, and aging (see Rosenmayr, 1963, 1970, 1976a; Rosenmayr, Köckeis, & Kreutz, 1966; Rosenmayr, Haller, & Szinovácz, 1973; Rosenmayr & Rosenmayr, 1978).

To give an example: when agricultural laborers or domestics in central or eastern Europe began to work as children 60 years ago, their "development" took place under socially deplorable conditions. Their old age is characterized by the historical conditions that affected their childhood and youth, namely, lack of schooling, minimal health education, and often submissiveness to all forms of authority. No wonder that the most underprivileged do not understand and cannot sufficiently take advantage of the opportunities now offered by social and medical care. Paradoxically, those who seem to be most deprived socially and economically, because of their inability to perceive their real condition and their failure to articulate needs, are far from the ones with the highest rate of declared needs and complaints (Attias-Donfut & Gognalons-Caillard, 1976/1980).

Scanty training and deprived early school careers in the lives of today's old, sick people are often the reasons for the failure of these people to contact service institutions. The latter, because they are not adequately structured, cannot offer the potentially existing opportunities for necessary help. Different elements of deprivation have a tendency to add up and to lead to a state of *cumulative deprivation* in old age (Rosenmayr & Majce, 1978).

The internalization of socioeconomic disadvantages and the gradual acceptance of low standards depresses expectations even further and reduces or extinguishes aspirations. The individual, as the last part of this chain of causation, becomes instrumental in his or her own handicap, so that we may speak of "self-induced *social* deprivation." Such a notion is derived from a longitudinal view of aging and is based on the study of social conditions over time. Similarly, studies of the development of young married couples or of households with young members have shown such differentiation. For example, delays in the founding of a household occur in disadvantaged milieus; attitudes toward planning the future and self-determination in the development of the family (including family planning and the use of contraceptives) vary markedly according to social class and context.

Life course considerations are furthered by sociological research tied to social work and social policy. If the sociology of aging is to establish the needs of older people, it is not enough, according to Malcolm L. Johnson, to list "barren responses to swiftly delivered questions about 'what do you need,' delivered by clipboard interviewers eager to press their instant replies into a computer" (Johnson, 1976). To identify the basic problems of elderly people for whom social help is relevant, it is much more important to identify the paths of their life histories through biographical reconstruction. In this way, their present problems and concerns generated by their life histories can be discovered. Even priorities in needs cannot be recognized except through life history. According to Martin Kohli, life histories are necessary for the study of work roles in the aging process, especially in the decade before retiring. In the area of recreational research, Claudine Attias-Donfut has taken a similar position (Kohli, 1978; Attias-Donfut, 1978).

We hope that these approaches will be useful for an understanding of subjective fulfillment. In addition, the understanding of strategies for life satisfaction and happiness makes an investigation into the individual historical life context necessary (Rosenmayr, 1979). My own inquiry into family relations, their quality, and durability has shown that the relationship between grown-up children and aged parents-in-law can only be understood when the history of the relationship including the children's original choice of spouse is studied (Rosenmayr, 1977). In-law relations are economically, socially, and medically relevant to the elderly. The task of caring for the elderly makes it imperative to follow a life course approach under a perspective of clinical sociology.

Life Phases: Their Sociobiological Origin and Determination by the Division of Labor in Society

In order to develop life course theory, the sociologist must deal with the sociostructural determinants of life *phases*. Such a procedure rests on the assumption that the individual life course and even the historical unfolding of cohorts need to be studied in view of what may be called the "axes" of society at a given period. In order to study such fundamental problems we have to turn to sociobiology.

Forms and structures of social organization have a decisive influence on animal as well as human survival and their evolutionary chances. Survival and development of higher animals depend on differentiated experiences and learning processes, which are to be transferred to the young during a life phase when they need the protection of their parents. The higher the development of an organism, the more basic is its need for a socially guaranteed phase during which its learning abilities can be developed.

Human parents live long past their procreative phase. Thus aging as a period for transmitting experience has an important social meaning, even when physical strength of the elders is already declining. Generally speaking, the transmission of experience has, in the history of the division of labor, changed from transmitting a knowledge of physical and economic production to applying a knowledge focussed more on handling the human factor and integrating social existence.

In recent years sociobiological and anthropological studies have added to our understanding of the social nature of aging. We know that in many animal societies life phases are connected with a differentiation of tasks and that this corresponds to the social organization of the respective animal society. In certain primate societies, for example, the Hamadryas baboons, the young males without families have a clear escort function of flanking the horde (Kummer, 1968; Washburn & DeVore, 1961). They are the first ones to be engaged in battle and are generally eaten up when leopards attack. The middle-aged unit leaders with their females and small offspring are well protected in the middle. The few older surviving individuals, again without families, are eventually highly esteemed as qualified food finders or vanguards (Kummer, 1968; Rosenmayr, 1978b).

Human society has developed an extremely long postprocreative phase. No mammals except humans continue to live a significant period after menopause (Campbell, 1974; Portmann, 1969, 1976). Humans have done so for a very long time and have transmitted inherited experience to their offspring who—differing in this respect also from animal species—have the chance to be "young" for a protracted period of time. The interplay of genetic factors with cultural learning in humans created a specific survival profile that proved to be functional to the evolution of intellectual and spiritual capacities and values (Rosenmayr, 1978a).

There seems to be evidence from the developmental physiology of aging that the postreproductive individual confers a survival advantage to younger animals and human individuals (Timiras, 1972). Tribes and families might have had a

> survival advantage if through the thousands of years of selection they had wise members to advise them. Thus the complex trait such as wisdom could have evolved in the period when individual storage of learned information was critical without a written language. . . . The clear inference can be drawn that successful adaptive behaviors in postreproductive organisms have had the potential for determining our genetic heritage. (Birren, 1980, p. 37 ff.)

Different from animal society, the *planned organization of production* for survival (be it even on the level of hunting and early cattle raising or primitive farming) formed a linkage between the genetically determined behavior and the cultural variations that arose. This planned organization or planfully evolving division of labor in the process of production became a prerequisite not only for the reproduction of the race but also for its creativity. The dignity of human aging is not solely based on a moral imperative. It is intimately connected with the phylogenetic destiny of man.

Age is the product of internal social necessities; it is not just the result of a role system in society. The age structure and often conflicting and changing *age norms are derivates of production, instruction, and school systems* at all levels and (at an increasing rate in the development of human history) of the support provided by medicine and social care. Age norms regulate access and are also the result of the power conflict over the fruits of production.

In intergenerational social life, when young individuals become sexually mature before completion of their learning phase and continue to live with their parents, the incest problem must be solved. This was particularly important since in the development of early humans the readiness to mate, to be sexually aroused and to copulate spread out beyond special estrus periods. The compelling result is the introduction of the controls, norms, and regulations that we actually find in the prohibition of incest. With the inception of human culture it is supposed that incest restrictions of and for the family were created gradually (Rosenmayr, 1976b). These norms were necessary because of the overlap of two cohabitating sexually mature generations, one being the offspring of the other, and the younger needing the older for learning the rather elaborate packages of survival techniques and modes of interindividual cooperation.

The prolongation of the learning phase made possible the preparation for production and the application of acquired knowledge. This prolongation was protected—as was the parental generation—by the crucial social regulation of the exogamy rule. This rule played a decisive role in forcing the development of interfamilial exchange. According to Claude Lévi-Strauss and further anthropological literature based on his writings, exogamy was connected with exchange, the introduction of various traditions from outside the group by the marriage to women from another tribe or clan. Culture, according to Lévi-Strauss, is based on such exchange activities. Culture in its origin is viewed as the replacement of accident by the deliberate organization of exchange (Lévi-Strauss, 1949). Generational separation, in order to constitute an exogamous family, is connected with the victory of the incest taboo. Generational cooperation, basic for cultural stability and dynamics, could become a principle only in an exogamous society.

As we have seen, the evolutionary utilization of survival chances determines the structure of phases in the life course. Evolution and division of labor determine which phases can be patterned in which way. Yet at the same time, the representatives of these life phases have to regulate their cooperation and coexistance and must mutually acknowledge their statuses. Not only the establishment of phases and their patterns but also the social interconnection and societal recognition and sanctioning of these phases are dependent upon the development of a society or its subunits. Human beings in their accumulation of power and knowledge, with their manifold reproduction and creativity, produce from this general basis ever new needs as prerequisites for their further development. Patterns that subdivide the life course have to be explained in terms of this societal development. They are designed socially to enable progress, or at least to facilitate new solutions to emerging problems. Therefore, essentially immutable sequences in life spans, that is, uniform periods of aging that appear in different fashions but are "always" occurring, cannot exist for humans. The essential conflicts in aging individuals or between representatives of age groups and generations and their specific prejudices can adequately be understood only in their macro- and microhistorical context and through the changes of social structure and of values.

Social organization tends toward "utilization" and standardization of the biologically anchored yet ontogenetically and phylogenetically modifiable human ages. The assessments especially suited for making the formation of societal structures as well as their changeability visible, is one that considers the division of labor. The latter specifies economic and social productivity and determines the distribution of the biological potential over the phases of the life cycle. The division of labor as it establishes itself through technological development and the (economic) power connected with the control and exploitation of technological progress, designs the division of life spans. Surely, ritual and symbolic interpretation (and the institutionalization thereof) name and sanction "youth," "maturity," "old age," and so on. Yet the *foundations* of life course stages in the division of labor must always be considered for explaining any set of life course or age positions in a given society.

Remarks on the Historical Genesis of New Life Phases

Elsewhere I have tried to exemplify the dependency of life phases on the division of labor in various phases of European history (Rosenmayr & Allerbeck, 1979). Here I will only refer in a sketchy way to the rise of new life phases in the last third of the 19th century in economically developed European societies. In response to pressures from social reformers and the socialist working-class movement there emerged pension legislation that led to the establishment of a new life phase or age category—*retirement age*. At the other end of life, the expansion of primary school was made necessary by the need for greater literacy and new forms of societal organization and administration. The differentiated school system, with the *Gymnasium* and other forms of higher education, were first available only to a numerically limited privileged class; later secondary education became more generally available to the bourgeoisie. This allowed the rise of a second new age category—*adolescence*. Universal compulsory education spread during the last third of the 19th century, often in the face of resistance from the poorest classes who lost their children's income. The chances for transition to secondary education for the upper middle class went up. The state was instrumental in the definition of a fixed period between early childhood and the beginning of the productive phase: schooling began to become more and more general.

In secondary schools some of the most talented pedagogues, imbued with the rising tide of a search for *philosophical renewal*, created the milieu, external to the family, that was fertile ground for the *Lebensphilosophie* containing elements of early existentialism. Also, the pedagogues advocated *corporative self-determination* of life styles for youth. This philosophy contributed to the culture of the youth movement at the beginning of the 20th century. The boy scout movement was by no means the most typical arbiter for the modern meaning of adolescence. To hike, to camp, to sing together in groups—"away" from the family and the school—became a means to find and to articulate oneself together with others of the same age and situation.

The life phase of adolescence thus received special content and value. It was based on protest, self-affirmation, and moral elitism.

The youth movement became a *special social power* that was accepted by the churches and the political forces of the time, and adolescence was recognized as a *special phase* of the human life course (Rosenmayr & Allerbeck, 1979). Student youth had already been acknowledged as a social subgroup much earlier in history, and fractions of it had become a source of conflict with society since the Middle Ages (Rosenmayr, 1976a). Heroic or literary youth (often a blend of both) became key figures of rebellion in the period of romanticism and revolutionary nationalism in central and western Europe and in Russia. The youth movement of the late 19th and early 20th century, a movement of and for adolescents, to some extent used the reputation of medieval students. The values of "migration," of independence and a mercenary type of life were underlined by games and songs; the wearing of uniforms, knives, and so on, gave youth an air of independence. These ideas supported the notion that adolescence was more than just a passage from childhood to adulthood. It became a new category in the spectrum of life phases (Hareven, 1976).

The "favored adolescence" of secondary schools emerged as a period free of work obligations, in this respect similar to the retirement phase. Here one can see very clearly how life phases are connected with the division of labor and with institutional or legislative changes: the school development, following the need of society for certain skills and qualifications was one and the emergence and politically supported legal definition of retirement was the other important determinant of change.

The sociostructural determination of life phases through the division of labor might also prove useful in studying the ambiguities and crises leading to alternative life styles in present-day society. Martin Kohli tried to trace the vaguely defined "midlife crisis"; he sees it as the result of a "discrepancy between aspiration and reality" of which individuals become aware during a certain phase of adulthood. Kohli linked this subjectively felt discrepancy to the conflict between norms of equality and the existence of inequality that production circumstances systematically enforce. In early work life, unrealistic aspirations concerning occupational and social mobility arise, but the disappointment of the aspirations in midlife leads to the manifestation of these social discrepancies within the individual (Kohli, 1977).

According to Kohli, capitalist society does not fulfill the promise it gives to young individuals. Youth does not sufficiently realize career limitations and does not anticipate barriers to occupational fulfillment; the mature person is then afflicted. This is an interesting theoretical conception. Midlife frustrations, however, need to be interpreted in the framework of a more general theory of personality discontinuity, connected with problems of sexual and love relationships. Furthermore it is questionable that work alienation and frustration with careers in midlife are limited to capitalist society. It is true, however, that in Western societies self-interpretations are "coached" through the mass media, the movies and the interpretative subculture of professional sociopsychological diagnosticians. Life styles develop a manipulated dynamics of their own, going far beyond the classical Marxist concept of an interpretative superstructure.

The Changing Bases of Memory: Theoretical and Empirical Issues

We can now extrapolate from the preliminaries of the previous sections: The structural variation in the social division of labor creates "objective chances" for life course subdivisions (life phases) which are subjectively perceived, evaluated, socially approachable, and seized as opportunities.

We must now deal with the recognition of subjectivity, the reconstruction of which William I. Thomas and Florian Znaniecki treated in *The Polish Peasant in Europe and America* at the beginning of this century. There they deplore the difficulties in the study of subjectivity "not only because of the schematic tendencies in our everyday understanding, but also because of the science itself" (Thomas & Znaniecki, 1927). Thomas and Znaniecki suspected that science might be inadequate for approaching and expressing human subjectivity. This was one of the sobering results of their gigantic study. Does this mean that the idea of science should and could be changed to suit the content of biography? Or does it mean that biography and autobiography actually involve dimensions of human creativity that entail a broader notion of science? Even if the notion of science is broadened I suspect there will remain an incompatibility between scientific procedures on the one hand and certain principles of biography on the other. How do we approach this problem?

Wilhelm Dilthey's early conceptualization of subjectivity at the end of the 19th century may still be the best starting point for theorizing about the interpretation of subjectivity and its application to problems of the life course. Dilthey was concerned with biography throughout his own scientific life course. Most of his mature thinking on this subject was expressed during his lectures at the Academy of Sciences in Berlin from 1900 to 1910. These lectures were published posthumously in 1927 in Volume 7 of Dilthey's collected works. Especially relevant are his *Categories of Life* (Dilthey, 1927) and *On Biography* (Dilthey, 1927).

What are the basic theoretical perspectives? Dilthey starts from the assumption that the subjectivity of human experience cannot be defined in objective terms. Life "from within" ought to be considered as a category that cannot be explored any further (Dilthey, 1927). The development of the humanities, based on an understanding of life different from the one developed by the natural sciences, rests on a "deepening of experience" but cannot rigorously explain the content of these experiences (Dilthey, 1927).

To some extent, however, in order to communicate their results, the humanities must "objectify" these experiences. They may achieve this by taking account of a three-pronged process: *experience, expression, and understanding.* Experience is a very precarious process. It is different from "explanation"; it can even be ruined through "observation" and the attempt to explain. Thus, *expression* as the tangible "substance of experience" requires careful consideration (Dilthey, 1927). Expression, through the communication and shaping of the content of experience, becomes something independent and permanent. Starting from these definitions, Dilthey emphasized the use of diaries, poems, letters, and other forms of self-descriptions. Charlotte Bühler and Siegfried Bernfeld, both influenced by Dilthey in their research, some 15 or 20 years later, preferred the "nonobtrusive methods" of collecting such materials to all forms of interviewing (Rosenmayr, 1962; Bernfeld, 1962).

All real *experience*, according to Dilthey, is brought forward from the *self* and is constituted as a part of the self (Dilthey, 1927). The manifold nature of experience relates to the unity of the self. Dilthey did not go on to tell us about philosophical roots of this unity as Kierkegaard or Hegel and Kant had done. Dilthey was content to affirm the "singularness of existence." This claim makes sense in terms of a scientific ethic, one that demands that no scientific effort should establish the illusion of "complete understanding." The idea of singularness and irreplaceability is an important element in Dilthey's approach to the life course: The "meaning of the individual existence" is "totally singular, and as such is not accessible to explanation" (Dilthey, 1927). The unyielding and unexhaustible regard of continuity and the persistence of the individual in respect to his or her own death is ineffable; it is more basic even than hope for an infinite continuation of the self, and it causes this hope to rise (Adorno, 1966).

As a heuristic research principle, this view of singularity does not lead much further, just as the formal establishment of the *general* idea of a unity of experience through a theory of the self does not lead much further. In recent research in which life course narratives are used, the concept of unity of life is frequently represented. But it is not translated into operational and to some extent empirically observable categories like style of problem resolution, of handling loss and despair, of shaping relationships or developing modes of self-reflection. It is the *heterogeneity of experience*, however, the appearance of divergent elements in the life course, happening in different degrees of connectedness with the self, that is necessary for designing life course research.

Methodologically, for Dilthey the life course is closely related to the elaboration of biography and autobiography. Thereby he understood the oral or written *exposure of a connection* that had become visible in the course of time and which had its own *particular actual meaning*. Writing the biography of somebody, for Dilthey, meant *verstehen*, that is, a certain form of selection that he called a tracing of a "formation process out of boundlessness" (cf. Misch, 1931). Autobiography as well as biography (the understanding of self and of the other) must involve an elaborate and laborious effort of the "energy of reflection." This effort is needed for a reconstruction of the constitutive processes of life itself. Reconstruction demands a recall of (selected) "meaningful moments" (Dilthey, 1927).

In much the same way, Sigmund Freud had emphasized psycho-analytic reconstruction of the past as *work*; different from Dilthey, however, Freud had insisted on the guiding principle of association in reconstruction work. The selection of issues has to be done by the patient in cooperation with the therapist, in a dialogue with a trained analyst. And Freud used a theory of personality, dynamics, and development to justify this method, and vice versa.

For Dilthey it was through a reflection directed by some pre-conceived elements of meaning that the past should acquire a "second life" (Dilthey, 1927). Parallels between Dilthey's biographical her-meneutics on the one hand and recollection through psychoanalysis on the other are obvious. Psychoanalysis and *verstehend* biography in their epistemology both focus ideographically on the individual. Yet psychoanalysis elaborated general categories for causal and quasi-causal analysis and thus represents a mixture of understanding and explanation. In psychoanalysis the search for regularities is in the service of operative therapeutic change. Moreover, in psychoanalysis rather rigorous procedures were established. In spite of the differ-ences of psychoanalytic schools, these procedures can be described relatively clearly (Becker, 1975). This is not true for psychological and sociological biography up to now. Dilthey saw biography in the end as *art*. He conceived of understanding as an irreplaceable in-dividual act of, in a way, reliving an experience through deciphering the objective *expression* of this experience. The problem that still re-mains unsolved is how Dilthey's biographical "understanding" could be stretched to include several or even many individuals and how these individuals are to be compared. Such comparison is necessary for sociological and sociopsychological approaches.

In spite of the manifold subtleties of his thinking, Dilthey's study of biography did not escape illusions. Edmund Husserl's theory of the consciousness made a step forward to more refined and critical think-ing about life history. Since 1906 Husserl, in developing his ideas about *roots of memory in actual consciousness*, was concerned with the continuously reciprocal transformation of actuality and inactuality within consciousness. The continuously flowing experiences of the ego, according to Husserl, are surrounded by a medium of inactuality. Consciousness may switch from a modus of actuality to inactuality or vice versa (Husserl, 1976). This oscillation from present to past necessarily has an important bearing on biography and autobiography. Husserl's theory of the intertwining of past and present emphasizes the human capacity to transpose even complex content from actual experience to memory—and to some extent even vice versa. Thus he points up the mutual influence of the actual and the remembered spheres of experience, an interdependency of great importance for biographical research. Important roots of recall are to be sought for in an evaluational frame of actual (present) consciousness. *The mutual or comparable use of biographies or statements about life course must therefore take into consideration the actual situational and structural foundation of the consciousnesses of those who produce statements about their life histories or phases and areas of their past experiences.*

Let us now consider whether (and in which way) this theoretical consideration is borne out by empirical research. We may find some examples in recent studies by Daniel Bertaux and Isabelle Bertaux-Wiame. They have shown that differences in conditions of the actual social situation that individuals live in are interrelated with differences in the retrospective evaluation of life phases. They report the results of their study of two major groups of 60-year-old bakers in France, in which they found important differences between the groups in the verbal representation of their early career phases. The evaluation of the bakers' past depended heavily on whether or not they had managed to become self-employed, that is master or patron. Those who remained in other people's employ described their apprenticeships and early careers differently from those who became self-employed and owners of small family firms. The accounts of those who remained employed, even at age 60, emphasize the important discouraging role that the bullying of their former masters had played in their lives (Bertaux, 1976). Accounts of this sort are completely absent from bakers who became masters. Moreover, in the latter's autobiographical reports all experiences were seen as pivotal to their upward social mobility. This result is not trivial since the alternative hypothesis could also claim to be meaningful, namely, that those who rose to an independent position presented their learning phase as marked by special difficulties. Having been bullied might have created a more effective description of their achieved success. Thus, one would presumably have to take into account the self-aggrandizement of those with higher education who have made significant advances in social mobility. For example, the small shopkeeper's child who becomes a manager in industry, politician, well-known artist, or scientist would paint earlier difficulties in his or her life in very dark colors as a contrasting background to dramatize success.

Other research by Isabelle Bertaux-Wiame should be taken into consideration in the formulation of hypotheses about the different languages used in life course narratives. From her study on bakers, Bertaux-Wiame reports that men use the active "I" more frequently than women, whereas women report situations and scenes. Instead of "I" a woman says "we," as if referring to her husband and herself. Impersonal report forms such as "then *one* could even . . ." dominate among women. The reports by males point out the tendency to present *actions*; the women emphasize *relationships* (Bertaux, 1978).

The results of Bertaux and Morin show the necessity of considering matrices of significance that are present in the personality of the narrators at the time when they describe and analyze their lives (Bertaux, 1976). This finding ties in with Husserl's emphasis on the actual consciousness as a frame for recall to open up theoretical perspectives for biography, which we have discussed earlier. But from Husserl we cannot learn *how* the significance matrix is constituted. On the one hand, it takes place through the socialization of individuals, the sociologically influenced life situations they are going through, and the life practices resulting therefrom. On the other hand, the significance matrix is being constituted through a continually reformulated self-image. There is a circular process between the *significance matrix*, on the one hand, and the results of the *remembrance processes*, on the other. He who *remembers* with the intention to discover himself also *changes* his self-image, when and if defense mechanisms permit him to do so. The changed self-image leads to changes of the significance matrix and thus to new perspectives for recall.

New values may enable people to see new facets of their past. This may bring about new elements for the significance matrix, new remembrance processes, and perhaps further changes. Remembering is psychological *action* not just passive mirroring.

From what has been said so far, it should be clear that the subjective data of interpreting self-reports are of a high psychosocial complexity that social researchers must study along with the content of the reports. If only the latter is studied, this analysis risks violating an important principle of psychological and historical method: of relating "all data" to the "context" they originate from. In biographical or oral history research, the historical and social context of the "lived life" is often accounted for, but not the historicosocial context of the "reporting situation." It may lead to basic errors if people are taken in the historical and sociological context at the time only *on* which and not *in* which they report.

To summarize, the life course method may be unmanageable and confusing, especially with a large number of individuals, unless a very carefully worked out research goal and data analysis are established for the material evoked. This is true especially when theoretical concepts are available but not precise enough, such that a gulf exists between theory and data (Gagnon & Jean, 1975). Combined methods of biographical techniques and enlarged questionnaires are recommended. Difficulties with biographies reappear in oral history research. Even with personnel who are scientifically trained in the documentation of life history, theoretical preconceptions will develop an enormous self-momentum, resulting in a heterogeneity of results. To illustrate, some interviewers emphasize everyday occurrences, others stimulate statements about value problems (Gagnon & Jean, 1975). Furthermore, the life history method using biographical and autobiographical materials for a considerable number of people shows a surprising paucity of statements. Thus, in a review of a Canadian research project at the Institute for Human Sciences of the University of Laval, Louis Morin (1974) remarked on the paucity of information and the repetitiveness of personal narratives. We are reminded of the reasons that led Paul Lazarsfeld, for example, to return to the questionnaire in his study of proletarian life course development in Vienna in the 1920s, although he had been a disciple of Charlotte Bühler and Siegfried Bernfeld who emphasized biographic and unobtrusive methods (Rosenmayr, 1962, 1976b). Similarily, Samuel A. Stouffer switched from qualitative biographical methods to quantitative research on the basis of his familiarity with the shortcomings of results obtained by Thomas and Znaniecki in their studies of the Polish peasant (Paul, 1979).

Life course analysis need not necessarily be approached only by biographic methodology. Age-group comparison or longitudinal research using questionnaires including projective techniques permit the investigation of class- and milieu-specific forms of development (Rosenmayr & Allerbeck, 1979). On the basis of such methods it becomes possible to study origins and conditions of cumulative disadvantages in developmental and aging processes. This can be shown by various types of data. Demographic, survey, and longitudinal research point out how disadvantages cumulate, how they may become internalized, and even how they lead to self-destructive processes (Rosenmayr & Majce, 1978). Sociological research thus cannot refrain from quantitative perspectives and methods. Life course research has to be defined as one of a mixture of quantitative and qualitative research and the relationships of the two to each other. This latter aspect of the problem is the crucial one, and the topical and theoretical bridge between quantitative and qualitative elements is difficult to build.

In the study of cumulative disadvantages, low income and a bad state of health often lead to avoidance–wastage behavior. Examples are never consulting a physician, ignoring medical advice or not following dietary regulations, buying unnecessary gadgets, spending foolishly after persuasion. This self-infliction, however, is socially dependent: In the course of the lifelong socialization processes, class-specific attitudes are developed that may be substantial impediments to planned and rational behavior from which the individual might have benefited, or might still benefit, given different social encouragement and support.

The social devaluation not only generally reduces the chances of social participation and of access to resources, but it also works as a multiplication of factors in terms of *cumulative disadvantages* of the economically weakest and socially most isolated groups of the aged (Rosenmayr, 1976c; Rosenmayr & Majce, 1978). Differences among socioeconomic strata are thus greater among the elderly than among the younger- and middle-aged cohorts. This is because of greater differences in their *initial* social situations and of biographically created conditions that lead to a progressive reduction of chances of the deprived of coping with their aging processes. The state of health is substantially worse in the lower socioeconomic classes, and the difficulty of activating the deprived, be it in their ecological setting, in medical institutions, in clubs of the aged, or day centers, becomes obvious.

The deprived tend to retreat to the social fringes. Applying the concepts of *socially dependent self-infliction* and the mechanism of *cumulative deprivation* (Rosenmayr & Majce, 1978) to the isolated widowed, we show that these groups practically never go on a vacation, often are too weak to move, and lack the initiative to leave their usually poor living environment. In cases where help is needed most, it is usually most expensive, most time consuming, and most difficult to furnish. The greater the need in one dimension, the more this need is coupled to other types of deficiencies. The resources of society are being wasted because of the self-inflicted, society-dependent resistance against individual intentions to help and because helpful social action is not being properly realized. Cumulative deprivation is *multifactorial* (bad health, poverty, low education, little access to resources, low mobility, psychic depressiveness, etc.) and longitudinal, that is, the result of drawn out processes that have added up.

Conceptual and Methodological Intricacies
of the Biographical Approach

After having underlined the necessity of continuing the effort to relate mutually quantitative life course data and nonquantifiable biographic methods in social research, I now want to turn to some special problems of biography in the hands of social scientists. We will again consider Bertaux who proposes to redefine sociological biography by overcoming what he calls the "ideology of biography."

Bertaux criticizes the "unity" postulate of the total life as a singular, coherent destiny. While we may agree with him on that, we should admit that there are *aspects* of unity that may be found, for example in coping styles, or in various areas of attitudes toward life, or in structural interconnections of problem solving in different life sectors. *Coherence* (in the sense of a certain form of unity) may bind together divergent obligations of public and private spheres of a subject. Integrative efforts to overcome discrepancies between the demands of various personally desirable activities, reconciling one set of aspirations with another, are forms or aspects of unity. It is justified to speak of *integrative tendencies* and to show them empirically rather than reify "life as a unity." Another aspect of the concept of unity is *continuity*, which may also be operationalized. Continuities may prevail as forms of self-perception and self-disclosure among individual informants. Continuities exist according to the values that subjects report directly or implicitly in speaking about their religious experience, work, family, or other aspects of their personal lives. Integrative aspects and/or continuities may lie in the *style* and *manner* of remembering, in the *verbal representation* of remembrance. Integration may attempt to *combine various segments* or fields of experience and action. Both integration and continuity may be because of an ascription of an (explicit) *meaning* as a linkage with one's past or in the search for *"threads" in the life course*, and thus in the establishment of a meaningful relationship between life phases. One may regret, as Erik Erikson does, that our civilization does not harbor a concept of the whole of life (Hareven, 1976). This certainly is a pertinent topic for future theoretical developments of the life course.

Bertaux would like to see biographies written not of persons or destinies in isolation but individuals tied up in class relations and determined by these: "Une vie particulière n'est que l'effet des rapports sociaux." I cannot agree with this type of reductionism. We may start as Bertaux does, with Marx's polemic directed against Feuerbach, namely, denying the idea of an abstract, unhistorical human nature because it does not express the social association abilities of individuals. Even if we want to see the individual "in his reality as an ensemble of the societal conditions" (sixth thesis of Marx against Feuerbach, 1845), however, we must not dispute the individual's ability to focus and form societal influences (third thesis).

The "ensemble" of the person, as Marx characterized it, is the "sensual human" and "practical–critical activity" (first thesis). The individual according to Marx is not just the result of mirroring or of coining processes of society (third thesis against Feuerbach). With the increase of mass education, the widening of the scope of choice behavior, of options offered—and even if only in a stereotyped form through mass media and commercialism—new life styles are created and thus new expectations and needs, which in turn cannot be overlooked in economics, the consumer market, and also in politics. In this way preferences based on values obtain historical momentum. New cohorts are capable of opening new types of approaches to culture, as Karl Mannheim stated. For a theory of the life course the concept of "formability," introduced in the discussion by Dilthey, has to be taken into account, along with an understanding of personal tensions and dynamics, as obtained by psychoanalysis describing the introjection of social reality into personal life. Instead of id, ego may develop, and the superego may in principle be revised. Resources and capabilities for selection and intrapersonal revision are, however, unequally distributed. Such capabilities must therefore be examined sociologically, as has already been emphasized in our discussion of different social paths of development, particularly with reference to cumulative effects of deprivation.

Finally Bertaux suggests a careful consideration and working out of what he calls *troncons*, that is, portions or chunks of the life span. Bertaux sees the continuity between such life span *troncons* in an individual's specific constellation of social relationships. Dividing lines *between* the chunks of the life span may range from entering or leaving school, getting married, joining a political or ideological organization or leaving it, suffering from blows of an accident or from a severe illness.

Furthermore, institutional obligations in occupational or political life ought to be studied as related to the *whole* network of personal relations of the individual. Change in institutional obligations of the individual may create significant life phase divisions. I would suggest that this cannot be determined without knowing how the subject *interprets* such changes. To be firmly grounded in the important and meaningful companionship of a marriage and in friendship reference groups may permit a more relaxed view of being exposed to the changes of forced retirement. All important issues of health, economics, and power changes are experienced and evaluated individually. This perception and evaluation, however, is not independent of the emotional resources available in and through significant others. Macrohistorical events (such as the outbreak of wars, revolutions, important changes in government and styles of policy) may create important divisions in the life course of individuals. The interplay between macro and micro levels is important to be aware of, and we increasingly need to define it.

Cross-sectional subdivisions in the life course are a necessary complement to longitudinal subdivisions in chunks and life phases. The mere classification of sections may seem trivial if, for example, a professional career is sectionally compared to the family career. The question of *complementarity* or *polarization* in the sectional careers of one and the same person (or of a group in various sections of their lives), however, permits the formulation of more concrete hypotheses. The consideration of *alternative "careers"* in the life span ought to play an important role in interdisciplinary research on aging, especially in view of rehabilitation problems. How can, for example, an especially ego-involved career in athletics, emotionally characterized by a strong socially approved self-image, be compensated when sickness or physical handicaps appear? This may still be more dramatic if the physical capacities (in the case of a dancer or singer) are profoundly connected with his or her sense of creative obligation and self-fulfillment. Resources to develop an *inner distance* are required, as J. Munnichs asserts. The problem cannot be reduced to simple substitution of one activity by another. Here we hit upon the question of a psychosociological "flexibility" (Munnichs, 1979), the capability for emotional balance, the identification with new tasks and groups and their aims.

The necessity *of balancing and revising the fields of activities in career, family, and other ego-involved relationships* ought to become a special field of study. Reorientation ought to be connected with self-determination in the second half of life. Which sectional careers, or life course threads, as I would like to call them, are especially relevant to self-esteem? Are they those that are socially visible and supported through *public* recognition? Or perhaps they are areas of *intimate* experience that are only known to the individual or to a very small group? Which possibilities for exchangeability, for the shifting of self-satisfactory activities from one area to another arise? Does education—as I would assume—influence the ability to "shift"? How is it possible to shift emphasis (and satisfaction) from one sectional area (for example, professional recognition) already established and well known to the individual to others to be newly created or revived by the individual? Under which social conditions of emotional "support," for example, mutually rewarding partnership and friendships, may a shifting or switching of activities occur? Can predictions about specific flexibilities be made for certain professional groups, educational levels, and cultural levels? Do ethnic backgrounds and other sociocultural traits determine chances of transitions? Which theoretical understanding proves to be useful in overcoming inhibitions and blocks in the process of self-fulfillment? Can psychoanalysis be useful in a theory of value change as it helps to explain superego revision?

If we accept these multidisciplinary considerations, life course research leads to general concepts and hypotheses of developmental psychology and sociology. Widely known models like those by Erik Erikson and Lawrence Kohlberg have been taken over into the sociological discussion of identity (Habermas, 1976). The dominant theory of identity, particularly as linked to the Eriksonian model, implies a rather a-historical anthropology. It requires a single, even if complex, *invariant model* with quasinormative fixed consequences. This, however, stands in contradiction to the empirically founded sociological hypotheses of life course research that stipulates the *societally dependent self-formation that varies greatly according to different social contexts, social class, networks, and so on.*

Many new insights that have come from aging research and social gerontology show that Erikson's normative formula of "integrity versus doubts and disgust" as a psychomoral assignment for the advanced phase of the second half of life is not free from subtle regressiveness. Even with health or social handicaps, activation with the necessary inner and outer encouragements *and* the consent of the individual concerned has to be induced in order to achieve "integration" (Rosenmayr & Rosenmayr, 1978). This seems to be important for intellectual and emotional developments and also for attitudes and behaviors concerning rehabilitation and health issues in the broadest sense. Metamorphosis may become an important notion to describe both the necessity of transitions and of the creation and the conscious integration of a *new* Gestalt, a *new* configuration of attitudes, behavior, and life style related to the self. Integration alone is not enough. Renewal as revision, rejection of earlier life habits (Rosenmayr, 1978a), perusal of freshly introduced aims is the agent to achieve the "meta" in the complex expectation and hope necessary to achieve metamorphosis.

REFERENCES

Adorno, T. W. *Negative Dialektik*. Frankfurt/Main: Suhrkamp, 1966.
Attias-Donfut, C. Freizeit, Lebenslauf, und Generationenbildung. In L. Rosenmayr (Ed.), *Die menschlichen Lebensalter: Kontinuität und Krisen*. Munich: Piper, 1978.
Attias-Donfut, C., & Gognalons-Caillard, M. *Nouvelles données d'une politique de la vieillesse*. Paris, August 1976 (mimeo.). (Now published under the title: Attias-Donfut, C., & Gognalons-Nicolet, M. Après 50 ans la redistribution des inégalités. *Documents d'Information et de Gestion*, 1980, No. 46–47.)
Becker, A. M. Psychoanalyse (in chapter "Techniken"). In H. Strotzka (Ed.), *Psychotherapie: Grundlagen, Verfahren, Indikationen*. Munich–Berlin–Vienna: Urban & Schwarzenberg, 1975.
Bernfeld, S. Ein Institut für Psychologie und Soziologie der Jugend (Archiv für Jugendkultur): Entwurf zu einem Programm (1917). Reprinted in L. Rosenmayr, *Geschichte der Jugendforschung in Österreich*. Vienna: Österreichisches Institut für Jugendkunde, 1962.
Bertaux, D. Histoire de vie—ou récits de pratiques? *Convention C.O.R.D.E.S.*, 1971, No. 23 (mimeo.). (Final report [Vol. 1], 1976.)
Bertaux, D. On the working paper by I. Bertaux, in the reports on the working group "Biography" at the Ninth World Congress of Sociology, Uppsala, August 1978. *MHS Informations*, Bulletin de la Fondation Maison de Sciences de l'Homme, November 1978, No. 26 (mimeo.).
Birren, J. E. Progress in research on aging in the behavioral and social sciences. *Human Development*, 1980, **23**, 33–45.
Campbell, B. G. *Human evolution: An introduction to man's adaptations*. Chicago: Aldine, 1974.
Dilthey, W. *Gesammelte Schriften* (Vol. 7). Leipzig–Berlin: Teubner, 1927.
Elder, G. H. *Children of the Great Depression*. Chicago: University of Chicago Press, 1974.
Elder, G. H., & Rockwell, R. C. Historische Zeit im Lebenslauf. In M. Kohli (Ed.), *Soziologie des Lebenslaufs*. Neuwied: Luchterhand, 1978.
Ferrarotti, F. *Sur l'autonomie de la méthode biographique*. Contribution to the ad hoc working group "L'approche Biographique" at the Ninth World Congress of Sociology, Uppsala, August 1978 (mimeo.).
Freud, S. Die endliche und unendliche Analyse. In *Gesammelte Werke* (Vol 16). Frankfurt/Main: S. Fischer, 1950.
Gagnon, N., & Jean, B. Les histoires de vie et la transformation du Québec contemporain. *Sound Heritage*, 1975, **4**, 1 (Review of Oral History, Provincial Archives of British Columbia, Victoria, B.C., Canada).
Habermas, J. *Zur Rekonstruktion des Historischen Materialismus*. Frankfurt/Main: Suhrkamp, 1976.
Hareven, T. The last stage: Historical adulthood in old age. *Daedalus*, 1976, **Fall**, 13–27.
Husserl, E. *Husserliana* (Vol. 3/1). The Hague: Nijhoff, 1976. (First edition, 1913.)

Johnson, M. L. That was your life: A biographical approach to later life. In J. M. A. Munnichs & W. van den Heuvel (Eds.), *Dependency or interdependency in old age.* The Hague: Nijhoff, 1976.

Kohli, M. Lebenslauf und Lebensmitte. *Kölner Zeitschrift für Soziologie und Sozialpsychologie,* 1977, **29**, 625–656.

Kohli, M. Unpublished research exposé, 1978.

Kummer, H. *Social organization of Hamadryas baboons: A field study.* Basel–New York: Karger, 1968.

Lévi-Strauss, C. *Les formes élémentaires de la parenté.* Paris: Presses Universitaires de France, 1949.

Misch, G. *Lebensphilosophie und Phänomenologie.* Leipzig–Berlin: Teubner, 1931.

Morin, L. Première lecture exploratoire d'un sous-échantillon d'histoires de vie, mise au point d'une stratégie d'analyse. *Cahier de l'ISSH,* 1974, **13**.

Munnichs, J. M. A. Orientierungen bzw. Modelle der Psycho-Gerontologie. Ein kurzer Überblick. *Aktuelle Gerontologie,* 1979, **9**, 191.

Paul, S. *Begegnungen: Zur Geschichte persönlicher Dokumente in Ethnologie, Soziologie, Psychologie* (Vol. 1). Hohenschäftlarn: Renner, 1979.

Portmann, A. *Biologische Fragmente zu einer Lehre vom Menschen.* Basel–Stuttgart: Schwabe, 1969.

Portmann, A. *An den Grenzen des Wissens: Vom Beitrag der Biologie zu einem neuen Weltbild.* Vienna–Düsseldorf: Econ, 1974.

Riley, M. W., & Foner, A. *Aging and society: An inventory of research findings* (Vol. 1). New York: Russell Sage Foundation, 1968.

Riley, M. W., Johnson, M., & Foner, A. *Aging and society: A sociology of age stratification* (Vol. 3). New York: Russell Sage Foundation, 1972.

Rosenmayr, L. *Geschichte der Jugendforschung in Österreich.* Vienna: Österreichisches Institut für Jugendkunde, 1962.

Rosenmayr, L. *Familienbeziehungen und Freizeitgewohnheiten jugendlicher Arbeiter.* Vienna: Verlag für Geschichte und Politik, 1963.

Rosenmayr, L. Cultural poverty of working class youth. In P. Townsend (Ed.), *A concept of poverty.* London: Heinemann, 1970.

Rosenmayr, L. Schwerpunkte der Soziologie des Alters (Gerosoziologie). In R. König (Ed.), *Handbuch der empirischen Sozialforschung* (Vol. 7). Stuttgart: Enke, 1976. (a)

Rosenmayr, L. Jugend. In R. König (Ed.), *Handbuch der empirischen Sozialforschung* (Vol. 6). Stuttgart: Enke, 1976. (b)

Rosenmayr, L. Die soziale Benachteiligung älterer Menschen. In W. Doberauer (Ed.), *Scriptum Geriatricum.* Munich–Berlin–Vienna: Urban & Schwarzenberg, 1976. (c)

Rosenmayr, L. Über das "Anwendbarkeitsdefizit" der Soziologie. In A. M. Becker & L. Reiter (Eds.), *Psychotherapie als Denken und Handeln.* Munich: Kindler, 1977.

Rosenmayr, L. Fragmente zu einer sozialwissenschaftlichen Theorie der Lebensalter. In L. Rosenmayr (Ed.), *Die menschlichen Lebensalter: Kontinuität und Krisen.* Munich: Piper, 1978. (a)

Rosenmayr, L. Die soziale Bewertung der alten Menschen. In L. Rosenmayr & H. Rosenmayr (Eds.), *Der alte Mensch in der Gesellschaft.* Reinbek: Rowohlt, 1978. (b)

Rosenmayr, L. Progress and unresolved problems in socio-gerontological theory. *Aktuelle Gerontologie,* 1979, **9**, 197–205.

Rosenmayr, L. Achievements, doubts and prospects of the sociology of aging. *Human Development,* 1980, **23**, 46–62.

Rosenmayr, L., & Allerbeck, K. (with a contribution by M. von Freyhold). Youth and society. *Current Sociology,* 1979, **27/2–3**, 1–335.

Rosenmayr, L., Haller, M., & Szinovácz, M. *Barrieren im beruflichen Aufstieg.* Vienna: Bundesministerium für Soziale Verwaltung, 1973.

Rosenmayr, L., Köckeis, E., & Kreutz, H. *Kulturelle Interessen von Jugendlichen.* Munich: Juventa, 1966.

Rosenmayr, L., & Majce, G. Die soziale Benachteiligung. In L. Rosenmayr & H. Rosenmayr (Eds.), *Der alte Mensch in der Gesellschaft.* Reinbek: Rowohlt, 1978.

Rosenmayr, L., & Rosenmayr, H. (Eds.). *Der alte Mensch in der Gesellschaft.* Reinbek: Rowohlt, 1978.

Rosow, I. What is a cohort and why? *Human Development*, 1978, **21**, 65–75.

Thomas, W. I., & Znaniecki, F. *The Polish peasant in Europe and America* (2nd ed; 2 vols.). New York: Knopf, 1927.

Timiras, P. S. *Developmental physiology and aging.* New York: Macmillan, 1972.

Trifonov, Y. *Widerschein des Feuers [Fires' reflection].* Neuwied: Luchterhand, 1979. (First edition, Moscow, 1966.)

Washburn, S. L., & DeVore, I. Social behavior of baboons and early man. In S. L. Washburn (Ed.), *Social life of early man.* Chicago: Viking Fund Publications in Anthropology, 1961.

3 Discontinuities in the Study of Aging

LEONARD I. PEARLIN

In recent years there has been a remarkable expansion of research on aging and the life course. This surge of interest has undoubtedly extended and enriched our knowledge, but it has also added confusion and conflict. Indeed, this is precisely what might be expected when a field is going through intense growth, for in these circumstances competing strategies for research are likely to surface, agreement concerning the identification of important issues becomes increasingly difficult to find, and an overproduction of new concepts that are difficult to distinguish from old concepts occurs. Furthermore, intellectual growing pains are particularly pronounced when the field attracts scholars from a variety of academic backgrounds. Though such developments need not be viewed with either surprise or alarm, they do impose a constant challenge to reappraise what we think we know, to strive after greater conceptual clarity, and to disentangle our assumptions, no matter how plausible and reasonable they may seem to us, from our systematically verified knowledge.

Clearly, it is necessary to pause occasionally and to take stock of past efforts and future goals. This chapter represents such a pause—a brief and modest one. It questions some of the ways we think about aging processes and the ways we commonly go about studying them. It focuses on three issues: first, the nature of the interconnections between life cycle transitions and the aging process; second, the need for certain comparative strategies in research on aging; and, third, the incorporation of coping and social support into our efforts to form an overview of the life course.

Research Perspectives

My own understanding of aging and the life course has to a large extent grown out of my longitudinal research on the social origins of stress. In observing strains and stresses as they surface and recede through time, I found that I was also observing important elements in the aging process. Since my discussions in this chapter draw heavily from my research, a brief discussion of its aims and substance is useful.

A fundamental goal of the work on stress is the identification of social circumstances that contribute to various forms of psychological distress. In pursuing this goal, my co-workers and I sought to ground the research in the actual experiences and perceptions of people, and for this reason we conducted a large number of exploratory interviews. It became evident from these interviews that an important source of psychological disturbance is typically overlooked by investigations of social stress, specifically, the low-keyed and rather chronic problems and conflicts that people often experience within the context of normal social roles. The relatively durable hardships and frustrations that arise out of being a worker and breadwinner or a marriage partner and parent, for example, can have a profound effect on psychological well-being. In 1972 we surveyed a large sample of people, with much of our interview schedule organized around the assessment of the relatively persistent strains that people encounter in their major social roles. The sample consisted of 2300 people representative of people from the Chicago area between the ages of 18 and 65.

Four years after the first inquiry we conducted a follow-up interview with a subsample of the same respondents. Many of the questions asked initially were repeated, thus enabling us to evaluate changes in the problems people were experiencing in their various social roles. The second interview was expanded, however, to include questions about a variety of life events. A number of these events are closely linked to the life cycle, such as marriage, birth of children, departure of children from the parental household, and death of a spouse. Interwoven with such family changes are the occupational transitions that are normally involved in movement into and out of the labor force. These family and occupational events typically involve transitions from one role or status to another. Transitional events involve experiences in moving between roles as opposed to the more chronic strains which involve experiences within roles.

Since transitional events are intimately connected to highly scheduled life cycle changes, there can be found among the members of a society a remarkable normative consensus about the optimum timing of such events (Neugarten, Moore, & Lowe, 1965).

Events that are bound to family transitions represent only one part of the range of events to which people are exposed. There are also the more eruptive and less predictable events of life, which stand in sharp contrast to the normative events that can be forecast far in advance of their actual occurrence. Being the victim of an accident or of a crime are rather extreme examples of unforeseen life events that stand outside scheduled transitions. But even those events that are more common, such as divorce or illness, can be considered as unscheduled. Although events of this type may be widespread and although they may not descend on us entirely without warning, we still do not plan for such exigencies in the same way that many people plan some day to be married and have children. A number of questions in the follow-up interview were designed to learn which less predictable events had been experienced by respondents during the preceding four years.

In sum, we have information about relatively durable strains that extend through daily life; about scheduled, transitional life events; and about some of the less-expected, unscheduled vicissitudes that people often experience. Together, these constitute the important forces that can converge on people and affect their well-being.

This three-part conceptual distinction of the types of conditions that regulate emotional well being has been analytically useful in several respects (Pearlin & Lieberman, 1979). In addition, one of its major aims is to provide an alternative to the usual inventories of life events (Holmes & Rahe, 1967) that tend to treat important social experiences as a series of unrelated random events. What is needed, of course, is a schema that goes beyond the mere enumeration of a host of events and seeks, instead, an understanding of how experience is organized through time and space. Indeed, I shall be arguing below that having an experience is only part of the story; the other, and equally important part, is how the experience becomes organized with other elements of life. It is the way it is organized that determines the effects that the experience will have.

In attempting to identify sources of psychological distress—the major goal of our research—it is necessary to ask not only what the hardships are that people experience but also how they deal with these hardships. Predictions of distress based solely on knowledge of the problems and frustrations people face are at best incomplete. People's coping repertoires and their access to and use of support systems are capable of blunting some of the distressful consequences of life problems. Thus, psychological functioning through the life course depends not only on the circumstances that impinge on people at any point in time or the changes that occur across time, but also on the adjustments and responses to these circumstances and changes. For these reasons our work devotes considerable effort to learning how people attempt to intervene in their own behalf when confronted with the challenges and vicissitudes of life. A more detailed discussion of some of these issues is presented later.

I would like to emphasize that I shall not be presenting a systematic or comprehensive report of our work. Instead, I shall selectively draw upon those of our findings that bear most directly on the issues I wish to address.

Adult Development and Family Development

The first issue concerns the connections between family cycle and processes of individual aging and development. It makes good sense to link the aging of individuals to the clearly defined stages of family development (Hill, 1964). There is, first of all, a close correlation between age and family transformations, despite the variations that have been observed in the timing of family stages (Elder & Rockwell, 1976). Consequently, the different family transitions come to be distinctly associated with broad age groups. We are married and have children when we are young; we typically see our children leave home in the middle part of our lives; and we become widows or widowers usually when we are old. With these kinds of connections existing between the individual life cycle and the family cycle, it is small wonder that when we think of one we are likely to think of the other. It is difficult to be interested in aging without also being interested in the phases of family life.

Many of the transitions and changes that take place in the normal course of the family cycle carry with them dramatic changes in the structure of the family. It is obvious that having a child and launching a child, for example, are really quite pivotal events in transforming family organization. While the impact of these events on the family structure is obvious, however, their impact on the emotional development of individuals is less clear. In fact, the many studies that examine the linkages between family transitions and their psychological effects report inconsistent results (Burr, 1972; Dyer, 1963; Glenn, 1975; Hobbs, 1976; Lopata, 1975; Russell, 1974; Spanier, 1975). Our own data, though, through which we are able to assess a variety of states of emotional distress, show that transitional events have little or no effect. As reported elsewhere (Pearlin, 1980b), extensive analyses reveal that transitions such as being married, giving birth, seeing a child enter school, having a child leave home, and becoming a grandparent are unrelated to changes in emotional states. It makes no difference, furthermore, whether a first, middle, or last born is involved in the transition. In each instance, no emotional consequences of family transitions can be detected.

Among the several psychological states that we measure, depression holds some special interest, for it has been shown to vary closely with a number of social and economic circumstances (Pearlin, 1975; Pearlin & Johnson, 1977). Nevertheless, when we evaluate the impact of transitions on depression, the only one discovered to elevate it appreciably is being widowed. Anxiety, another psychological state highly responsive to environmental conditions, is even more impervious to transitions than is depression, for there is no family transformation associated with the elevation of this dimension of distress. Thus, conditions that make us sad do not necessarily also make us nervous.

In a separate analysis, Menaghan (1978) traced the consequences of family transitions, not on the psychological functioning of individuals but on the quality of their marital relations. She scrutinized the family transitions, looking for possible effects on elements of marriage such as the exchange of affection, reciprocity, and the fulfillment of role expectations by one's spouse. She found that in the marital domain (as with psychological functioning) transitions are essentially without impact.

Finally, we explored the possibility that the transitions, even if they do not affect emotional distress or marriage, may still have important influence in the realm of self-attitudes. In order to assess this possibility, we sought to learn if self-esteem and mastery fluctuate with family change. In neither case did we find that transitions have an appreciable influence.

What do these results indicate about family transitions in relationship to developmental changes and aging? They certainly suggest that it would be easy to attribute to these transitions more capacity to affect our psychological well-being than they possess in reality. Everything we are learning indicates that the role gains and losses that are entailed in family transitions do not, with some limited exception, explain alterations in the emotional well-being of individuals, in their marital relations, or in shifts in their self-attitudes. Perhaps this should come as no surprise. Elsewhere (Pearlin, 1980a) I have emphasized that because family transitions are scheduled life events, adjustments to them are able to take place far in advance of the events themselves. Although the experiences we actually encounter in a new role may be quite discontinuous with our earlier preparation and socialization for the role (Benedict, 1938), we are not likely to confront circumstances that were completely unforeseen prior to the transition. On the contrary, the data indicate that these scheduled, family transitions are typically taken in emotional stride.

But in pointing out that family transitions are generally unrelated to emotional well-being, to marital discord, or to key self-attitudes, I do not mean to suggest that they are unimportant events in the lives of people. They might produce some short-lived effects that cannot be observed by ordinary longitudinal studies, or their effects may be so slowly cumulative that they escape observation. We also cannot determine how family changes may influence functioning that is not embedded within the boundaries of our work. We know nothing, for example, of how alterations in values or in goals and aspirations might follow from alterations in family structure. Similarly, it seems plausible that some transitions would help to shape our judgments of how much time we have left to live. It is even more certain that as children mature and eventually leave the parental household, the increased availability of time, energy, and resources can result in altering parental life styles. The significant issue here, then, is not that family transitions are of no consequence to aging but that the particular consequences they might have need to be specified and observed. They cannot be assumed to be so pervasive that they cut across all important aspects of people's lives.

In order to detect whatever influence transitions do have on the lives of people, we need to consider not only where people are located in the life cycle but also the experiences they are having as a result of their locations. Let us consider widowhood as an example. Previously, I noted that of all the transitional events examined, this is the only one found to be related to an increase in depression. There are certain factors that come to mind as significantly contributing to this relationship. First, widowhood usually involves the loss of an important relationship, and, second, it involves movement out of one status and into another one, movement that by itself may test the adjustment capacities of people. But it often happens that along with widowhood there are also alterations in the social and economic foundations of our lives, and we have some indication (Pearlin & Lieberman, 1979) that it is the adverse changes in the more persistent conditions of life that account for much of the depression that accompanies widowhood. Below, I will discuss the ways people are affected by changes and events in their lives; the point here is that family transitions should neither be accepted nor rejected as representing crucial junctures in aging and development. Instead, we should consider this an empirical question, without taking for granted that because transitions involve major family transformations they must also result in major psychological transformations. We also should not assume that the effects of family transitions are universal; on the contrary, there is every reason to believe that the same transitions can have very different effects under different social and economic conditions.

The Study of Aging versus the Study of Ages

Within the rather vast terrain covered by the field of human development there is an established tradition of dividing research turf according to the ages of people being studied. Infants have been a constant favorite; adolescents have had a fair share of attention; the aged were discovered some time ago and seem to be riding a wave of rediscovery; the middle aged seem to be the group most recently recognized. This division of the life span into age groups has produced a rather large body of knowledge. But it also may have produced some problems.

Most important is that in separating out specific age groups for study, the development of theories and the accumulation of information having some general relevance to the total life span are made more difficult. If there are processes extending through the entirety of life—or large portions of it—they cannot be captured by placing side by side studies of different age groups, each addressing itself to different problems and using different conceptual frameworks. Such studies tend to look for conditions and experiences thought to be unique to the group under observation. And even if the conditions and experiences are really not unique, we may think they are simply because the design of the research permits no opportunities for comparing one age group with another. Whatever gains might result from the focused study of particular age groups, there are losses to be considered, too.

Some of these losses stand out with special clarity in research into the crises and transitions of the middle aged (Gould, 1972; Levinson, Darrow, Klein, Levinson, & McKee, 1978; Sheehy, 1976; Vaillant, 1977). There is no doubt that there are particular types of crises experienced by people who are in the midrange of their lives. What is doubtful are suggestions that crises are especially likely to surface in the middle part of the life span or that they are somehow more severe than those arising at other times in adult life. Within the limits of the life strains we are able to examine, middle age simply does not emerge as the age at which people are outstandingly exposed or vulnerable to problems and crises. Indeed, although it cannot be described as a quiescent period, it is actually less demanding than other periods of adulthood.

There can be no disputing that the salience of different life tasks changes with age; however, in the absence of studies permitting cross-age comparisons, there is no way to determine reliably the nature and extent of such changes or to ascertain whether certain tasks have a greater effect on some people than on others. It is tempting to assume that the particular cohort and the particular set of conditions we happen to be observing capture the most intense and dramatic of life's struggles; but these assumptions are best put to test in comparative analyses. Otherwise, we are left with discrete studies of separate age groups whose reliability may be limited and whose relevence to more general concerns with aging and the life course is ambiguous.

The Multiple Patterns of Aging

It is my position, then, as well as that of others (Riley, 1971), that in order to understand a particular segment of the age span, it is useful to examine it in relationship to other segments. As important as such comparisons across age ranks are, however, comparisons within age ranks are at least equally important. Without such comparisons, we can easily fail to see that which is crucial to recognize: There is not one process of aging, but many; there is not one life course that is followed, but multiple courses.

This assertion is based on the rather frequent finding that important life circumstances are unevenly distributed. Put another way, adults of the same age but differing in other social and economic characteristics will be exposed to very different conditions of life that lead, in turn, to different patterns of change and development. It cannot be assumed, therefore, that people of identical age share the same experiences or move through the same aging process. On the contrary, we know that a cohort may be deeply divided by the economic conditions its members have experienced and that these divisions have a remarkable tenacity through the life course (Elder, 1974). While moving an equal distance across the life span from the same temporal starting point may provide a basis for some common experiences, such commonalities are not sufficiently powerful to erase the profound differences that result from people having different origins and from the variations in their current social and economic experiences. Sex roles are a good illustration of this point, for men and women of the same age will have had very dissimilar pasts, strikingly different ongoing experiences, and largely divergent developmental futures. Essentially the same statements can be made about people who are divided by income, by social status, by race, and so on. It is misleading, therefore, to think of movement across the life span as entailing a unitary process or to think of a life stage on which all people of the same age stand. There is a variety of ways to age and to traverse the life course; there is not one sequence of stages, but many. The variety is as rich as the historic conditions people have faced and the current circumstances they experience.

I do not suggest that the life tasks that are peculiar to an age should be ignored; I wish only to emphasize that whatever may be unique to a cohort does not diminish the many differences that crisscross it. We have analyzed some of these differences; since most of our findings have been reported elsewhere (Pearlin & Lieberman, 1979), I shall only present some illustrations here. Consider first the untoward events that can happen in people's occupational lives, namely, the involuntary loss of a job. In each age group—young adults, middle aged, and older people—exposure to this vicissitude is unequally distributed among those having different status characteristics. Specifically, people with limited educations and low occupational prestige are considerably more likely to experience job loss than their age-mates in higher status positions. Indeed, it can be reported that regardless of age, most of the unwanted conditions and events of job and occupation are predominantly found in the lower strata of society, and those that can be considered as desirable and sought after are disproportionately found at the upper levels. When it comes to occupational experiences—careers, dissatisfactions, dreams, and vulnerabilities—the intracohort differences that exist are abundant.

The family is also an area in which it is difficult to find meaningful circumstances that are uniformly experienced by socially differentiated people of the same age or at the same point in the family cycle. Differences between men and women are particularly striking in the family domain, more so than differences in class and status. Thus, in marriage, women are more likely than men to experience a sense of inequity, to feel that they give to their spouses more than they receive from them. Women are also more apt to state that their mates neither recognize nor accept them as they really are. While these differences exist at each age level, they increase with age.

This small sample of illustrations of differences within age cohorts is selected in support of a rather fundamental point: Because people are at the same age or life cycle phase, it cannot be assumed that they have either traveled the same route to reach their present locations or that they are headed in the same future directions. Earlier I argued that we need a comparative perspective in looking across ages, for such a perspective might reveal that there is less distinctiveness among people at different locations in the life span than would otherwise be supposed. Now I am arguing that we need also to maintain a comparative perspective within cohorts, for such a perspective is likely to reveal fewer similarities among age-mates than might otherwise be realized.

In general, it might be productive to direct some of our research effort against the grain of established practice by giving some emphasis both to elements of experience and development that unite people of different ages and to those that separate people of the same age.

Are Life Changes Bad for People?

By their very nature, aging and the life course involve change. If people's lives remained unaltered, there would be no social aging but only that which is strictly biological. In a very real sense, therefore, the study of aging is also the study of change and its consequences. From social and psychological perspectives, aging may be viewed as representing the cumulative effects of alterations in life circumstances through time. Clearly, our ability to assess such alterations and their effects is quite limited at this time.

There are, however, various lines of research which, though not necessarily concerned directly with aging, have some influence on our thinking about the process. I refer specifically to work which, following the lead established by Selye (1956), essentially views stress as a manifestation of responses to environmental changes. Under ordinary conditions, inner forces are in harmony with one another and with the environment. Alterations in the environment, however, intrude upon this harmony and create a situation of disequilibrium and instability. Within this framework, life events can be regarded as environmental sources of personal dislocation. Indeed, a number of researchers, using an assessment instrument developed by Holmes and Rahe (1967), sought to show that the sheer number of life events people confronted was related to various indicators of stress. A number of methodological problems have been identified in connection with this instrument (Rabkin & Streuning, 1976), but what is of primary interest here is that there is a widely held view that life events create instability among inner forces and that stress is a signal that the organism is struggling to reestablish stability and equilibrium.

Such a view has some interesting implications for the aging process. If, in fact, life events and other life changes are sources of stress, then stress must be an inevitable concomitant of aging simply because the quintessence of aging is change and stress is the inescapable companion of change. Even those most skilled at adaptation could hardly avoid the cumulative burden of change as they progress along the life course. Aging, from this position, must certainly be inimical to well-being. The data we are able to muster do not, however, support such a position; on the contrary, quite the opposite seems to be true.

A broad overview of age and stress reveals that in the role areas that we are able to examine, younger people experience greater challenges to adjustments than their elders. That is, when we look at the circumstances that people encounter on their jobs, in their efforts to earn a living, and in raising children, we find that those conditions most likely to lead to depression, anxiety, and symptoms of situational stress tend to be concentrated among adults who are not yet 40 years of age. As observed elsewhere (Pearlin, 1980b), life is most demanding of those in the process of becoming established in occupational, economic, and family roles and is least demanding of those who have been in these roles for a period of time. Marriage is the only exception to this general tendency; younger people are not more apt than others to experience stress-producing problems. Since divorce and separation are concentrated in the younger age ranks, however, this finding may be misleading. The marriages that survive intact, that is, may represent those who earlier were least beset by marital problems.

At any rate, the thrust of the findings are inconsistent with any assumption that there is an accretion of social and economic problems and a decline in psychological well-being that take place with aging. It should be understood that older adults certainly are not free of problems. Our data only emphasize that the relationship between age and stress is quite different from that commonly assumed, at least up to the age of 70—the upper limit of our sample at the time of the follow-up interview. Furthermore, it is only because we are able to make comparisons across age ranks that it is possible to observe these kinds of relationships.

It appears, then, that neither the hardships of life nor their effects accumulate with age. Furthermore, we are beginning to learn from our research that the effects of life events probably do not depend on the magnitude of the changes they demand from people. Instead, our data consistently indicate that life events impinge on people by first altering the more persistent, less eventful conditions of life, and these alterations, in turn, adversely act upon emotional well-being. Reference to such indirect effects was made earlier in discussing widowhood. Divorce provides another illustration. Consistent with a large body of research, we found that people whose marriages were disrupted in the four-year interval between interviews were significantly more distressed than people in stable marriages. Initially it seemed reasonable to hypothesize that the distress stemmed from the change of status—the loss of one status and the painful readjustments involved in the passage to another status. It is not the change of status that matters, however, but the circumstances faced by the newly single in their daily lives. Thus, among the divorced people whose circumstances are relatively benign, judged especially by the level of their economic resources, there is virtually no emotional distress associated with divorce; and among those who have gone through the same marital disruption but who have ended up in difficult and demanding economic straits, distress is likely to be intense. Other conditions also enter into this picture, such as the displacement of friends and—especially among single parents—an inability to establish activities and interests outside of the household. Together, these conditions indicate that it is not the changes embodied in the event itself that matter but the nature of the changed circumstances with which the newly divorced have to deal.

Similar analyses, with similar findings, have been made of other changes that involve the gains and losses of roles, such as in retirement. These analyses are consistent in pointing to the importance of social and economic contexts in determining the effects of events, and they are equally consistent in underscoring the futility of merely taking inventory of life events without seeing how they fit with other elements of life circumstances. From what we have been able to observe thus far, we have concluded that

> emotional disturbance is most likely to surface when events adversely reshape important life-circumstances with which people must contend over time. Thus, the event does not act solely or directly upon inner life, but through the reordering of more enveloping circumstances. The impact of events, we submit, is largely channeled through the persistent problems of roles. (Pearlin & Lieberman, 1979, p. 235)

To what extent can these findings concerning personal change be extrapolated to more broadly based social and cultural changes? I raise this question partly as a result of a recent opportunity to observe Papua, New Guinea, a country being catapulted out of the Stone Age by rapid, ubiquitous change. Speculatively, it would seem that people can easily accommodate even to a profoundly new way of life as long as the social and economic resources on which they depend for support and security are left intact. This is entirely consistent with what Mead (1971) was able to observe in Manus after two decades of widespread cultural and technological upheaval. It is certainly consistent with what I was able to see during my stay. The destructive and disorganizing impact that we would ordinarily expect to result from such bewildering and rapid change seems to occur primarily where there is a breakdown in the social institutions on which people depend. On the other hand, where their communities, families, and other support systems do not disintegrate, people are not necessarily injured by alterations in technology, communications, occupational structure, patterns of consumption, popular culture, and so on. It is my strong guess that whether the changes we encounter are on the vast scale of those underway in New Guinea or on the order of those people confront during the ordinary life course, the change itself matters less than the conditions under which it takes place.

Coping with Change

The emotional fates of people as they move through the life course depend on the conditions, events, and vicissitudes that impinge on them. This is only part of the story however; the other part concerns the manner in which people reach out and respond to the demands of life. Most people do not simply remain passive in the face of the forces that adversely affect them. Instead, they actively react either (1) by seeking to alter the situations that give rise to the adverse forces, (2) by attempting perceptually and cognitively to reshape the meaning of the forces in a way that reduces their threat, or (3) by establishing devices that enable them to live with distress without being overwhelmed by it. People engage in these functions in at least three distinct—though certainly not mutually exclusive—ways: by the selective use of their own coping activities and responses; by calling upon resources residing within personality, especially mastery and self-esteem; and by establishing and employing social support networks. The conditions, transitions, and events of the life course do affect psychological functioning, but these effects are often mediated by coping and social and psychological resources.

Let us first consider individual coping behavior. We have reported elsewhere the results of earlier analyses of how people cope with relatively enduring problems and conflicts (Pearlin & Schooler, 1978). Briefly, we learned from that earlier work that individuals' coping responses can help buffer the stressful impact of life problems. There is no assurance, however, that the efficacy of one's coping is in direct proportion to one's efforts at coping. In particular, the chronic problems and strains that arise in impersonal contexts, such as those that are faced on the job or in earning an adequate living, are not as responsive to coping as are difficulties confronted in the closer interpersonal relations of the family. Thus the more directly life problems are rooted in large, impersonal social and economic organization, the more resistant they appear to be to individual coping efforts. It should also be noted that although a number of coping responses were found to be efficacious, there is no single mode of coping that stands out as preeminently powerful. The range and diversity of one's coping repertoire is probably more important to effectiveness than any single coping response that could be identified.

How is coping related to aging? There are some significant variations in coping behavior among people of different ages. No age rank seems to have an advantage however, when it comes to making use of the more effective coping responses. In this regard we noted the following:

> There seems to be a balance in the coping efficacy of younger and older people, each being about equally well-equipped with effective elements. These results certainly do not support views of aging as a process in which people inexorably become increasingly vulnerable, unable to cope effectively with life-strains. Although there are substantial relationships between age and coping, neither the younger nor the older appear to have any overall advantage in coping effectiveness. (Pearlin & Schooler, 1978, p. 16)

Earlier I pointed out that older people are not exposed to more stresses than younger. In addition, when problems and stresses do arise in their lives, they are no less able to cope with them.

Turning now to the use and effectiveness of support systems, we discover a number of complex issues, one of them being the very use of the term "support systems," a phrase that assumes that we know when a system is being supportive. We tend to think that if a person is part of a social network, then he or she is automatically able to draw support from that network. Our findings are not consistent with this assumption. Neither the presence of friends or family nor frequent interaction with such groups insures that supportive functions will be performed. It is the quality of interaction rather than its other properties that seems to underlie support. The quality that in this respect is especially outstanding is expressive exchange. That is, relationships that are marked by the communication of important and intimate feelings are those that are most likely to stand as barriers to distressful consequences of life problems.

Another of the complexities in understanding support systems concerns the ways in which their efficacy is judged. We have learned that it is not possible to ascertain whether people are being helped by a relationship simply by asking them if they seek help from it:

Getting help and asking for help may be quite independent. Thus, there is some good evidence that people may typically be the recipients of help and support without seeking it or without any awareness of what has taken place. This is a consequence of the support being a natural and spontaneous product of interactions embedded in the social network of which we are a part (Brown, 1978). Correspondingly, if we actively seek help from those about us, there is a good chance it will not be forthcoming, for if we must solicit help, our network probably is not functioning in a solidary and supportive fashion. Thus, we cannot be sure who is receiving support from knowledge of only those who are asking for it.

In trying to understand how people deal with problems as they move through the life course, it is important to recognize that coping and the use of social supports are selectively used according to the nature of the problems involved. For example, there is no reason to suppose that people would deal with problems arising out of discrete events in the same manner they would deal with the more continuous and chronic problems. From very preliminary and incomplete analysis, it appears that some of the coping responses that develop out of efforts to deal with persistent problems are either not used at all to cope with life events or are used ineffectively. There are several reasons why this would be the case. Consider first life cycle transitions, events characterized by their scheduled, predictable appearance. Because transitional events can be foreseen, coping with them may begin not with the emergence of the event, but with its anticipation. The trying out of future roles in our fantasies, the use of role models, and the mass media are among the mechanisms through which we can prepare for such future events. It will be recognized, however, that not all events are so amenable to prior preparation. Thus, changes that are more eruptive or unexpected are not so easily accommodating to anticipatory coping. Second, this type of prior adaptation is most apt to occur with changes and events that the society prizes rather than those it attempts to discourage. While even young children may learn what it is like to be married or to go to work, there is less in the socialization process that prepares us for divorce or unemployment.

How, then, do we cope with the unscheduled and often undesired events of life? Very little is known about how people attempt to deal with vicissitudes of this kind, and even less is known about how modes of adjustment to problems of this order might change developmentally. We do know, nevertheless, that not infrequently what begins as an eruptive event eventually results in rather durable, continuing problematic circumstances. When this happens, the many coping responses that we have shown to be employed in dealing with chronic problems will be invoked. It would seem, however, that during the time that we are most sharply experiencing unexpected changes or life crises, we would also be most disposed to exercise whatever access we have to social support systems. I submit that we are most apt to turn to others for support and guidance at those junctures of the life course where we face new conditions with which we have neither prior experience nor enough opportunity to establish appropriate coping through trial and error. In the absence of such supports, we may indeed find ourselves in trouble.

Although we can at this time only speculate about coping and the use of social supports within the context of the life course, the importance of this behavior is self-evident. We simply will not be able to understand the experiences and changes of people through time until we are able to understand how people respond to the conditions they encounter along the way. It is rather urgent that as we continue to research the processes of aging and adult development, we try at the same time to come to grips with the ways people cope with different types of problems. We need a view of the interplay across the life course of the demands that impinge on people and their attempts to deal with these demands.

One final implication of coping needs to be underscored, namely, its part in further differentiating cohorts. Earlier I argued that despite their having traveled the same distance across the life span, people of the same age are likely to be divided by variations in their social and economic circumstances. This observation can be carried a step further: Not only is a cohort likely to be divided by different conditions of life, but even when conditions are similar their impact may differ because of variations in coping responses. All in all, it seems untenable to speak of either ages or life stages as though they are made up of undifferentiated people following a uniform life course. Far from it.

Conclusion

There is certainly no theoretical consensus in the broad field of aging. Its boundaries are too unclear, and the scholars working in and around it are too diverse for perspectives to emerge that would be fully shared. Nevertheless, there are assumptions and conceptual leanings that appear to have some general currency. This chapter sought especially to identify a few that are not entirely consistent with findings that are beginning to emerge from our own research. Thus, we find the following: (1) family transitions do not represent important benchmarks and turning points of adult life when judged by their impact on emotional well-being; (2) it is doubtful that we can discern processes of aging by extrapolating from studies of specific age groups; (3) research results suggest that we be concerned with similarities among people of different ages and differences among people of the same age; (4) people seem to adapt to social and personal changes with more ease than might be supposed; (5) aging itself, at least until it leads to infirmity, may impose less distress than having to contend with the demands faced by young adults; and (6) the same circumstances faced by different people in the life course will have effects that vary with their coping responses and their use of social and psychological resources. These observations will be uncongenial with the views of some researchers, acceptable to others, and—justifiably—seen as incomplete by all.

In emphasizing discontinuities between commonly held views and emerging empirical information, I have ignored one of the salient features of research into aging and the life course: the sheer challenge and excitement that we can find in this field. It is my guess that this is especially the case where our intellectual appetites are for rather large and multidimensional problems. A major part of the attractiveness of studying aging and the life course derives from its absorption of a variety of disciplinary interests and backgrounds. Thus, we have learned enough to know that the twists and turns of the life course are determined by the convergence of many different kinds of processes: historical, social structural, cultural, normative, and personality. To deal with aging and the life course from the perspective of one of these processes is complex enough. But to see how they come together in giving shape and focus to people's lives through time is indeed a challenge to theoretical and methodological ingenuity.

It is both wise and necessary for us to be aware of the problems and obstacles to knowledge in the area of aging. It is no less desirable that we be aware of the exciting rewards to be gained by searching for the connections between social change and personal change.

REFERENCES

Benedict, R. Continuities and discontinuities in cultural conditioning. *Psychiatry*, 1938, **2**, 161–170.

Brown, B. B. Social and psychological correlates of help-seeking behavior among urban adults. *American Journal of Community Psychology*, 1978, **5**, 425–439.

Burr, W. R. Role transitions: A reformulation of theory. *Journal of Marriage and the Family*, 1972, **34**, 407–416.

Dyer, E. E. Parenthood as crisis: A restudy. *Journal of Marriage and the Family*, 1963, **25**, 196–201.

Elder, G. H., Jr. *Children of the Great Depression*. Chicago: University of Chicago Press, 1974.

Elder, G. H., Jr., & Rockwell, R. C. Marital timing in women's life patterns. *Journal of Family History*, 1976, **1**, 34–53.

Glenn, N. D. Psychological well-being in the postparental stage: Some evidence from national surveys. *Journal of Marriage and the Family*, 1975, **37**, 105–112.

Gould, R. The phases of adult life: A study of developmental psychology. *American Journal of Psychiatry*, 1972, **129**, 521–531.

Hill, R. Methodological issues in family development research. *Family Process*, 1964, **3**, 186–206.

Hobbs, D. F., Jr., & Cole, S. P. Transition to parenthood: A decade replication. *Journal of Marriage and the Family*, 1976, **38**, 723–732.

Holmes, F., & Rahe, R. H. Social readjustment rating scale. *Journal of Psychosomatic Research*, 1967, **11**, 213–218.

Levinson, D. J., Darrow, C. N., Klein, E. B., Levinson, M. N., & McKee, B. *The seasons of a man's life*. New York: Knopf, 1978.

Lopata, H. Z. Widowhood: Societal factors in life-span disruptions and alternatives. In N. Datan & L. H. Ginsberg (Eds.), *Life-span developmental psychology: Normative life crises*. New York: Academic Press, 1975.

Mead, M. *New lives for old: Cultural transformation—Manus, 1928–1953*. New York: Dell, 1971.

Menaghan, E. G. *The effect of family transitions on marital experience*. Unpublished doctoral thesis, University of Chicago, 1978.

Neugarten, B. L., Moore, J., & Lowe, J. C. Age norms, age constraints, and adult socialization. *American Journal of Sociology*, 1965, **70**, 710–717.

Pearlin, L. I. Life strains and psychological distress among adults: A conceptual overview. In N. J. Smelser & E. H. Erikson (Eds.), *Themes of love and work in adulthood*. Boston: Harvard University Press, 1980. (a)

Pearlin, L. I. The life cycle and life strains. In H. M. Blalock, Jr. (Ed.), *Sociological theory and research: A critical appraisal*. New York: The Free Press, 1980. (b)

Pearlin, L. I. Sex roles and depression. In N. Datan & L. Ginsberg (Eds.), *Life-span developmental psychology: Normative life crises*. New York: Academic Press, 1975.

Pearlin, L. I., & Johnson, J. S. Marital status, life-strains and depression. *American Sociological Review*, 1977, **42**, 704–715.

Pearlin, L. I., & Lieberman, M. A. Social sources of emotional distress. In R. Simmons (Ed.), *Research in community and mental health*. Greenwich, Conn.: JAI Press, 1979.

Pearlin, L. I., & Schooler, C. The structure of coping. *Journal of Health and Social Behavior*, 1978, **19**, 2–21.

Rabkin, J. G., & Struening, E. L. Life events, stress, and illness. *Science*, 1976, **194**, 1013–1020.

Riley, M. W. Social gerontology and the age stratification of society. *Gerontologist*, 1971, **11**, 78–87.

Russell, C. S. Transition to parenthood: Problems and gratifications. *Journal of Marriage and the Family*, 1974, **36**, 294–303.

Selye, H. *The stress of life*. New York: McGraw-Hill, 1956.

Sheehy, G. *Passages: Predictable crises of adult life*. New York: Dutton, 1976.

Spanier, G. B., Lewis, R. A., & Cole, C. L. Marital adjustment over the family life cycle: The issue of curvilinearity. *Journal of Marriage and the Family*, 1975, **37**, 263–275.

Vaillant, G. E. *Adaptation to life*. Boston: Little, Brown, 1977.

4 Historical Experiences in the Later Years

GLEN H. ELDER, JR.

What I remember most is what the Depression did to the spirit of people.[1]

[Mother] always said life was just one disappointment after another.[1]

I'm a person of life. I don't feel old.[2]

A recurring theme in the human drama of rapid change centers on the fragmentation of lives and their internal discontinuities in a transformed environment. When such changes occur midway in life, initial purposes and directions lose meaning for the anticipated future. The ends of life may "become obscure" (Redfield, 1955). Migration to urban areas from the rural countryside and economic cycles are potential sources of disjuncture in the life course. Americans who grew up in Depression scarcity soon faced the problems and temptations of prosperity, while their postwar offspring now must cope with a period of retrenchment that calls for the scarcity virtues of thrift and conservation. In various ways, historical change thrusts people into new situations that can challenge the means, pathways and ends of accustomed life.

An alternative or supplementary account of social change in life experience stresses the preparatory influence of certain historical

1. From an interview with an old woman in Westin (1976, p. 127).

2. From an interview with an elderly woman in the Berkeley Guidance Study (Maas & Kuypers, 1974, p. 137).

transitions for subsequent life adaptations. Examples of this outcome are suggested by the military and homefront demands of wartime America. Military service in World War II and the Korean War opened up developmental experiences and educational opportunities for some veterans that enhanced career prospects. Wartime employment opportunities also enabled some women to acquire the skills and confidence of self-support. Most occasions of social change defy a simple account of life effects by giving rise to contradictory or varied consequences, both continuous and discontinuous in the life span.

This chapter explores a continuity theme that connects one type of social change and life experience: a theme of loss and adaptation in the economic collapse of the 1930s and the life course development of a small number of women who were born at the turn of the century (from about 1890 to 1910). Building upon the prevalence of loss in the Depression and later years of these women, this study investigates the hypothesis that their health in old age is partially a function of how they dealt with the problem of human and material loss during the 1930s. Early and later adaptations to loss are contingent on both the severity of the deprivation and on the resources brought to the situation. These conditions favored the life course and well-being of women from the middle class, in contrast to those of lower status.

Women in this study started their families during the prosperous 1920s and experienced the bust and boom of the 1930s and 1940s as wives, mothers, and earners. All are members of the well-known Berkeley Guidance Study (Macfarlane, 1938), a longitudinal investigation of normal development in a sample of 211 middle- and working-class children and their families. The children were systematically selected from a list of Berkeley, California, births in 1928–1929. Approximately 82 of the women were interviewed in 1969–1970 (mean age, 70). As might be expected from class differences in mortality and social participation, high-status and well-educated women were more likely than other women to be contacted in old age (Maas & Kuypers, 1974). These differences remain even with the deceased excluded from the comparison—about half of the attrition sample. Nevertheless, the participants resemble other women in the incidence and severity of economic loss in the 1930s.

The Great Depression both increased and diminished some problematic aspects of the later years.[3] The unparalleled crisis gave birth to social insurance as a buffer for life's misfortunes and fostered unknown strengths, but it also drained many families and lives of physical and emotional well-being. Economic downturns are known to increase the rate of mental hospitalization (Brenner, 1973). These contrasting sides of the 1930s are part of the challenge in tracing the implications of Depression life for women in old age. Their hard-time experience may offer valuable clues as to why some have adapted better than others to problem situations in this life stage.

The analysis first examines the social and personal resources of the Berkeley women from the 1930s to old age, and then examines their physical and psychological health during the later years. Economic variation during the 1930s represents a starting point in tracing the long-term effects of the Depression experience. The strategy entails systematic comparisons of the effects of economic loss among women who entered the 1930s from the middle and working classes. Class position and age are attributes that shaped women's losses and adaptations. Before taking up the analysis, some preliminary conceptual and design issues warrant brief discussion. I hypothesize that the adaptive benefits of Depression hard times are most likely to be expressed in the lives of women from the middle class. Conversely, hard times are most apt to become bad times in the lives of working-class women.

Problems of Loss and Adaptation:
The Later Years and Prior Hard Times

Loss represents a common human experience during the later years of life, from the departure of children and the death of parents to disabling illness and the death of a spouse. Learning to manage or cope with these events and transitions assumes primary significance as a developmental task. Successful aging may be linked to early experience that tests and develops a person's mettle in coping with the disruption of losses, with the problem of lost attachments and

---

3. Achenbaum (1974) offers an insightful analysis of historical change in attitudes toward and concepts of old age up to World War I in America; Chudacoff and Hareven (1979) explore demographic evidence on historical change in the transition to old age; Uhlenburg (1979) extends this research to a comparison of old-age cohorts; and Calhoun (1978) investigates the redefinition of old age and retirement between 1940 and the 1970s in the United States.

purposes. Bereavement can be viewed as a process in which the life made unmanageable and meaningless by acute loss becomes controllable and purposeful once again, though on different terms. As Marris (1974) observes, a sense of continuity between past and present can be restored following a disruptive loss by "detaching the familiar meanings of life from the relationship in which they were embodied and re-establishing them independently of it." Mastery of grief comes not from rejecting the past but from recasting it in terms appropriate for the present and future.

The Great Depression has unique relevance for women's lives in old age through the common and profound experience of loss. Decremental events are common to Depression life and to life situations in old age, and such changes are generally beyond personal control. An example is a husband's loss of job in the 1930s and at retirement many years later. Family experience in the 1930s often entailed severe income reductions and prolonged unemployment; the loss of a home and furnishings; the end of plans for a first child or more children; the trauma of financial dependence and shared living quarters; the disability, death, or separation of a spouse (Elder, 1974). A way of life had come to an end for many. The challenge of surmounting the life problems posed by such losses can be viewed as an adaptational orientation for the constraints of infirmity and limited resources during old age. Depression hardship offered a potential form of apprenticeship for women in learning to cope with the inevitable losses of old age. These losses include departure of the youngest child from home, widowhood, major illnesses, and retirement of self and spouse.

The central idea relating Depression experiences to well-being in old age assumes that successful coping with loss builds confidence and resources for dealing with future trials. Health is relative to the problems encountered. As Sanford (1966) points out, a person may be quite healthy in a protective environment and yet not have what it takes to persevere under very trying circumstances. Accordingly, women who managed to keep their families going on little more than $1.00 a day in the early 1930s are likely to have an advantage in knowing how to get along on little income after retirement. In the words of a wife and mother who knew first hand the deprivations of the 1930s, "What you can't change you learn to live with" (Westin, 1976). Likewise, women who experienced the trauma of losing a family home in the 1930s may be better equipped to accept the residential changes of old age. One woman from the Depression era in Westin's (1976) oral histories recalled how hard it was on a woman to lose her home but quickly added that strength came out of it. We just "kept on going during those years." Along the same line, Scott and Howard (in Levine & Scotch, 1970) conclude from studies of life change that mastery of a problem leaves the organism in a superior state in the "sense that if the same problem arises again, the organism will be able to deal with it more efficiently than before."

The daily round of Depression life for women expanded as the world of their unemployed or deprived husbands shrank. When men lost jobs, income, and meaning in life, their wives became central figures in an undermanned field of obligations and activities, from home production and management, to caretaker of a relative and child rearer, to breadwinner and head of household (Elder, 1974). Survival needs pushed the managerial skill of women to more demanding levels. They were drawn into the financial transactions of borrowing money from banks and relatives. They managed to get along on less by reducing purchases to the barest minimum and entered the labor force despite adverse public opinion on women employees. Concerning her Depression experience, an older woman exclaimed (Westin, 1976), "It's absolutely surprising the number of things a woman can do to manage. . . . You accepted what you had and you made the most of it rather than to think—if I had something better, I'd such and such."

Coping with loss in the Depression and learning the managerial skill of running a deprived household represent two plausible developmental linkages between the 1930s and healthful adaptations to old age among the Berkeley women. Two other temporal connections are also worth noting as possibilities: the value and lesson of being independent and personal involvement in meeting the needs of others. A number of events underscored the value of a woman's independence: the need to share a cramped household with relatives, the risk of depending on the economic achievements of a husband, the domestic burdens that fell upon women as their husbands withdrew into themselves. Whatever the lessons drawn from such experiences, a large percentage of the Berkeley women assumed more responsibility for family income by entering the labor market. Nearly half of the women in hardpressed families worked at some point during the 1930s, and a sizeable proportion continued to hold a job in the 1940s. Though most jobs in the 1930s were part-time, they placed women more on their own and provided skills that foster successful aging. Recovery from the death of spouse is especially problematic among older women who are highly dependent on their husband and do not have a worklife of their own (Weiss & Parkes, 1978). Through male default and pressure to work, Depression realities may have shaped a model of self-reliant womanhood that is uniquely suited to the living requirements of widowhood.

Hard times in the 1930s frequently strengthened the social ties of married women and mothers, while diminishing the social relations of men (Bakke, 1940; Elder, 1974). Deprivation pushed women into paid work and enlarged their traditional care-taking functions relative to husband, children, parents, and other kin. The Depression world of women favored a constructive response to losses of one kind or another by centering on the welfare of others. Meaning, significance, and inner resources could be found through the necessity of meeting such concerns. This psychology differs from that of men in deprived households. Economic misfortune was not the exclusive fault of men, yet they consistently focused the blame on themselves. Despair, withdrawal, and prolonged disability were common events in the self-defeating response of men to their deprivation. Depressed feelings led to withdrawal from community and family affairs (Elder, 1974). Unlike the response of men, women's social adaptations in the Depression established a pattern of coping with loss that could prove healthful in the later years of their life.

A "strong woman" image of Depression life appears in oral histories of the decade and in studies of families during this period (Elder, 1974). Memories depict women as seemingly able "to develop the strength to survive anything . . . they carried such a load" (Westin, 1976). Often paired with this central figure is a characterization of beaten or victimized men. Recollections of the harsh toll of the Depression on men are commonplace among the women in Westin's sample (1976): "Hard times hit father more than mother—he couldn't walk down the street and hold his head up. . . . I think hard times is harder on a man. . . . It's just a worry for him, and he feels so terrible he can't take care of his family. . . . [Loss of a steady job proved to be] such a tremendous blow to his ego that he developed asthma. . . . [Mother] accepted things as they came . . . she always had work to do."

This sex difference is documented by historical analyses of the relation between economic downturns and hospitalization (Brenner,

1973) and points to three conditions that bear upon the long-term effects of economic deprivation: (1) *the degree or severity of the loss*, (2) *adaptive resources brought to this new situation* (education, problem-solving skills, etc.), and (3) *responses* (employment, social withdrawal, etc.) *to the economic change.* The first two conditions influence the third. Drastic change and minimal resources increase the likelihood of ineffective coping and adverse consequences for health (Lieberman, 1975). In various combinations, these class-linked conditions undoubtedly shaped different pathways from the 1930s to old age in women's lives—from growth and resilience under stress to no effect and a life stunted by impaired self-worth and confidence.

Each type of factor plays a role in Brown and Harris's (1978) explanatory account of emotional depression among working-class women. Especially among large families (three children or more at home), they found severe life events and major difficulties (chronic problems) to be most common in the working class. Housing, children, marriage, and money posed difficulties that took more time to resolve in the working class than in the middle class. Class-linked resources also contributed to the depressive reactions of low-status women—less know-how on where to seek and obtain help in crises, lower feelings of self-worth and mastery. In their formulation, "response to loss and disappointment is mediated by a sense of one's ability to control the world and thus to repair damage, a confidence that in the end alternative sources of value will become available. If self-esteem and feelings of mastery are low *before* a major loss and disappointment, a woman is less likely to be able to imagine herself emerging from her privation." Given feelings of inadequacy, grief over a severe loss is more apt to become exceedingly painful, leading to denial, a failure to work through grief, and, eventually, clinical depression.

The class positions of the Berkeley women before 1930 illumines their Depression experience (severity of loss, adaptive resources, modes of response) and later life in the 1960s. According to the Oakland study (Elder, 1974), loss of status was especially painful to middle-class women, but they had more resources than lower-status women for dealing effectively with family hardship. Their educational, economic, and status advantages were expressed in stronger feelings of personal worth and more developed skills in problem solving. The long-term significance of this advantage is suggested by research that links maladaptive behavior in deprived circumstances to feelings of low self-esteem and mastery. Among persons of this type, economic strain tends to increase reliance upon heavy drinking (Pearlin & Radabaugh, 1976). The resource handicap of working-class women in the Berkeley sample gains importance for life outcomes when considered in relation to the severity of Depression losses in this stratum. Especially among the unskilled, income and job losses during the early 1930s were often followed by more of the same before the economic boom of war mobilization. These issues suggest an "interaction" hypothesis: *Low socioeconomic status among women before the 1930s increased chances that hardship would impair their life prospects in old age (economic, health). Any beneficial effects from Depression losses are most likely among women who entered the 1930s from the middle class.*

The most obvious path for the negative effects of family deprivation on health is through economic circumstances in old age (Shanas, 1962). Unemployment and heavy income losses during the 1930s forced unknown numbers of families to give up security assets—a home of their own, other real estate, stocks and bonds, insurance policies. We do not know how prevalent these losses were among the Berkeley women or whether they represented more or less permanent reductions in their material status up to old age (about four decades after the stock market crash). But persistent strain seems most likely among members of the Depression working class. Better educated Americans are more successful in building security assets for old age than are the less educated (Henretta & Campbell, 1978); the net worth of the better educated in the later years is greater than expectations based on earnings, while the reverse pattern holds for the less educated.

Other plausible linkages for the negative effects of economic deprivation include the wear and tear of women's heavy obligations in deprived families and a reduction in their social support during the later years through fertility control in the 1930s and loss of spouse by means of an early death, separation, or divorce. Economic losses caught the Berkeley women in the midst of childbearing and may well have led to a change of plans regarding more children. Consequently, the deprived women may have fewer children to call upon than elderly women who lived through the decade in the privileged sanctuary of a nondeprived family. Considering the significance of children in a widow's network (Lopata, 1979), this question brings up a noteworthy connection between two widely separated periods in the life course. Fertility control was clearly an adaptive response for women and families in the scarcity climate of the 1930s, yet its benefits are likely to be outweighed by the costs of having only one child or no children during the last years of life. Among American women who were born around the first years of this century (NIH, 1978), 22% have no children and 23% have only one.

Two general sources of life course variation structure the design of the analysis. Class position in 1929[4] as a proxy measure of the resources women brought to the 1930s (Kessler & Cleary, 1980; Kuypers, 1974), and exposure to drastic income loss between 1929 and 1933. Not all women experienced such loss. Indeed, some were spared misfortune altogether. Taking into account the sharp decline in cost of living within the San Francisco Bay area (about 25% by 1933), the correlation between income and asset loss and past measurement decisions in the study, we classified all families that lost at least 35% of their 1929 income as economically deprived. Less hard-pressed families were defined as nondeprived. In the middle class of 1929, slightly more than one-third of the women were members of deprived households. This percentage increased to over one-half of the women from the working class.

The analysis is organized in two phases. First, we begin with women's resources in the life course, as charted from the early 1930s when they were childbearing age to the later years. Do we find differences in social support and problem-solving skill between women from high- and low-status families, from the economically deprived and nondeprived? Are there postwar differences between these groups on socioeconomic career, residential setting, and social network—contact with children, grandchildren, confidante? The most general issue here is whether social class and economic loss produced different pathways for women and life outcomes. According to the interaction hypothesis, the health effects of Depression hardship are more positive and developmental in the lives of middle-class women than among lower-status women. The second part of the

4. High-status or middle-class women in 1929 are defined by membership in strata I and II on the two-factor Hollingshead index (education and occupation) and in stratum III by marriage to a man with at least come college. Ordinarily, all three strata define the middle class. Considerations of sample size, however, called for a more restrictive definition, one that would place the wife of a high-school-educated sales clerk in the working class. In lieu of this decision, we would not be able to investigate the life course of women from the lower socioeconomic strata.

analysis puts this hypothesis to a direct test by comparing Depression effects on the physical and mental health of elderly women from the middle and working class.

Women's Resources from Childbearing to Old Age

The Berkeley women are members of an age group that spans in its lifetime what Cain (1967) has called an "historical hinge" or "watershed" at the end of World War I. Their 20th-century cohort is distinguished by a smaller family of origin and a smaller proportion of the foreign born. They experienced greater educational opportunity, led the way on an "early marriage" trend that became more pronounced in the 1940s, and experienced a longer postparental span with their husbands. They reached the middle years of life at a time of rising wages, social insurance, and liberalized social constraints. These distinctions begin to tell us something about the resources women brought to the 1930s and to the later years of their life.

As a generational bridge between large families and the fertility constraints of the 1930s, the Berkeley women may possess a kin network for old age in which siblings play a more important support role than offspring. The demographic facts shown in Table 4-1 document this kin potential, especially in the working class. The Berkeley women had fewer children on the average than their mothers; those in the working class were more likely to have only one child. Three out of four of the women had a daughter on whom to rely in old age. It is clear that social class matters more than Depression hardship as a source of kin variation. Lower-status women entered the 1930s with more siblings than higher-status women and experienced a lower probability of Depression births and marital stability. Economic hardship made little difference in fertility and marital permanence and thus in the social support of elderly women. Class standing is far more important as a determinant of these conditions.

A similar conclusion applies to women's problem-solving resources in the 1930s. Using seven-point ratings by interviewers, we see that middle-class women rank well above lower-status women on qualities that could make a difference in the management and solution of Depression-related problems. Consistent with their higher education, these women were judged brighter, more verbal, and more articulate by the interviewer. The former also stood out on

Table 4-1. Women's Potential Resources in Old Age from the Perspective of Their Early Life Course, by Socioeconomic Status in 1929 and Economic Deprivation

Indicators of potential resources	1929 status		High status		Low status	
	High (n = 49)	Low (n = 34)	Nondeprived (n = 31)	Deprived (n = 17)	Nondeprived (n = 15)	Deprived (n = 19)
Kin support						
Family of origin						
Mean size	3.5 **	4.6	3.6	3.3	5.0	4.3
Only child (%)	15 *	10	16	13	0	19
Own children						
Number ever born ($\bar{x}$)	2.8 **	2.1	2.7	2.9	2.2	2.1
One child (%)	6	24	10	0	27	21
Marital stability						
Broken, 1929–1946 (%)	8	17	3	18	15	19
Problem-solving resources						
Ratings, 1930–1931 ($\bar{x}$)[a]						
Intelligence	5.03 **	4.13	4.98	5.12	4.10	4.16
Energy output	4.95 *	4.31	5.03	4.82	4.59	4.08
Self-assurance	4.38	3.94	4.42	4.31	3.97	3.92
Emotional instability	3.59	4.27	3.64	3.51	4.36	4.18
Ever employed (%)						
1930–1935	15	50	10	24	39	59
1936–1939	21	47	10	41	45	49
1940–1945	35	76	32	41	72	79

[a]All ratings include seven points and represent an average of two assessments.
*p = .05; **p = .01 (two-tailed test of difference).

vitality and activity level, on poise and self-assurance, on a positive
sense of self (not shown in table), and on emotional stability. In
combination these variations suggest that middle-class women had
more in reserve when they entered the 1930s, a decade that magni-
fied many times over the life stresses that ordinarily pile up during
the early childbearing years. Emotionally stable women were less
reactive to minor frustrations and displayed less of a tendency to
"borrow trouble." Before the Depression, these women seemed less
vulnerable to setbacks, barriers, and criticism, factors that soon became commonplace. At least on these ratings, economic misfortune
was not simply a continuation of misfortune. Resourcefulness is
linked to a woman's education and family status, not to her economic
fate in the Depression.

Women's entry into the Depression labor market represented an
important indication of resourcefulness at the time and perhaps in
subsequent crises that call for independence, initiative, and management skills. Intellectual flexibility, self-confidence, and a sense of
autonomy are fostered by challenging jobs and work settings (Miller,
Schooler, Kohn, & Miller, 1979). In spite of dismal job opportunities
and hostile community sentiment toward the working mother, nearly
two-fifths of the Berkeley women were gainfully employed at some
point in the 1930s, a percentage that is consistently higher in the
working class than in the middle class and among deprived families in
each stratum. During the early 1930s, the pressures of young children
countered economic need as factors in the work decisions of mothers.
With household burdens and limited options, part-time employment
was the rule. Only at the end of the decade do we find a sizeable
proportion of full-time workers; for the most part, child-care demands
and Depression hard times had become matters of the past.

Our perspective on the 1930s questions two accounts of Depression hardship as a detrimental factor in women's health during old
age: (1) *lack of kin or primary resources and support* and (2) *the notion that
Depression "misfortune" is earned or deserved by the less able or healthy.* Loss of
future kin support (through fertility control in the 1930s) is clearly not
a plausible link between economic hardship and women's health status
many years later. Whatever the availability of offspring, most women
had two or more brothers and sisters on whom to rely in time of need.
It is class position and not actual Depression loss that influences
women's coping resources. Middle-class women had more resources
to draw upon in the 1930s, and their paid employment represents a

potential source of growth. Paid employment enabled women in deprived households to gain more control over their life situation.

When we turn to the postwar years and old age, economics, marital history, and the social network yield a complex picture of the Depression's legacy, one that does not correspond with our inter-action hypothesis on class and deprivation (Table 4-2). Early economic hardships among the Berkeley women suggest more of the same in the later years. The well-documented severity of the Depression among working-class families points to a substantial disadvantage from in-come losses during the 1930s, but we find that this disadvantage is largely because of the chronic deprivations of lower social class.

Women from the lower strata rank well below those from the middle class on economic status at the end of World War II and on financial circumstances in old age. Using a three-item measure of financial strain in old age, we estimated the independent effects of five conditions that bear upon economic welfare at this time of life: retirement of wife and spouse if living, marital status, Depression hardship, social class in 1929, and women's career stage in 1930 (born after 1899 or earlier). The five factors account for approximately 40% of the variance in reported financial strain.[5] The best indicator by far of women's material well-being in old age is their socioeconomic position before the Great Depression (beta = −.51 vs. .10 for depriva-tion). Retirement is the next most influential factor. The economic costs of Depression hardship, as seen in old age, are not more pro-nounced in the working class.

Another contributing factor to old-age hardship is the high rate of widowhood among women from the deprived middle class; only one-fourth of the 1929 marriages in this group survived to 1969. This figure is well below the survival rate for middle-class women who were spared major setbacks in the 1930s and may reflect the devas-tating effects of job and income loss on men, often lasting months and even years (cf. Cohn, 1978). A woman in Westin's study (1976) conveys something of the tension that jobless men experienced in her

5. The codes and beta coefficients for the variables are (1) retirement—0 = husband or wife works, 1 = retired (beta = .25); (2) marital status—0 = unmarried, 1 = married (beta = −.14); (3) economic deprivation—0 = nondeprived, 1 = deprived (beta = .10); (4) social class in 1929—scores from 1 to 5 (beta = −.51); and (5) career stage—0 = birth before 1900, 1 = birth 1900 or later (beta = .15). The financial strain index represents the sum of three standardized interview items: (1) economic status—affluent, no worries, hardship; (2) home status—superior, all other; and (3) neighbor-hood status—superior, all other (R^2 = .40).

Table 4-2. Women's Potential Resources in Old Age from the Perspective of the Postwar Years, by Socioeconomic Status in 1929 and Economic Deprivation

Indicators of resource status	1929 status		High status		Low status	
	High ($n=48$)	Low ($n=34$)	Nondeprived ($n=31$)	Deprived ($n=17$)	Nondeprived ($n=15$)	Deprived ($n=19$)
Socioeconomic pattern						
Socioeconomic status, 1945 ($\bar{x}$) (1=low, 7=high)	4.29	2.50	4.48	3.94	2.47	2.53
Women's worklife						
Postwar to 1969	21	38	7	47	47	31
1969–1970	8	35	6	11	32	37
Retired, H and W (%)	69	47	68	71	53	42
Perception of retirement						
Mostly losses	15	21	19	7	18	23
Mostly gains (freedom, etc.)	55	46	50	64	55	38
Both	30	33	31	29	27	38
	100(40)	100(24)	100(26)	100(14)	100(11)	100(13)
Socioeconomic status, 1967–1970						
Some hardship or more	39	50	29	29	53	47
Generally satisfied with present economics (more pluses than minuses) (%)	65(48)	35(34)	65(31)	65(17)	40(15)	32(19)
Residential setting						
Lives in own home, 1969–1970	71	59	81	53	60	58
Retirement community	12	6	13	12	13	0
Lives alone	37	32	19	41	33	32
Satisfied with home (more pluses than minuses) (%)	77	50	84	65	67	37

recollections of her husband during a labor strike of the 1930s: "You should see him come home at night, so tired like he was dead, and irritable. . . . He's so nervous and his temper's bad. And then at night in bed, he shakes."

Much of the literature on economic stress gives support to the observation that Depression men who experienced prolonged hardship were subject to the high probability of ill health and an abbreviated life span. The same conditions that pushed women into more demanding life situations undermined the personal worth and resourcefulness of men. According to this account, we should expect an association between deprivation and widowhood in both the middle and working class. Widows, however, are not unusually common in households of the deprived working class (Table 4-3).

A number of factors could account for this disparity, including biases in sample attrition. A disproportionate number of working-class women dropped out of the study between 1930 and old age, and some were from the most deprived working-class families in the 1930s. Another potential reason for the disparity involves age variations in class origins and economic deprivation. The high rate of widowhood among women from the deprived middle class might reflect their older age, relative to that of other subgroups, and the much older age of their first husbands. But no reliable differences of this sort were found. Whatever explanation, loss of husbands through death or divorce in the postwar years tended to place the Berkeley women more on their own. A marital break made a substantial difference in women's lives by prompting their labor-force participation. Women were more inclined to be employed during the postwar era when their marriage ended through divorce or death of spouse.[6]

The principal conclusion across these fragmentary data on life situations in old age is the irrelevance of Depression hardship. Novel hard times in the 1930s did not forecast economic difficulties during the later years of life. Is this because we do not have information on financial matters that bear upon the 1930s, especially in the realm of securities and property? Perhaps. We do not know how many of the

6. With 1945 socioeconomic status, economic deprivation, and 1929 social class in the equation, single status during the postwar era predicted women's employment at some point during the period from 1945 to 1970. The beta coefficient for marital instability among women from high-status families is .34—in the low-status group, the coefficient is .26.

women turned in life insurance or lost a house or lot. But even in the subjective realm of economic status, we find little evidence of a Depression legacy. Economic dissatisfaction is not more common among women from deprived families, and it does not appear to be a major factor in their more critical evaluation of present living accommodations.

More women from deprived households do not own their residential unit in old age, and lack of ownership is a source of housing dissatisfaction. Scattered evidence suggests that much of this housing discontent is symptomatic of more generalized feelings toward independence and dependence. The lessons of "being dependent" on another person's income were frequently vivid memories as were the tensions, conflicts, and deprivations of multigeneration households. The desire to remain independent occasionally took the form of housing judgments and employment. One of the Berkeley women put it this way: "I do not want to become dependent upon anyone which may partially explain the fact that I am working full time at age 75 and travel a total of three hours a day."

This brings us to a final observation on women's social resources in the life course, that of social networks made up of spouse, children, grandchildren, siblings, and close friends or confidantes (Table 4-3). The Depression did not make a consistent impact on the social networks or significant others of women. The only apparent social disadvantage of Depression hardship appears in the large number of widows from the deprived middle class. But even this outcome may be inconsequential, for as Lopata (1979) points out, "a husband in memory can also provide a form of support" in a widow's life. Most women have at least two living children and several grandchildren as part of their social world; nearly half see one of the children every month. Siblings and confidantes appear to be especially significant as social supports in the lives of deprived women, especially when compared to their status among women from nondeprived circumstances. They helped to fill the void created by a spouse's death. Adequate social resources can be mobilized in different ways and combinations.[7]

This section began with the notion that women's social resources would provide insights into the connection between Depres-

---

7. Apart from kin ties and relations with a close friend, we find no evidence that deprived women were less socially involved than women from nondeprived homes, and this applies to both the middle class and working class. The two groups are very similar on formal group and religious activity, and they are equally close to people—they were judged equally likable, trusting, and open.

Table 4-3. Women's Social Network and Resources in Old Age, by Depression Hardship and Family Status in 1929 (%)

Social network and resources	1929 status		High status		Low status	
	High (n=48)	Low (n=34)	Nondeprived (n=31)	Deprived (n=17)	Nondeprived (n=15)	Deprived (n=19)
Marital situation, 1969–1970						
1929 marriage still intact	54	47	71	24	33	58
Married now	69	59	84	41	47	68
Widowed, not remarried	29	29	16	53	40	21
Children						
Two or more living children	92	76	90	94	80	74
Proximity of children: within 30 min. walk/drive	52	68	48	59	73	63
Contact with most seen child: once a week or more	29	23	26	35	20	26
Contact with most seen child: at least once a month but less than once a week	46	50	42	53	60	42
Satisfaction from visits more plus than minus	35	26	32	41	27	26
Grandchildren						
Three or more grandchildren	92	85	97	82	93	79
Contact with most seen grandchildren: once a week or more	21	18	19	24	13	22
Satisfaction with grandchild more plus than minus	71	79	71	71	80	78
Siblings						
Two or more living siblings	38	59	29	53	60	58
Relationship with closest sibling more plus than minus	39(33)	62(29)	32(19)	50(14)	54(13)	69(16)
Closest friend						
Confidante	48	50	42	59	47	53
Proximity of closest friend: within 30 min. walk/drive	50	59	52	47	53	63

sion hardship and health in the later years—kin support through siblings and own children, problem-solving resources, employment as a mode of adaptation to family need, the postwar socioeconomic career, and marital history to old age. Resources brought to the 1930s provide reason to expect a negative effect of economic deprivation on old-age health in the working class and a less adverse or even a positive outcome in the middle class. The greater coping resources of the middle class established some opportunity for beneficial learning from Depression losses. Beyond this expectation, the picture is less clear. Depression hardship is correlated with more adverse outcomes in the middle class, especially widowhood. Even so a large percentage of middle-class women from deprived families undoubtedly achieved some measure of independence and confidence through household management and employment in the Depression and postwar years. Having coped with the strain of the 1930s, these Depression women may share the belief that they can survive any adversity that old age offers.

Managing Losses and Health in Old Age

Preparatory experiences for the inevitable losses occurring during old age suggest that learning how to deal with loss is an essential step toward learning how to live in the fullness of good health. Especially vivid documentation of this point comes from the Depression decade. Consider the proud men who angrily denied the realities of economic loss and rejected help that might have eased the burden of severe hardship. A widow in Westin's (1975) study recalled the pain caused by her husband's stubborn pride: "When a man is that proud it makes it hard on his family. Can you understand that?" Though few jobs were available, her husband was too proud to look for one or to accept the overtures of kin. Her man was a hard worker who just "never learned to give an inch." As a result, the family had to suffer a precarious existence when "it wasn't really necessary." With lives more firmly anchored in the family and its welfare, wives were no doubt better able to work through the problems and feelings of loss, a contrast that may also apply to old age and its multiple transitions.

    The notion that early Depression losses better prepared women for the deprivations of old age is put to its most severe test by the Berkeley survivors of the deprived middle class. Broken marriages, widowhood, and economic pressures are more common events in their lives when compared to the privileged middle class. Neither group held an advantage as to physical health before the 1930s, according to sketchy information in the archive, and the same conclusion about health applies to women from the working class. This similarity on health ends, however, as we move to the later years. Even with no statistical adjustments on situational variations (Table 4-4), older women from the deprived middle class stand out on physical well-being, as indexed by limited interview measures, 1969–1970. These women rank higher than any other group on good physical health and on satisfaction with health. Bodily concerns are least prevalent in their lives. By comparison, the health status of women from the privileged middle class has more in common with

Table 4-4. Women's Reports on Health Status, Activities, and Attitudes during Their Later Years, by Socioeconomic Status and Economic Deprivation in the 1930s

Factors, 1969	High status, 1929		Low status, 1929	
	Nondeprived ($n=31$)	Deprived ($n=17$)	Nondeprived ($n=15$)	Deprived ($n=19$)
Good physical health, self-reported $(\bar{x})^a$	4.08 **c	7.28	4.66	4.72
Saw doctor for treatment last year (%)	52	24	60	37
Went to hospital last year (%)	42	29	40	11
Health has declined since the 1940s (%)	48	35	33	37
Generally satisfied about health (%)	39 **	76	40	47
Preoccupied with body, health $(\bar{x})^b$	5.54 **	4.36	5.08	5.28

[a]The physical health index represents the sum of five standardized items on the 1969–1970 interview: general health as compared to others the same age, degree of disablement, present health or illness proneness, self-care difficulties, and energy level. To obtain positive mean scores, we added a constant (5) to the values.
[b]Two related nine-point Q-ratings (based on the 1969 interview) were averaged to form this measure: "concern with own body" and "anxiety finds outlets in bodily symptoms." This index is correlated ($r=-.60$) with the index of good physical health.
[c]With statistical controls on financial strain and marital status in old age, birth year, and class position in 1929, economic deprivation produced much greater variation in the physical health of middle-class women than of working-class women ($b=.72$ vs. .06, probability of same slope = .10). The symbol b refers to the unstandardized regression coefficient, the amount of change in physical health per unit change in economic deprivation.
**$p<.01$ (t-test).

that of lower-status women. Economic security and stable marriages may have favored the health of women from the nondeprived middle class, but we see little evidence of this in their reported health.

How can we explain such health contrasts in the middle class and their seeming reversal of common beliefs about healthful circumstances? Using available information on physical well-being before the Depression, we find no health difference between nondeprived and deprived women at the time. The superior physical health of the latter only appears 40 years later, a finding that is at least suggestive of developmental effects from the Depression experience.[8] Comparison of the married and not married also points to the Depression's impact. Consistent with the health benefits of marital support, married women from hardpressed families are healthier than the unmarried. Both groups, however, rank higher on physical health than their counterparts in the nondeprived middle class.

Our interview measures of physical health leave much to be desired as an empirical base for interpretations, but the index at least identifies women for whom health is a problem. Women who reported ill health were also most likely to be considered highly preoccupied by bodily concerns ($r = .60$). These concerns were indexed by an average of two clinical ratings: "concerned with own body" and "anxiety finds outlets in bodily symptoms." For another link to the Depression experience, consider the lower percentage of women from deprived backgrounds who reported hospitalization or outpatient care by a physician. Extreme economic pressures during the 1930s forced a good many women to postpone medical care whenever possible, occasionally to the detriment of their health or that of a family member. The data suggest that some deprived women carried this attitude into their later years, especially those in the lower stratum. Deprivation is not a factor in the reported physical health of these women, and yet those who experienced heavy income losses are less likely to report incidents of medical care during the past year.

8. Middle-class women ranked higher than working-class women on ratings of poise, emotional stability, and intelligence in 1930–1931. Two of these factors are correlated with physical health in old age among women who experienced economic deprivation in the 1930s. The correlation coefficients, however, are relatively weak ($r_s < .15$) and do not compare with women's education ($r = .27$), husband's occupational status in 1929 ($r = .33$), and a standard of living index for 1929 ($r = .45$). In other words, we know far more about the physical well-being of Depression women in old age from knowledge of their life situation before the 1930s than from personal attributes at the time.

The reported physical health of the Berkeley women tells us something about their health attitudes or preoccupations, but it does not reveal much about their psychological status. Consider, for example, an index based on eight nine-point items from the 1969 California Q-sort and interview (Maas & Kuypers, 1974). In the 100-item California Q-sort, clinical judgments take into account the relative salience of each item within a forced normal distribution (nine categories) on each person, a procedure that avoids problems of temporal and ecological change in frame of reference. The position of an item on the distribution indicates its salience as a descriptor of the individual when compared to other items. Note that an individual's normative standing (position relative to other individuals) is not clearly indicated by item scores. Fearfulness could stand out among the descriptors of a relatively bland personality type, and yet this type might rank below the normative position of other age-mates on fearfulness. All ratings were made by professionally trained clinicians (at least two judges per case). The average composite interjudge reliability for the Q-sort as a whole is .70, with a spread from .60 to .74.

Four ratings tap resourceful, effective behavior—dependable, giving, insight into self-motives, and productive—and four index personal limitations—brittle, distrustful, anxious, and self-defeating (all reversed scored). The items were drawn from a clinical portrait of psychological health in Livson and Peskin (1967). Using average scores on the eight items, we find that psychological health does not predict physical health among women in old age $(r = .11)$. Depression hardship, however, is linked to *different* health outcomes in the two social strata (Table 4-5). Even with statistical controls (on marital status, financial strain, 1929 social class, and birth year), economic hardship during the 1930s increased the psychological health of elderly middle-class women and decreased such prospects among working-class women. The difference between the two effects approaches statistical reliability.

The most noteworthy feature of this contrast is not the Depression's enduring effect on health in old age, but its different consequences for middle- and working-class women. The positive effect on middle-class women is not statistically reliable and neither is the adverse effect on working-class women. But when combined, the two results clearly support our findings on physical health and point to a more general outcome and hypothesis: *When women encounter economic stress, the long-term health consequences of this change depend on the*

Table 4-5. *Women's Mental Health in Old Age, by Economic Deprivation in the 1930s and Socioeconomic Status in 1929*

Old-age indicator	High status, 1929 x̄ (SD)	Low status, 1929 x̄ (SD)	Deprivation effects[a]				Probability of same slope (high vs. low)
			High status, 1929 b	beta	Low status, 1929 b	beta	
Mental health	(n = 48)	(n = 34)					
Psychological health[b]	5.83 (1.19)	5.62 (1.34)	.72	.29	−.43	−.16	.08
Life satisfaction index[c]	19.2 (3.13) *	17.0 (3.56)	1.83	.28	−2.77	−.39	.002
Self-esteem[d]	4.58 (1.10) *	4.07 (1.13)	.80 **	.35	−.37	−.16	.04
Self-assurance, poise[d]	4.89 (.93)	4.79 (1.24)	.52	.27	−.81	−.33	.01
Intelligence[d]	5.25 (.74) *	4.40 (.97)	.15	.10	−.15	−.08	.47
Ego functioning[e]	(n = 42)	(n = 30)					
Coping behavior	30.7 (6.15) *	26.5 (5.64)	1.93	.16	−.65	−.06	.38
Defensive behavior	24.7 (5.35)	24.5 (5.53)	−3.14	−.29	.31	.03	.24
Disorganized behavior	11.83 (2.93)	11.85 (2.16)	−1.67	−.28	.32	.08	.12

[a] All regression coefficients showing the effect of economic deprivation are drawn from equations that include four other factors that bear upon old-age health: (1) economic status in old age, the financial strain measure; (2) marital status in old age, 1 = married, 0 = unmarried; (3) class position in 1929 (the five-point Hollingshead index for 1929—based on husband's education and occupation; and (4) birth year of woman—whether in the older cohort (before 1900) or in the younger cohort. Status in 1929 is part of this analysis since status variations are not eliminated by the two socioeconomic groups. Within-group status variations are related to economic deprivation and to financial well-being in old age.

[b] The index of psychological health represents a composite of eight nine-point items from the 1969 Q-sort (Maas & Kuypers, 1974). The items were selected from the set of Q-items that Livson and Peskin (1967) have identified as most and least characteristic of psychological health in middle age. The characteristic items include: dependable, giving, insight into own motives, and productive. The least characteristic items are: brittle, distrustful, anxious, and self-defeating (all scores reflected). The mean intercorrelation among the component items is .43; alpha reliability = .86.

[c] The total score on life satisfaction represents the sum of five ratings, each based on the 1969 interview (range from 1 to 5): zest versus apathy, resolution and fortitude, congruence of goals, self-concept, and mood tone (Maas & Kuypers, 1974).

[d] Seven-point ratings based on the 1969 interview.

[e] Following the work and codes of Haan (1969), we use these three scales to view women's adaptive capacity in old age in terms of ego functioning. According to Haan's formulation, 10 ego processes find expression as coping, defense, and disorganized behavior. Thus the ego process of "delayed response" may take the form of a tolerance of ambiguity (coping), of doubt (defense), and of immobilization (disorganization). In its various forms, coping behavior is flexible and self-adaptive, an approach to the social environment that is reality oriented. Defensive behavior is rigid and compelled, and does not show a realistic, tempered view of reality. Disorganized behavior is not responsive to situational pressures or constraints. Each scale represents an average of 10 five-point ratings.

*Difference between means: $p < .05$.

**Metric coefficient at least equal to twice its standard error.

severity of the event, the resources they bring to the situation (social class, self-worth, mastery, intelligence), and their adaptations—family leadership, gainful employment, and so on.

Adverse life changes are known to be more common in the working class, and working-class Berkeley women were less likely to feel good about themselves and to be in command of their life situation than higher-status women. Indeed, the most accurate prediction of psychological well-being in old age (index of psychological health) comes from knowledge of husband's occupational status in 1929 ($r = .55$) among women from deprived families. Their education does not match the predictive value of husband's status ($r = .42$), and, for that time, this is even more true of personal characteristics. Women's self-assurance or poise in 1930, for instance, is much less predictive ($r = .16$). Even less useful are early measures of intellectual functioning and emotional stability.

Problem-solving skills and coping behavior in old age tell us more about the social environment of women before the Great Depression (their education, husband's status) than about experience in the 1930s. Like our assessment of intelligence in old age, ratings of coping behavior during the later years have more to do with the initial class position of women than with economic deprivation. In this analysis, we used three measures of ego functioning during old age—coping, defense, and disorganization (Haan, 1969). Each measure includes 10 five-point ratings of specific ego processes; the ratings were made by at least two clinically trained workers using the 1969 interview transcripts.

Flexible, reality-oriented behavior is indexed by the coping measure; processes include a tolerance of ambiguity, empathy, concentration, suppression, and objectivity. Well-known mechanisms of defense are assessed by the defense measure—isolation, intellectualization, doubt, denial, regression, displacement, repression. Disorganization refers to pathological behavior, such as impulse preoccupation and immobilization. For an example of the three types of ego adaptation, consider the process of sensitivity. Empathy is coping; projection is defense; and delusion is disorganized conduct.

In old age the most adaptive women among the deprived are those who entered the 1930s from the middle class. They were not characterized by greater ego strength or health before the economy collapsed, and their lives up to old age have had no particular claim on good fortune. Even so they are more likely than women of privileged circumstances to display a hopeful, reality-oriented approach to life. Among all women with hardship experiences in the 1930s, the "copers" in old age standout on education and husband's status ($r_s = .56$). Much less predictive ($r_s = .30$) are their ratings on intelligence, self-assurance, and emotional stability prior to the Depression.

A more general view of aging among the Berkeley women comes from types of personality configurations that depict social competence and a coping life style. Using factor analysis and 100 items in the California Q-sort, Maas and Kuypers (1974) identified five groups of women on psychological functioning. Slightly more than three-fifths of the women were characterized by one of the two modes of competent functioning—autonomous and person orientation. The autonomous group stands out on dependability, initiative, high aspirations, and a relatively individualistic life style. They are not easily impressed by others and generally maintain a distant relationship to others. The person-oriented group is distinguished by dependability, charm and poise, and a straightforward style of interaction. Their interpersonal style is characterized by sympathetic understanding, warmth, a giving attitude, and a sense of humor. In combination, these forms of competence are most common among deprived women from the middle class: 81% as against 62% of the nondeprived from this stratum. Approximately 56% of the lower-status women are members of this psychological category, and the percentage does not vary by Depression experience.

Whatever their social standing before the Depression, socially competent women in old age rank well above other Berkeley women on measures of physical and psychological health. They report better physical health, score higher on life satisfaction, and display stronger coping skills (all differences between means exceed a probability of .01). The same story emerges from a comparison of the groups on ratings of self-assurance and self-esteem in old age. Even when troubled by health problems, the socially competent were more likely to make the best of their situation than to engage in self-pity. As one of the women put it (Maas & Kuypers, 1974), "I get in a little difficulty and I've had eight surgeries trying to correct it, but now I've just given up. Do the best I can and most of the time I get along very well."

The Depression's imprint on personality brings to mind constricted thought and feeling, a sense of vulnerability and apprehension, a feeling of being cheated or unfairly deprived by circumstances. In the classic study of Marienthal, Austria, during the 1930s, Jahoda, Lazarsfeld, and Zeisel (1970) documented some of these patterns as an emergent response to extraordinary hardships. With the closing of their only employer, a small textile mile, the residents of Marienthal experienced more than three years of extreme privation. The population's breadth of interest, wants, and claims on life narrowed sharply over this time period. Related to a victimized outlook is the strategy of ensuring a sense of importance by making others feel obligated. According to a 1930s study of Oakland, California, families (Elder, 1974), "deprived situations in the Depression were made to order for the long-suffering, martyr role. . . . Mothers with a martyr complex were remembered by their daughters as suffering from feelings of inferiority and insecurity; they felt victimized and ill treated." Consistent with these psychological adaptations is Smith's (1968) characterization of vicious cycles in life course development. A poor start and low self-esteem increases the likelihood of setbacks that make one "hesitant to try."

A small number of older Berkeley women are part of a cycle of self-decline. Maas and Kuypers (1974) label them the "fearful, ordering" type. They feel anxious, inadequate, and bereft of a sense of personal meaning. Favoring conservative values, they appear uncomfortable with uncertainty, are needful of reassurance, and are inclined to withdraw from conflict. This sense of alienation and a victimized life is powerfully expressed in the words of a Berkeley woman who claims to have had "a lot of sadness in [her] life." When asked about living life over again, she replied by stressing the unattractiveness of such an option. More appealing was the possibility of becoming somebody else, "someone real fancy and somebody whose father was rich." Everyday things proved too much for her: "don't have the energy or interest"; "it would be so much easier if we didn't have to struggle along." This type of woman is likely to be found in the working class, especially among those with a background of hard times.

By and large, the women who felt cheated by life, especially vulnerable to criticism, and inclined to give up are concentrated in the low-competence group. Table 4-6 displays the mean scores of six Q-sort items that index a woman's breadth of perspective and understanding and the average scores of 10 items on self-adequacy. The scores are not adjusted for variations in either Depression hardship or old age, such as marital status, financial strain, and retirement. Each score tells us how salient the attribute is in the subgroup personalities.

Table 4-6. *Mean Clinical Ratings of Women's Breadth, Understanding, and Self-Adequacy, by Status in 1929 and Economic Deprivation*

Q-sort items, based on 1969 interview	High status[a]		Low status[a]	
	Nondeprived $(n=30)$	Deprived $(n=16)$	Nondeprived $(n=15)$	Deprived $(n=18)$
Breadth and understanding				
Wide interests	5.6	5.8	4.4	4.4
Conservative on values	6.8	6.1	7.4 **	6.2
Generally fearful	4.3 **	2.8	4.0	5.0
Behaves in giving way	6.4	6.8	6.7	6.5
Insightful of own motives	4.0 **	5.5	4.3	4.3
Sees to heart of problem	4.6 *	5.5	4.2	4.6
Self-adequacy				
Feels cheated by life	3.2	2.7	3.5 *	5.1
Thin skinned	4.6	4.0	4.6	4.8
Lacks personal meaning	3.9 *	2.6	3.6 *	5.2
Turned to for advice	4.8	5.5	4.7	4.7
Gives up and withdraws	3.8 **	2.2	3.8	4.0
Reluctant to take action	4.2 *	3.1	4.0	4.2
Self-defeating	3.3	2.7	3.4 *	4.7
Productive, gets things done	6.3	6.8	6.3	6.4
Creates, exploits dependency	4.4	4.1	4.6	4.8
Brittle	4.5 **	3.0	3.9	4.4

[a]For each rating, the highest of the four cell scores is underlined.
$^*p < .05$; $^{**}p < .01$.

For all women, the most salient items in the set of 16 describe central themes in women's lives (behaves in a giving way) and in life adaptation generally (the ability to get things done and holding onto the past through its meanings, as in a conservative stand on values). The "conservative impulses" (Marris, 1974) are "means to defend our ability to make sense of life." Interestingly, this outlook is far less dominant in the lives of women who suffered Depression losses than among the nondeprived who knew the fear of what might happen but not the realities of extreme hardship.

To a remarkable degree, our results parallel the life experience of a younger group of women who were born in 1920–1921 and grew up in Oakland, California, in the 1930s. The assumption that "smooth sailing in a protected childhood may not develop adaptive skills which are called upon in later life" (Elder, 1974) is consistent with the lives of women from nondeprived families of the middle class. They ranked lower on psychological health and resourcefulness at middle age than women who encountered first hand the emotional trauma and pressures of hardtimes in the middle class. The latter were often described as "warm, vital persons with an understanding nature," a portrait that "bears little resemblance to their Depression experience or to traditional thinking on stress and illness." As in the Berkeley study, the health of Oakland women from the affluent middle class bears some resemblence to that of women who had a life of hardship—the deprived working class. Neither a privileged life of ease nor one of unrelenting deprivation assures the inner resources for successful aging.

By any standard, hard times in the Berkeley working class were not conducive to a healthful old age. Women in this group were disadvantaged on personal and social resources when compared to the middle class at the time of the economic collapse, and they experienced Depression losses in their most severe, prolonged form. Over two-thirds lost more than half of their 1929 income by the end of 1932. Four out of five husbands were unemployed or underemployed at some point in the 1930s. This pervasive change points to continuing hardship as a Depression legacy among working-class women and as a bridge between poor health in old age and deprivation in the 1930s. Depression losses may well have taken on a life of their own in the postwar era, but this connection has less to do with income losses than with the chronic privation of low status. As noted earlier, economic loss is not as predictive of financial strain in old age as socioeconomic position before the Depression. Poor health in old age is correlated with financial strain at the time only in the working class—$r = .33$ versus .02 in the middle class.

Initial resources and the severity of Depression adversity are plausible explanations for the differing health of women from the middle and working classes. Economic loss produced situations with developmental potential in the middle class that placed resourceful women more on their own—marital friction and separation, a disabled or withdrawn husband, a more influential role on household matters, and gainful employment. Each change underscored the necessity for a married woman to make her own life and may have enhanced effective aging in later life through greater self-confidence. Indeed, clinicians judged the "value of independence" as more characteristic of elderly women from the deprived middle class, when compared to the nondeprived ($\bar{x} = 6.2$ vs. 5.6 on a nine-point scale).[9] Nevertheless, specific linkages between hardship and health are stronger in theory than in empirical findings. No intervening factor, such as employment, made a reliable difference in the physical and psychological health of women. This unsuccessful effort may reflect our limited data. For example, a woman's employment status, the only work information we have, does not tell us much about the job itself or its complexity, pace, and autonomy.

The findings both support and challenge simple versions of life course development as continuity and accentuation: that early development mirrors its future course and that life experience tends to accentuate early developmental differences—they become more pronounced through the life course. Both accounts affirm the predictive value of early life patterns—that one's trajectory takes form early in life and persists over time. But how is a vicious cycle reversed? One clue is suggested by recollections of a middle-class woman in the Berkeley study (1973 interview):

My memory of the Depression is one of humiliation and frustration. It all started in 1931 when my husband, an outside salesman, returned home from a successful business trip to find a telegram stating that he no longer had a job—no explanation. We had two young children, the youngest but a few months old. Soon all our savings were gone. I remember the day when the last can was gone from the shelf and the last bit of flour had been used the night before to make biscuits with bacon for shortening. Mother became aware of our plight and gave us money each week until I was able to get a typing position with the WPA. My husband did very little until he got into the shipyards sometime later.

When asked how all of this affected her life, the woman replied: "It humbled me considerably. In fact, it was a contributing factor to an inferiority complex which I have had to work hard to overcome." Mastery experiences and problem-solving skills may account for why this woman worked hard through her own career and succeeded in repairing the psychic damage of Depression losses while other women

9. We find the very same difference on the valuing of independence among women from the nondeprived and deprived working classes ($\bar{x} = 6.3$ vs. 5.6). For the total sample, the difference between means approaches statistical reliability ($p < .10$).

gave way to conditions of this sort. Personal and social resources enabled some women to turn a setback into a growth-promoting experience.

Discussion and Review

Loss and adaptation represent a theoretical bridge between the Depression and aging experience of women in the Berkeley study. The implications of an early loss depend on its severity or degree (the value lost, etc.) and on what women brought to the 1930s (their options and resources). Middle-class women from deprived families experienced less severe hardship, had more in the way of intellectual, emotional, and social resources, and came through the Depression experience with more coping skills and better health than working-class women from deprived families. Though Depression hardship is linked to financial strain and early widowhood in the middle class, these women of deprivation rank well above the nondeprived on physical health, psychological well-being, and life satisfaction. In the lower strata, hard times left its damaging imprint on women's life course and health up to old age. A large percentage resemble a women's observation on her husband at the end of World War II: "You know, he's never gotten over it."

The effect of the Depression on the lives of men underscores the importance of specifying the nature and meaning of loss. Without exception, the Depression literature yields contrasting images of men and women; more often than not these accounts point to the expanding life sphere of women and the demoralization of men.

A number of familiar explanations for this difference come to mind. Amidst the individualistic ethos of the times, men blamed themselves for loss of job and income, as did their wives on occasion. Addams (1932) observed in the winter of 1932 that "one of the most unfortunate consequences of the Depression is the tendency to call a man a failure because he is out of work." Men commonly interpreted lost jobs and earning power as symptomatic of personal inadequacies. Even when immensely upset by their husbands' trauma and burdened by the task of family care, women largely escaped the destructive impact of self-recrimination and public blame. Their life in hard times became one of valued courage and sacrifice, not one of personal failure and deficiences.

The different meaning of Depression losses for men and women has much to do with another plausible source of the Depression's contrasting effect on health in the two groups: the way people coped with or responded to the crisis. Brown and Harris (1978) refer to this variable as a key to the psychological consequences of loss. They found that women who lost a mother during childhood were vulnerable to depressed states because they were not old enough to work out the grief and achieve control. "The earlier the mother is lost, the more the child is likely to be set back in his or her learning of mastery of the environment." Likewise, we see that men were less able than wives in the 1930s to achieve control in hardpressed situations. They did not have the compelling options of women: their important and legitimate roles in the family and their employment options across wage levels and time schedules. Unemployed men could not turn as readily to the family for compensatory meaning and significance.

Much work remains in tracing out the long-term effects of social change on aging among men and women as expressed through the 1930s and into the postwar era.

Other cohorts and generations are needed to test the generality of our findings. Even among women who shared the same birth year, those from the deprived middle class have a very different life story to tell than those from the deprived working class. Life reviews of the former are likely to emphasize good times in hard times (raising my family), the setbacks endured and overcome, the challenges successfully met, and the lessons learned. This is hardly the outlook of women who faced the barest margins of survival in deprived working-class homes. Their past has a bitter edge in recollections, and their hard times are mainly bad times. They often represent themselves as victims of unfair circumstances, not as actors making the best of a difficult life.

The model set forth in this study outlines two causal chains that link economic change in the 1930s to behavior and life styles in old age: one among women who entered the Depression in the middle class and the other among working-class women. Our analysis to date has centered on the differential effect of economic deprivation in these strata and, consequently, ignores some basic questions on life span development. Is physical and psychological health in old age highly dependent on comparable health states in prior decades, and does this dependency vary according to social position and career? Between early and later adulthood, is "real" continuity (without measurement error) in psychological functioning greater in the middle class than in the working class? What social changes account for temporal variations in psychological continuity. The next research stage will construct, test, and compare causal models that link the 1930s to old age, including adaptations to economic loss such as women's employment. The major question is whether and how these models or formulations vary by social class and gender.

The life course is marked by discontinuities and contradictions. The young enter the full-time labor market without work experience; career opportunities for women coincide with the usual timing of parenthood; and some old people experience the heartbreak of losses without first-hand experience in dealing with such events. All too often, the wisdom to make appropriate decisions and to live fully comes at a time when the most important choices have been made. Encounters with loss as preparation for loss is a problem worthy of life course research.

REFERENCES

Achenbaum, W. A. The obsolescence of old age in America, 1865–1914. *Journal of Social History*, 1974, **8**, 48–62.
Addams, J. Social consequences of business depression. In F. Morley (Ed.), *Aspects of the Depression*. Chicago: University of Chicago press, 1932.
Bakke, E. W. *Citizens without work*. New Haven, Conn.: Yale University Press, 1940.
Brenner, M. H. *Mental illness and the economy*. Cambridge, Mass.: Harvard University Press, 1973.
Brown, G. W., & Harris, T. *Social Origins of depression: A study of psychiatric disorder in women*. New York: The Free Press, 1978.
Cain, L. D., Jr. Age status and generational phenomena: The new old people in contemporary America. *Gerontologist*, 1967, **7**, 83–92.
Calhoun, R. B. In search of the new old: Redefining old age in America, 1945–1970. New York: Elsevier, 1978.
Chudacoff, H. P., & Hareven, T. K. From the empty nest to family dissolution: Life course transitions into old age. *Journal of Family History*, 1979, **4** (**Spring**), 69–83.
Cohn, R. M. The effect of employment status change on self-attitudes. *Sociometry*, 1978, **41**, 81–93.
Elder, G. H., Jr. *Children of the Great Depression*. Chicago: University of Chicago Press, 1974.
Elder, G. H., Jr. Historical change in life patterns and personality. In P. Baltes & O. Brim (Eds.), *Life-span development and behavior* (Vol. 2). New York: Academic Press, 1979.
Haan, N. A tripartite model of ego functioning: Values and clinical applications. *Journal of Nervous and Mental Disease*, 1969, **148**, 14–30.
Henretta, J. C., & Campbell, R. T. Net worth as an aspect of status. *American Journal of Sociology*, 1978, **83**, 1204–1223.
Jahoda, M., Lazarsfeld, P. F., & Zeisel, H. *Marienthal*. Chicago: Aldine, 1970.

Kessler, R. C., & Cleary, P. D. Social class and psychological distress. *American Sociological Review*,1980, **45**, 463–478.

Kuypers, J. A. Ego functioning in old age: Early adult life antecedents. *International Journal of Aging and Human Development*, 1974, **5(2)**, 157–179.

Levine, S., & Scotch, N. A. (Eds.). *Social stress.* Chicago: Aldine, 1970.

Lieberman, M. A. Adaptive processes in late life. In N. Datan & L. H. Ginsberg (Eds.), *Life-span developmental psychology: Normative life crises.* New York: Academic Press, 1975.

Livson, N., & Peskin, H. Prediction of adult psychological health in a longitudinal study. *Journal of Abnormal Psychology*, 1967, **72**, 509–518.

Lopata, H. Z. *Women as widows: Support systems.* New York: Elsevier/North-Holland, 1979.

Maas, H., & Kuypers, J. *From thirty to seventy: A forty-year longitudinal study of adult life styles and personality.* San Francisco: Jossey-Bass, 1974.

Macfarlane, J. W. Studies in child guidance. I: Methodology of data collection and organization. *Monographs of the Society for Research on Child Development*, 1938, *3*, 1–254.

Marris, P. *Loss and change.* New York: Pantheon, 1974.

Miller, J., Schooler, C., Kohn, M. L., & Miller, K. A. Women and work: The psychological effects of occupational conditions. *American Journal of Sociology*, 1979, **85**, 66–94.

National Institutes of Health. *The older woman: Continuities and discontinuities* (Report of the NIA and NIMH Workshop, September 14–18, 1978). Washington, D.C.: U.S. Government Printing Office, 1979.

Neugarten, B. L. Dynamics of transition of middle age to old age: Adaptation and the life cycle. *Journal of Geriatric Psychiatry*, 1970, **4**, 71–87.

Pearlin, L. I., & Radabaugh, C. W. Economic strains and the coping functions of alcohol. *American Journal of Sociology*, 1976, **82**, 652–663.

Redfield, R. *The little community.* Chicago: University of Chicago Press, 1955.

Sanford, N. *Self and society.* New York: Atherton Press, 1966.

Scott, R., & Howard, A. Modes of stress. In S. Levine & N. A. Scotch (Eds.), *Social stress.* Chicago: Aldine, 1970.

Shanas, E. *The health of older people.* Cambridge, Mass.: Harvard University Press, 1962.

Smith, M. B. Competence and socialization. In J. A. Clausen (Ed.), *Socialization and society.* Boston: Little, Brown, 1968.

Uhlenberg, P. Demographic change and problems of the ages. In M. W. Riley (Ed.), *Aging from birth to death.* Boulder, Colo.: Westview, 1979.

Weiss, R. S., & Parkes, C. M. *Some determinants of the quality of recovery from bereavement.* Paper presented at conference "The Older Woman: Continuities and Discontinuities," sponsored by the National Institute of Aging and the National Institute of Mental Health, Washington, D.C., September 14–16, 1978.

Westin, J. *Making do: How women survived the '30s.* Chicago: Follett, 1976.

5 Resistance at Forty-Eight: Old-Age Brinksmanship and Japanese Life Course Pathways[1]

DAVID W. PLATH

The man who is a pessimist before forty-eight
knows too much; the man who is an optimist
after forty-eight knows too little.

Mark Twain

Testing the Limits

Old age has become a cultural nightmare for postmodern human-kind, and people approaching the transition into old age are assumed to suffer insomnia. By cultural nightmare I mean a condition that we make extraordinary efforts to avoid or deny, for it places a fearsome strain upon our heritage of ideas that bind together human effort and reward. Death, disease, and disaster have always been the most frightening conditions. And old age, as a prelude to death, probably always has been unsettling. But there may have been a time when old age was credible as just one more "predictable crisis of adult life" as the soul continued its pilgrimage toward coming of age in the universe. Our secular era, having defined death as a transition to nowhere, an alchemy that turns something into nothing, a no-fault accident on life's limited access highway, is left to symbolize old age with metaphors of disaster and terminal disease. And the season of years before old age, once known as "life's prime," now is named a

1. Some of the material in this article has been excerpted or adapted from *Long engagements: Maturity in modern Japan*, by David W. Plath, with the permission of the publishers, Stanford University Press. © 1980 by the Board of Trustees of the Leland Stanford Junior University.

"crisis." It is a time for brinksmanship, for testing the limits of a dangerous condition.

In this chapter I look at old-age brinksmanship as it is portrayed in a modern Japanese novel that has become a perennial best seller in its homeland. I follow the usual logic of cultural comparison: to draw lessons from the similarities and differences that the Japanese experience may afford us. Like the West today in technology, so near in the forms of her major social institutions, postindustrial Japan remains distant in her heritage of life course pathways. By these I mean sets of ideas (and symbols for them) about the "self" or entity of human growth and aging, about the states of being that a self may achieve or cannot avoid, about what "it" is that is in transition along the biographical time line. Where we find differences in Japan they may help illuminate areas that are shaded in our own archetype of life course change. Where we find similarities, they may alert us to existential barriers: boundaries to the human condition (or at least its postmodern version) that we are unlikely to surmount no matter how strenuously we redefine old age as "the completion of being."

Nishimura's "Resistance"

In Japan as in the West the mass media frequently take up the topic of "middle-age crisis." Most of the middle-aged men and women I interviewed a few years ago in the Osaka-Kobe area were acquainted with the notion. Some of them commented that Japanese tradition may have a loose analogue in its concept of *yakudoshi* or "danger years." These are calendar years of life during which a person is believed to be abnormally vulnerable and so should conduct his or her affairs circumspectly (Norbeck, 1955)—the worst years being 33 for women and 42 for men. However, nothing in the lore about danger years ties them directly to the transition into old age. And my interviewees were skeptical about the suggestion that any one event or year during midlife is a universal threshold of crisis. Or if there is any threshold—some men said with a wry smile—then maybe it's "resistance at 48."

Resistance at Forty-Eight is a novel by veteran writer Ishikawa Tatsuzō.[2] First published serially in the national newspaper *Yomiuri* from November 1955 to April 1956, it remains available in Japanese bookstores today, having gone through more than 20 reprintings. Its title has become one of the standard phrases in the vernacular vocabulary that Japanese use when talking about old-age brinksmanship.

The book portrays a white-collar worker's struggles along the margin. Nishimura Kōtarō, having served for two dozen years as a minor executive in a Tokyo insurance company, hungers for an escape from his overroutinized daily round. Just once he wants to fulfill his vision of *kaishō*, of virility, by having an affair with a younger woman. "Or if my youthful vigor is gone," he says, "then I must know the extent of my senile decay."

The general theme—of the decline of vigor, or fears of it, of finding that years of effort have not been adequately rewarded—is familiar enough in world fiction. Of recent Western examples I think of James Gould Cozzens's *By Love Possessed* or of Doris Lessing's *The Temptation of Jack Orkney* and *The Summer before the Dark*. The classic of the genre is, of course, Goethe's *Faust*, and in writing *Resistance*, Ishikawa borrowed blatantly from Goethe. The bored protagonist happens to reread Faust, and at times after that his adventures border upon Faustian burlesque.

Unlike Doctor Faustus, however (who had studied "Philosophy and Jurisprudence, Medicine and even, alas!, Theology from end to end"), Nishimura is a very ordinary man. His years of working for the Showa Fire and Marine Insurance Corporation have carried him to the post of deputy manager for fire insurance. But he knows that he never will be named to the Board of Directors. He will remain a deputy manager until the day when he is issued his severance pay— at age 55 as is the norm in Japanese corporations and bureaus.

And his body is weakening. In the opening scene we find him lingering in bed, troubled by a stiffness in his hips. "A mild neuralgia?" he wonders. Later we learn that he is troubled with hypertension. No longer can he play mah-jongg all night with the younger men or match drink for drink with them all night without suffering for it the next day.

> If he got too little sleep his blood pressure soon went up. His head grew heavy and his shoulders ached. . . . He couldn't concentrate on his work. His patience flagged. Cigarettes tasted flat. After everybody else had gone out to lunch he would stay at his

---

2. The only available English translation of Ishikawa's novel is a pedestrian one published over 20 years ago (Ishikawa, 1960). The passages that I quote are my own renderings from the Japanese edition of 1958. Since the curious reader may wonder: I have written this chapter in my 48th year.

desk dawdling. His mind was busy with all sorts of plans but his body would not pick up on them. Maybe it was a sign of getting on in years. When the body won't do what you want it to the mind becomes flustered. Probably that's why old men are so crabby. (pp. 173–174)

And as he sits in the barber's chair, Nishimura can't believe how large his bald spot has grown:

Physical decline is like a bald spot on your head. While you aren't aware of it, in places you don't notice, secretly and inexorably it spreads over you. And you can't do a thing about it. (p. 13)

Nishimura resists with an armament of pills. One nostrum is said to reduce blood pressure, another to prevent the formation of fat in the liver while at the same time to protect against hangover. He takes hormones and vitamin pills to build stamina and potency. He also goes for a walk every Sunday. A senior colleague told him that walking is the key to vitality, that a man always can compensate for failing teeth or eyes but not for failing legs. And he wishes he could quit smoking since that might cure the persistent dryness in his mouth:

There was an ancient Chinese sage—he mutters to himself—who said that to stay sound in mind and body a person should swallow twelve gallons of saliva a day. Profuse saliva is proof of health. (p. 63)

Nishimura has been a dedicated and diligent employee. The socialist views of his student years have yielded to a recognition that insurance is a business and not an act of social welfare. His work habits have become part of his very being. Even as Nishimura and his section chief attempt to relax in the bath at a spa, he cannot help but mentally calculate the worth of the building and its fixtures and the cost of insurance premiums for them:

They were seriously worrying about how to preserve the profits of the stockholders and board of directors. To worry about such matters was their main occupation. They had been doing it for years. Years of work had made it habitual and had warped their ways of thinking. Like a boxer's broken nose or a jockey's bowed legs, their minds were permanently bent. (p. 44)

However, the work no longer holds challenge. And Nishimura no longer can sustain the illusion that someday he will blossom as a great financial wizard. So is he to be chained to seven more years of wage slavery?

Nor can he draw excitement from his future in his family. His wife looks young for her years; her teeth and complexion remain good. But she is putting on weight; her fertility is gone and her sexuality is fading. Biologically she is a hollow shell. Perhaps as a sort of apology for it all she has become a better cook. But if she remains faithful to him she also has become defiant, extravagant, more and more jealous about his expense-account evenings on the town. She nags him to take his medicines and to quit trying to carouse with the younger men.

Nishimura's daughter has a lover whom she insists she will marry despite parental disapproval. She attacks her father's views on arranged marriage as being hopelessly antiquated. And this signals the end of another stage in his family career:

> So long as they remain grateful to their parents they're still in infancy. Once parents get to be in the way it shows that growth is over and the age of independence has arrived. His time as a parent was ending. (p. 137)

On the other hand, a young woman at the office remarks that she could easily fall for a mature man like him. A masseuse admires his "romance grey" hair and tells him it indicates that he is in his virile prime. With his daughter leaving, why should he stay with his wife when they have so little to talk about anymore? A wife should be an ally in a man's resistance. Instead his wife compares Nishimura to his future son-in-law and snorts, "You haven't got that kind of fight left in you any more, have you."

> The enviable thing about Doctor Faustus—Nishimura tells himself—is that he seems to have been single. An old man without a wife or kids. So he could afford to abandon his house if he wanted to, and rush off anywhere adventuring with the Devil. (p. 38)

Nishimura tries to imagine bachelorhood but knows he could not tolerate the inconveniences and the loneliness.

Retirement will be upon him in seven years, a silver wedding anniversary in two. He can expect to live 20 years more. Adding it all up Nishimura only can conclude that he is poised at the top of the slope that speeds downhill into senility. I am too old for debauchery, he says to himself, but not too old for desire. What I need is a way to disappear—even if only temporarily—into another life that nobody will know about or even suspect.

Into these sessions of silent desperation comes Nishimura's tempter, a man known as Sōga Hōsuke. Soga is a mysterious junior executive in the fire insurance division. But he may be—and the author sustains this ambiguity throughout the book—no more than an imaginary alter ego. The Chinese characters, "Sōga Hōsuke" make up a plausible patronym and personal name, but they also can be read as "one's former self as guide." Or to translate it with a fundamentalist flourish, "led by the Old Adam." Young, handsome, utterly manly, Sōga is wordly wise and unattached. He seems able to read Nishimura's every thought and is fond of quoting *Faust* at every turn of the plot.

Sōga opens new doors to pleasure. He brings pills and nostrums to restore Nishimura's vitality, coaxes him into eating grilled pig's heart and other "hormone broil" dishes to strengthen stamina. Even in amusement districts, which Nishimura thought he knew well, Sōga steers him into new bars and cabarets. And in time Sōga takes him to meet his "Marguerite," a winsome young hostess who seems not to be tainted by the corrupt cabaret world in which she works.

Nishimura believes that he can marshall his wits and win her love. After all, he tells himself, he has the advantages of experience. Still, he hesitates:

> If he were ten years younger at least, people might forgive him; but they are not going to forgive a man who falls in love with a girl younger than his own daughter. Even though ours is the age of many freedoms, freedom has its limits; and at some point Nishimura Kōtarō's realm of options had faded away. (p. 118)

This could be his last chance to keep a woman. But that requires money. Sōga shows him how to pad expense accounts and assures him that all the smart executives in the corporation are doing it. Even so, padded accounts will not yield the amount Nishimura calculates that he needs. There is a family nest egg but it is in his wife's custody, and it has, after all, been earmarked to pay for his daughter's wedding. Nishimura decides that he is not bold enough to embezzle any large sum; instead, he opts for blackmail. He will extort from a hotel owner who, Nishimura feels certain, deliberately set fire to his building in order to collect the insurance.

Ashamed that he will be committing a crime, Nishimura argues that his motives are of the purest. He is extorting money, but to sustain an unsullied love for an innocent woman. Fate, however, saves him. Or perhaps he was the sort who would fail anyway. When Nishimura goes to threaten the hotel owner he finds the man bed-ridden with a paralytic shock that had been triggered by the fire, incapable even of talking. His hostess, "Marguerite," had accom-panied him on the journey, but she elected to sleep in a separate room and was gone by the time Nishimura woke up the next morning. Sitting there, Nishimura looks ahead to see uneventful years, prob-ably lonely ones. Still, part of him feels relief that the episode is safely behind.

The excitement of it all brings on a severe attack of pneumonia. In his weeks of quiet recuperation, Nishimura reconciles himself to the idea that he has crossed the threshold. He has learned the extent of his senile decay. His wife turns out to be an ally in his resistance, after all, though it irks him to see her being so downright cheerful as she fusses over his food, bedding, and medicines. And it dismays him to think that in a few months his daughter will give birth, for that means that he will be called "Grandpa" even before he retires from the corporation.

> Nobody knew how unpleasant the word was to him. He wanted to run away from it. But he would have to come to terms with it. Every man gets to be a grandfather some day. He was coming around to the idea of waiting calmly and serenely for the word to be visited upon him. Perhaps that shows how enervated he had grown. (p. 315)

Nishimura has seen his fate and has acceded to it. After all, he muses to himself, even Confucius was not able to submit to Heaven's will until he was 50.

Thresholds

We are born alone and we die alone, each an organism genetically unique. But we mature or decline together: In the company of others we mutually domesticate the wild genetic pulse as we go about shaping ourselves into persons after the vision of our group's herit-age. Perhaps the growth and aging of an organism can be described well enough in terms of stages and transitions within the individual as a monad entity. But in a social animal the life course changes have to be described in terms of a collective fabricating of selves, a mutual building of biographies (Plath 1980a, 1980b). And this is all the more so for the symbol-stuffed animal that is *Homo sapiens*.

The human life course entity in transition is both an *individual*, a mortal center of initiative and integrity, and a *person*, a moral actor in society's dramas. Aware of morality, we are under a biographical imperative: to own responsibility for a line of continuity that connects our conduct—our efforts and rewards—past, present, and potential. Aware of mortality, we are under an existential imperative: to sustain hope that despite the probability of decline and the certainty of death we may nevertheless achieve a fair share of "the promise of adulthood" (Rohlen, 1978).

As we struggle under these imperatives, we sustain ourselves by feeding, so to speak, on nurturant others and on nourishing ideas. The most significant others, from a life course point of view, are people in our convoy of intimates, those whose lives run close and parallel to our own, who grow older with us. (Hareven, 1980, speaks of the "schools of fish" who swim the river of biography with us.) The most significant ideas are those contained in our cultural pathways: ideas that we can draw upon to plot where we are in the tangled currents of change and to project where we yet may go; or what an earlier era would have termed a philosophy of life and what a contemporary anthropologist would call an ethnotheory or folk theory of the life course and its transitions.

In examining the life course dynamic, I have found it useful to posit three core units of analysis. First, the *self* or reflexive entity of change and continuity, which "authors" a behavioral biography of successive actions. Second, the *convoy* or circle of others who share in the actions of the self and who have the power to decide which actions are culturally "authorized." And, third, the *pathways* or long-term guidelines that self and convoy mutually apply to their actions as they pilot their collective course down the biographical current. (For a similar scheme, see LeVine, 1978.)

Transitions can serve as strategic points of analysis, for a transition often exposes what may be obscure in the trivia of daily routine: the intricate fabric of timing woven by self, convoy, and pathways. There are problems of definition (how do we know a transition from a threshold?). And these are linked to problems of placement (has he crossed enough thresholds that he is over the brink?). In life course placement, there usually is ample room for uncertainty and dispute. Self and convoy have their several vested interests in placement because of what they portend for each person's biographical and existential imperatives.

I must know where I am, cries Nishimura Kōtarō, whether the verdict be that I am youthful or worn out; only then can I decide whether to resist or to yield. Or to take a more distant example, in East African tribal societies that are organized into age sets, men in their prime may resist initiating a new cohort of young warriors. The entry of a new cohort automatically advances those above it by one grade and so places the senior men into the respected—but terminal—grade of elder. Nor should the outside observer pretend to be coolly neutral in these matters. He may rightly strive for dispassion, but where he places others in their life courses will reflect back upon where he sits in his own. Much of the ethnographic record, it seems to me, is tinged with an age bias, perhaps unintended but pervasive, ethnography being an enterprise mainly conducted by young adults.

To the extent that it has age–place implications, almost any item of human behavior can be taken as a threshold. Self and convoy may use it as raw material for their refined social rhetoric of life course placement. The number of potential thresholds appears to be astronomical. (For studies that explore a few of these age norms see Neugarten, Moore, & Lowe, 1968; Plath & Ikeda, 1975.) So for any major transition, built upon a compound assembly of thresholds, the scope for brinksmanship opens wide. In *Resistance at Forty-Eight* we see Nishimura measure himself against an array of thresholds—hair loss, impotence, career doldrums, daughter's fractiousness—as he surveys the terrain across which he may yet be able to mount a resistance campaign.

In any society some thresholds are more standardized than others, more hemmed by norms, less open to negotiation. For example, once Nishimura's daughter is pregnant he sees no option but to begin anticipatory self-socialization to grandfatherhood. (However, I interviewed one woman who told of her rather Quixotic attempt, when her first grandchild was born, to force her convoy not to address her as "Grandma.") Again, in industrial Japan, age 55 has become a strongly sanctioned threshold for severance from working careers. And people in East Asia have for centuries used Confucius's life course yardstick to mark off certain ages as thresholds for self evaluation. "At 15 I thought only of study," goes the Confucian line, "at 30 I began playing my role; at 40 I was sure of myself; at 50 I was conscious of my position in the universe." (Translations vary; this is

Ware's [1955, p.25] rendition.) For purposes of dramatic presentation, then, age 48 is a good point by which the humble white-collar worker is likely to begin feeling himself pushed to the brink.

Thresholds such as these are part of the culturally standardized timetable in Japan. They are predictable, a healthy adult ought to be able to take them in stride. It is the unscheduled, not the predictable crisis, that may elevate stress to the point where it precipitates illness. Such is Neugarten's inference from her studies of life course timing (1979). Such, too, is Pearlin's interpretation—see Chapter 3 in this book—of the results of research on life course stress. And in *Resistance at Forty-Eight* what sends Nishimura to his sickbed is not the predictable crises (unless we want to argue that his campaign of brinksmanship gave him combat fatigue). He suffers a broken romance. That washes away his resistance, medical as well as social. He then must begin to try to accept his "position in the universe" graciously.

The novel's emphasis on heartbreak may seem curious to Western readers. There is a Western belief that assumes that European tradition holds a patent on the idea of romantic love. In point of fact, Japanese literature gave the world its earliest known romantic novel (and still among its best): the 11th-century *Tale of Genji*. In order to see Nishimura Kōtarō's brinksmanship in cultural perspective, we need to recognize him as heir to this venerable element of Japanese tradition. And to do this we must move out from the novel itself to consider the differences in Japanese and Western archetypes of life course growth.

Archetypes of Growth

I will posit that in evolving their ideas about the entity of life course change, Japan and the West began from separate starting points. The West began with the individual, Japan with the person. These imply rather different trajectories for human growth. In the Western view, individuality already is God given; in Japan it has to be evoked in relationships. Indeed the most common Japanese word for "human," *ningen*, is written with two East Asian characters that, read singly, denote "person" and "interval" or by extention "relationship."

To the West, all seeds of uniqueness are already present at the moment of impregnation. We enter into a social contract out of animal weakness and practical need. But social participation can only diminish us: Our highest self is realized in peak experiences (à la Maslow) that take us out of the social ruck. All life long we struggle to defend this uniqueness from the down drafts of collective conformity.

Viewing Japanese tradition through this lens, Western observers find it deficient. Failing to detect familiar cues of "individualism" in the Japanese milieu, observers tend to project its opposite. They see a collectivism that they then characterize with labels such as anti-individual, sociotaxic, sociocentric, or sociocultic. Japanese as individuals, they report, have "weak and permeable ego boundaries" or a "submerged sense of self." They concede that Japan is modern in technology and in social institutions, but this is historically incomplete as a transformation because Japanese are not yet "psychologically modern."

These cliches are a help in that they alert us to be wary of differences. They hinder to the extent that they remain rooted in Western assumptions and put the Japanese archetype as negative. To state it more positively—if again over simply—the Japanese archetype of growth centers on the cultivation of personal capacities for relatedness. It is not "sociocentric" if that means being attuned primarily to society as an abstract structure of roles. In the Japanese view, people enter into relations with one another not from animal weakness but from human strength. What is special about *Homo sapiens* is its capacity for sentience and spontaneity, for tears and laughter.

In early Japanese mythology all of the flora and fauna also shared some of these capacities. This, however, made the world *too* sentient and spontaneous; so civilization was created by dampening the expressive powers of the other entities (Pelzel, 1970). What is special then about a person is not that he or she has these capacities uniquely but what the person is able to do with them uniquely. The life course struggle is to carry out our obligations to others without diminishing our playful responsiveness toward them. The great fear is that we may fail to elicit "human feelings" (*ninjō*) from others and then be blocked from cultivating our individuality any further.

I am only pointing to a gross direction of difference in archetypes of life course change; there also are many similarities. But this difference does appear to underlie behavior that can be measured empirically. One example appears in a recent study of values preferences in Japan and the United States (Kusatsu, 1977, Part II). Men in the two countries were asked to rank 18 items (e.g., equality, pleasure, wisdom) in order of importance to them. There were several similarities; in both countries the highest rankings went to items such as "a world at peace," "family security," and "freedom." However, American men gave much higher priority than Japanese men did to "sense of accomplishment," "salvation," "wisdom," and "national security." Japanese men, on the other hand, saw much more significance in "mature love," "pleasure," "true friendship," and "an exciting life."

The Western archetype, in short, seems more aimed at cultivating a self that feels secure in its uniqueness in the cosmos, the Japanese archetype to a self that can feel human in the company of others.

If this general concern for emotional competence appears already in the earliest Japanese myths, the specific theme of romantic love may not have evolved until historic times. It was, at any rate, well adumbrated by 1000 years ago—as seen in the Genji story—at least among the courtly elite. By the 17th century it had been articulated in popular form for the urban masses: a key theme in the "townsman" (chōnin) lifestyle that emerged in the booming metropolitan centers of the Tokugawa period. Since the late 19th century it has been carried forward and further generalized as part of the middle-mass culture of an industrialized Japan.

Pursued to the utmost, heterosexual love could even rise to spiritual planes of pure action. The notion is familiar in the West; as part of the "townsman" pathway it has echoed through Japanese popular fiction ever since the 17th-century love–suicide dramas of Chikamatsu Monzaemon. In *Resistance at Forty-Eight* we see Nishimura, about to commit extortion after 20 years of professional propriety, excusing himself on grounds that he will use the money to sustain a pure love for an unsullied woman.

However, if romance has transcendant potential, in the "townsman" pathway it is basically meant to be an avocation, not a spiritual quest. It allows a man to cultivate his capacities for emotional expression. To reject these capacities—whether from Puritanical aversion to the flesh, as in the West, or from Buddhist aversion to any attachment, as in the East—would be to throw away opportunities for becoming more completely human. Nevertheless, the opportunities must be managed: The true townsman will not let them subvert his obligations to family and to society.

A "complete" townsman, then, should be competent enough to sustain both family and romance. Nishimura Kōtarō, alerted that he may be nearing the brink of old age, that he soon will undergo the age-50 placement test of his "position in the universe," sees that his capacity for romance has not been fully tried. He judges himself qualified in physique, social skills, savior faire, though short on cash. He has proved many times over his ability as worker and as head of household: If he is no paragon neither is he a dismal failure in those domains. If he cannot also win the love of a woman then he must confess that whatever potential he once may have had in the domain of human feeling, his capacity has shrunk. And so he may no longer be fit to reject the nightmare state of agedness.

Cultural Pathways

Every cultural heritage offers a pattern of ideas and symbols for dealing with self, convoy, and life course pathways. Some of these ideas are explicit and easily learned. A few will have been formulated into life philosophies, common sense maxims, and pop wisdom. Many remain implicit, accessible only through persistent inquiry, experience, analysis. A considerable amount of cross-cultural information already is on hand regarding these tacit theories of life span development and behavior, but typically it has been collected under other rubrics such as world view or values or social strategies. The challenge that a life course approach sends down to the anthropologist as interpreter of cultural systems is to reexamine our store of information, this time fixing our minds' eye firmly upon the biographical and existential imperatives. We need to identify the array of patterns that have evolved in different cultures for dealing with the common issues of human ontogeny. We need also to discover how each of these patterns had been woven within a long historical fabric of institutions, economies, and technologies.

I find it useful, in comparing cultural pathways, to class them according to the relative emphasis they give to each of three domains of life course change:

1. A personal domain of inner capacities. Here the mode of action is labor—seen as the natural operations of body and of

mind—and growth is measured by an expansion of strength, wit, and wisdom.

2. An interpersonal domain of capacities for relationship. Here the mode of action is love—seen as the natural flowing of human sentiment—and growth is measured by an expansion of mutualities of feeling.

3. An impersonal domain of capacities for affecting the outer world. Here the mode of action is work—seen as the natural flowing of human energy—and growth is measured by an expansion of power over objects and over people treated as objects.

Any cultural heritage of pathways will, I suppose, encompass all three domains and will strive for some balance among them. But it will set priorities. And in this regard the Western priority appears to be upon the impersonal domain, the Japanese priority on the interpersonal.

Resistance at Forty-Eight offers a representative example, with its emphasis on Nishimura's developmental disability in the interpersonal realm. (In the impersonal world of work he is shown as competent, but his future is blocked by the system. In the personal realm he has neither future nor past: He seems never to have been particularly contemplative or artistic or even athletic.) Nishimura has not done well at relating with his convoy, and his attempt to build a new love is a fiasco. Only as he regains physical health does he begin to regain a modicum of interpersonal health. He failed as a lover, he now comes to understand, because actually he had only been trying to exploit selfishly (impersonally) his partner; his had not been the pure love he had imagined. The implication is that he may be growing from failure and that he will in time put the lesson into practice in relating anew to wife, daughter, and grandchild-to-be.

Transitions and Mass Longevity

What does all of this have to do with the study of life course transitions and aging? In the postmodern era we confront radical transformations in the demography of the human life cycle, in the standardization of its stages, and in the value imputed to various forms of growth and decline. To cope with a problem of such magnitude we need to arm ourselves with a comprehensive understanding of the biographical flow of life in all three domains of change: personal, interpersonal, and impersonal.

The Western heritage has given us an archetype of ideas that deal best with the impersonal domain: a theory of an agent self, inherently alone, condemned to work upon an environment of refractory things. For the other two domains we would do well to learn from the heritages of archetypes that have evolved elsewhere. For the interpersonal domain I have suggested that Japanese tradition is one such, with its theory of self trying to vibrate sympathetically in a convoy of others. For the personal domain South Asian tradition may be a good candidate, with its theory of a self finding the whole cosmos within.

The humanist side of this agenda of inquiry calls on us to articulate a threefold archetype of the potentials for life course growth. No one of the traditional pathways by itself is sufficient, I believe, to meet the demands imposed by the postmodern transformation of the life cycle. Ethnic chauvinists may assert the contrary, insisting that the nightmare of old age is a peculiarity of Western culture. But for postmodern Japan, at least, the tide of recent jitters over problems of aging (Plath, 1972)—*Resistance at Forty-Eight* is no isolated phenomenon —is evidence that Japanese tradition has not provided all the answers either.

The social science side of the agenda calls on us to find ways to maximize the promise of the archetype amid the constraints of a high-technology, high-longevity milieu. In the early industrial era the key cultural nightmare was poverty. Mass productivity raised hopes that material want might now be overcome for all. Escape from poverty was the recurring dream: Dickens's novels are the type case. Popular culture in the United States formulated the figure of Santa Claus as patron saint of a new cargo cult of abundance. Economics, said Thomas Carlyle, was a dismal science if it could not guarantee affluence. But access to abundance, warned Marx, was blocked by the power relations of productivity.

Now mass longevity is transforming the social framework of the life cycle, as industrial production transformed the social framework of property. Mass longevity raises a hope that everyone born human may enjoy a full span of years, and by extension a full range of the opportunities for whatever growth the life cycle allows. Gerontology at times has seemed to be on the way to being the dismal science of

124 Old-Age Brinksmanship

the 20th century, absorbed in the study of human capacities for decline. The life course perspective has opened a fresh flow of optimism. But that optimism needs to be tempered by an understanding of the power relations of life course transitions and of ideologies of human development.

It seems too facile to twist the Marxian paradigm, as some have, and prophesy that the postindustrial era will witness a new kind of class struggle: age class pitted against age class in competition for control over the rewards of experience. But we certainly need to ask whose ("class") interests are being served by defining a life course threshold or transition in one way rather than another. The very word "transition" may be deceptively impersonal. Recuperating from pneumonia, perhaps Nishimura Kōtarō would accept a reclassification of his recent experience as "transition." But until then he was on the brink, fighting a campaign of resistance that was anything but affectively neutral. By using a word such as "transition" do we tacitly acknowledge that our interests are well served by the format of the postindustrial life course, so that we are not tempted to resist?

REFERENCES

Hareven, T. K. The life course and aging in historical perspective. In K. W. Back (Ed.), *Life course: Integrative theories and exemplary populations.* Boulder, Colo.: Westview Press, 1980.
Ishikawa, T. *Yonjū-hassai no teiko.* Tokyo: Shinchōsha, 1958.
Ishikawa, T. [*Resistance at forty-eight*] (N. Kazuma, trans.). Tokyo: Hokuseido Press, 1960.
Kusatsu, O. Ego development and sociocultural process in Japan. *Keizaigaku Kiyo*, 1977, **3**, Part I, 47–109; Part II, 74–128. (In English)
LeVine, R. A. Adulthood and aging in cross-cultural perspective. *Social Science Research Council Items*, 1978, **31/32**, 1–5.
Neugarten, B. Time, age, and the life cycle. *American Journal of Psychiatry*, 1979, **136 (7)**, 887–894.
Neugarten, G., Moore, J. W., & Lowe, J. C. Age norms, age constraints and adult socialization. In B. Neugarten (Ed.), *Middle age and aging.* Chicago: University of Chicago Press, 1968.
Norbeck, E. Yakudoshi: A Japanese complex of supernatural beliefs. *Southwestern Journal of Anthropology*, 1955, **2 (2)**, 105–120.
Pelzel, J. C. Human nature in the Japanese myths. In A. M. Craig & D. H. Shively (Eds.), *Personality in Japanese history.* Berkeley and Los Angeles: University of California Press, 1970.
Plath, D. W. Japan: The after years. In D. O. Cowgill & L. D. Holmes (Eds.), *Aging and modernization.* New York: Appleton-Century-Crofts, 1972.
Plath, D. W. *Long engagements: Maturity in modern Japan.* Stanford, Calif.: Stanford University Press, 1980. (a)

Plath, D. W. Contours of consociation: Lessons from a Japanese narrative. In P. Baltes & O. Brim, Jr. (Eds.), *Life-span development and behavior* (Vol. 3). New York: Academic Press, 1980. (b)

Plath, D. W., & Ikeda, K. After coming of age: Adult awareness of age norms. In T. R. Williams (Ed.), *Socialization and communication in primary groups*. The Hague: Mouton, 1955.

Rohlen, T. The promise of adulthood in Japanese spiritualism. In E. Erikson (Ed.), *Adulthood*. New York: W. W. Norton, 1978.

Ware, J. *The sayings of Confucius*. New York: Mentor, 1955.

6 The Life Course Approach as a Challenge to the Social Sciences

DANIEL BERTAUX

While a developmental focus has been part of the scope of psychology, sociology has yet to take its first step in this direction. The main stem of 20th-century psychology, behaviorism, has a synchronic orientation, but branches have grown from this stem (or against it): Piaget's research on the development of the child's intellectual capacities and, more recently, the whole field of developmental psychology, which grew out from the other end, the study of aging and senescence. Developmental psychology is now beginning to encompass aging as a lifelong process. And in the background of psychological research, psychoanalysis as a wisdom of the human soul, as a praxis of investigation into personal history, has always maintained the diachronic approach as a prerequisite.

Empirical sociology, on the other hand, has mostly turned toward the study of relations between variables, while theoretical sociology's focus is upon institutions and societal structures. Formerly, historical and social thinking went hand in hand, as can be seen in the works of Tocqueville, Marx, and Max Weber. The influence of the 19th century's German philosophy of history crossed the Atlantic, and the founders of American sociology in the early 20th century retained, at least, the view of society as an ongoing process. They were unable, however, to form from this general conception a theoretical framework having enough consistency, plausibility, and explanatory power to win consensus, first, among sociologists themselves, then, among historians, economists, and the general public.[1]

1. The key reason for this failure is, in my opinion, the refusal to develop Marx's central intuitions (for extrascientific reasons) and the vain search for an alternative to his social-historical framework.

Professional social thinkers were looking first and foremost for some sort of social legitimacy. Given the academic context, it was not Marx's conception nor the German philosophers' who could establish it, but the opposite conception: social thinking as a science, as a *physique sociale*, that is, the conception of Auguste Comte, who coined the term sociologie. It is this definition of social thinking as divorced from historical knowledge that was to bring recognition to sociology as a separate discipline and to confer on it a scientific legitimacy. Under widely different forms, from the theoretical frameworks developed by Durkheim and his distant pupil Talcott Parsons to the empirical practice of the survey research and to the level of middle-range theories defined by Robert K. Merton, it is the same epistemology that is to be found: the belief in a realm of social logic that could be completely divorced from history.

In the 1940s, the task was completed: Sociology (in the United States) was at last recognized as a social *science*, and sociologists were seen as professionals of social analysis. Economists had done it some 40 years earlier (with marginalism) and at the same cost: separation from history—and from politics which is one of the mediating fields through which social forces make history.

It eventually became obvious that this cost was much too high. In its rage to cut itself from history, "scientific" sociology lost sight not only of the *historical* side of social processes, but also of their *diachronic* dimension. As a consequence, while it was both necessary and quite feasible to take into account, within a purely structuro-functionalist or structuralist framework, the routine diachronic processes by which local parts of total structures are reproduced, academic sociology was very slow to develop an interest in these routine processes. There is, for instance, considerable literature on stratification but very little on career paths; and the same is true of, say, voting patterns versus the lifelong formation of political attitudes; social segregation in urban residence versus processes of moving from one part of the city to another following changes in income and status; inequality of school chances of children versus concrete processes by which differences in family background are transformed into differences in school achievement; structures of large organizations versus the actual flows over the years of recruitment, promotion, demotion, exit, of their employees; and so on.

Historical processes are, of course, of a completely different kind. Wars, revolutions, counterrevolutions, passages from dictatorship to democracy, from democracy to dictatorship, or from one form of dictatorship or democracy to another form of dictatorship or democracy, social movements, cultural breakthroughs, and the like, will never be understood by the kind of sociology that presupposes that "society" is a stable order based on commonly shared values (functionalism) or even by this related kind of sociology that sees social life as completely determined by underlying "structures" (structuralism). The main weakness is that "structures" are usually seen as forming *noncontradictory systems*. But, of course, as soon as we reintroduce the three *enfants terribles*, the ideas of *contradiction, praxis,* and *history*, we are led to the unescapable conclusion that the movement of societies is in fact *unpredictable*; and social thought, while becoming incomparably more intelligent and interesting, loses its pretention to the title of "science." Taking a hard look at it, it is rather obvious that all attempts of social thought at becoming 100% scientific (in the sense of a *physique sociale*) are bound to fail, simply because the life of societies, that is, history, resembles much more a football game than the movement of planets; and if science can predict the latter with utmost accuracy, it can in no way predict the course of the former. This rather obvious character of human history is not acknowledged (as it would lead to the loss of the status of science) by economics and sociology, because of professional interests.

On the other hand, within an overall historical conception of societal life,[2] there is room indeed for regional theories taking a nondialectical form. This is so because, if society as a stable form is to exist at all, it takes some routines to continually reproduce it; and if social life relies first and foremost on the basic production of material goods, this production necessarily obeys certain socially structured relations.

Opportunity for scientific studies exists when and where power relations have become stabilized, routinized, institutionalized. Thus the demography of the Armenian people in Turkey was predictable until 1896, or the economics of oil production and market until 1973, or the political system of Iran until 1978. But when large shifts in the balance

---

2. Social thought must meet head on the question of *power* (economy as *political economy*, sociology as the study of class relations). As the power game is not predetermined, all hopes of finding the ultimate determinations of social phenomena ("laws") are lost. Otherwise, social thought is forced to do away with the irritating question of power, in which case it becomes simply one more ideological system, consistent in form, universal in content.

of power occur, it seems that our social sciences have nothing to say, precisely when some elucidation of what is happening would be most interesting.

It is because the social sciences, including economics, limit themselves to regional areas of societal life (i.e., structures of relations and routine processes in power-stabilized social formations) that their observations and theories, conclusions and discussions are only of limited validity and interest. And it is because they desperately look for scientific legitimacy that, compared to the audience they should have, what they say is so little read and discussed. Science is not written to be read.[3] It is not simply a matter of jargon or of *form*; it is before all a matter of *content*. A body of thought about social life that aims at becoming scientific is bound to move away from what has always attracted the attention of people: drama, passions, wars, the power game, uncertain struggles. It is bound to focus upon what people by personal experience already understand best—the routines organizing ordinary life. From this the tragedy of contemporary social thought is derived. In its efforts to strive for scientific truth, science abandons the historic role it could play, that of helping to shape a consciousness of the world.

If there is some truth in this description of the situation, then we will better appreciate the formidable challenge that the concept of life course poses to sociology. If taken seriously, the life course approach should force social thinking to move, first, from structures to routine processes (i.e., from synchrony to diachrony). But this would be only the first step; the next one should be to extend social thought in such a way that it would become able to account for wars, crises, mass migrations, changes of political regimes, and other kinds of disruption of the routine social order. As most life courses have passed through such disruptions, sociology would have to follow them and move *from structure to process, from process to history*: a long walk indeed, full of disruptions for sociology itself. Only by following this path would sociology meet the call of the great C. W. Mills, reiterated by Tamara Hareven—that of analyzing the relations between history, social structures, and individuals' lives (Hareven 1977, Chapter 1, this volume).

3. For an attempt to understand what is wrong with the sociologists' style of writing, see Bertaux (1979).

A Study of the French Bakery through Life Stories

Although my main field is social mobility, or rather, the distribution of men and women in relation to the class structure, I have spent some time in the last 10 years, along with my wife, Isabelle, collecting life story interviews in the baker's trade. It is through this project that we became involved in life course analysis.

Initially, I wanted to learn how bread is made, not technically, but socially. What were the social relationships of production organizing the process of production of bread? Was it true that the structural relationships determined the practices and the values of people embedded in them (i.e., was the structuralist hypothesis valid)? Was it true that the goal of making profit, not bread, was the actual goal of production and its organizing principle (i.e., was the Marxist hypothesis valid)? Could it be shown that the relationship of production between master bakers and bakery workers was determining two different ways of life—"different" in a strong sense, that is, ways of life in which such concepts as work, income, leisure, family, children, illness, retirement, death, would take radically different meanings? These were some of the questions with which I started.

As can be seen, my epistemology was wholly structuralist–Marxist. This view was quite common in France in the early 1970s. Two specific features, however, characterized my own work: First, I was not satisfied with mere theorization and decided to get involved in fieldwork. Second, in order to collect data I tried a long-forgotten approach, never used by French sociologists: the life story. There was no other reason at that time than my deep enthusiasm for Oscar Lewis's works. Certainly it seemed bizarre to use such a qualitative technique within a structuralist–Marxist theoretical framework. But this research was a personal hobby (my main academic work focusing on social mobility), which also meant I felt perfectly free to do as I liked.

This decision to collect life stories appeared later to have been a good one. Not only did it allow me to get the information I wanted on the relationships of production and thus to prove that it is possible to use a reputedly qualitative approach to get at the core of social phenomena, but life stories, by their very nature, also shed light on many fundamental aspects that I had initially overlooked. Among these, the most important is the process by which the artisanal bakery reproduces its structure and its very existence over successive generations.

This research on the French bakery has grown over the years. Here I will merely present sketches, to illustrate some points relevant to the study of life courses.[4]

SATURATION

The first point is methodological. It is an answer to the question: How is it possible to *generalize* to the whole population of the bakery from information collected on a small (a few dozen) nonrandom sample? There are about 45,000 artisanal bakers in France, as many bakers' wives who sell the bread, and 80,000 bakery workers (industrial bread represents less than 10% of the total production of bread). Adding some 30,000 salegirls, we get a total of 200,000 persons (1% of the active population in France), most of them working within artisanal relations of production.

We interviewed about 30 bakery workers, as many bakers and bakers' wives, and apprentices—a total of about 100 life stories, focused on work life (but not restricted to it). Compared to the usual sample sizes in sociology, this is small; but even more questionable (from the empiricist point of view) is the fact that we did not choose our interviewees through a random process. Instead, we moved from one to the next, following the threads of acquaintance relations among the bakers themselves and among bakery workers. We tried to reach representativeness by diversifying our networks. We did fieldwork both in the Paris area and in a rural area in southwest France. We added to the bakery workers' union network another one of non-unionized workers. We looked for missing numbers not found through the networks (e.g., the very successful baker, the total failure, the young, the extremely busy, the friendless baker, etc.).

Despite this seemingly erratic character of our sample, we are now pretty sure of our sociological conclusions about the artisanal bakery. But on what grounds? How is it possible, from the study of a small number of cases, to draw a theory that is not merely a set of hypotheses to be verified by another (quantitative) method, a theory

4. More details on this study of the artisanal bakery are given in other works published in English (Bertaux, 1981; Bertaux & Bertaux-Wiame, 1981).

that already has its own validity with respect to the process studied? This is a key question in the life course field, as most studies are done on a small number of cases.

By experimenting with life stories in the loose way described above, we eventually found the answer to this question. We noticed that if the first life story of a bakery worker had taught us a lot; if the second and third and fourth had also brought new information and, by the mere effect of repetition, had stressed some crucial points that were present in the first life story but lost in the narrative; if each subsequent bakery worker's life story had something to add, especially about new topics such as family life and union life (which we were introducing because we felt much safer about our own understanding of the logic of work life); if, therefore, every new life story brought something new, the proportion of the new versus the already known was getting smaller all the time. After about 15 life stories we were pretty certain that we had a clear picture of the basic stucture of the work life, whether weekly or across the life course.

Most bakery workers are at their jobs at least six nights a week, at least nine hours per night (from 3 A. M., or earlier, to noon). Thus, no matter whether he is from rural or urban background, Catholic or agnostic, fat or thin, married or single, a bakery worker will work at least (6 x 9) 54 hours a week. This massive fact, a direct consequence of the artisanal character of the relationships of production, determines most of the rest of his life—his weekly time budget, his family life, (sleeping in the afternoon, after work), his health (which declines after age 40 because of long hours and working in front of an oven), his activities outside work—restricted in the young years to sports such as cycling, swimming, rowing, and boxing, which, by their character of violent physical efforts, correspond to the work activity. For bakery workers there is no reading, no participation in cultural activities, no movies; for, as they say, because of the chronic lack of sleep they tend to fall asleep "as soon as the lights are off."

As this *pattern of living* was coming up again and again and as it was obvious that it was re-created in every life not by some mentality or psychological tendency, but as a direct consequence of the relations of production themselves, confidence could be gained that it was the pattern underlying not only the lives of the first 15 men we had interviewed, but the lives of the 80,000 bakery workers (or at least the 75,000 who work within the frame of artisanal relations of production). It was the structure of relations of production that was determining the observed pattern. With 15 more life stories we were sure of that.

Hence, we have the answer to the methodological question discussed here; we call it *saturation*. When the interviews bring again and again the same elements of a recognizable pattern, when subsequent interviews with new persons confirm its presence in *every* life, then the pattern may be considered not merely fantasy of the researcher (in social-scientific language—mere hypothesis) but a structuring feature of the actual processes.

In the dominant epistemology of the social sciences, the use of quantitative data is the only way to *prove* a given hypothesis. This epistemology has been kind enough to admit that qualitative techniques could help to bring clues, insights, and hints and to lead to the formulation of hypotheses, but nothing more. The term "qualitative data" is in itself a product of the quantitative epistemology, where it is defined negatively by opposition to the term "quantitative data."[5]

The discovery of the saturation phenomenon gives a new legitimacy to so-called qualitative observations obtained on a small number of cases not chosen through some kind of random procedure. Saturation is the answer to the famous riddle of the validity of "qualitative data." It allows the development of an alternative to the neopositivist epistemology so prevalent in the social sciences. It questions its built-in principles, like the separation of the moments of theory, observation, and analysis; the inherent superiority of quantitative data; the emphasis put on proving assumptions by referring to related variations of quantitative measures; and so on. All of these principles are very useful in the natural sciences but have eventually proven sterile in the social sciences. The latter require an emphasis upon what Glaser and Strauss (1967) have aptly called "the discovery of grounded theory."

THE STRUCTURALIST INTERPRETATION

If the saturation phenomenon allows for the construction of a new epistemology, we are tempted to take an objectivist stand as to its

5. It could be argued that *the very idea of data* as observations gathered in a systematic way, which means also through a fixed instrument of observation, is part of the neopositivist epistemology. In contrast to the use of questionnaires, the life story guide we used in our interviews not only was different for bakery workers, bakers, and so on, but was also evolutive as new information led to new questions or to the focus on new areas of research.

conditions of validity. After all, it should not be too difficult to reach saturation on a given phenomenon. To the structuralist sociologist, however, remains the question of what it means, and this question may only be answered in terms of *social relationships (rapports sociaux)* not in terms of psychic traits, or interpersonal interaction, or commonly shared values. Saturation is a sign that one and the same process is at work in the lives of different people who ignore each other: The sociologist cannot help interpreting this sign as indicating the hidden work of some *sociostructural* process. To make this underlying structure, or structural process, explicit is the task of sociology.

The sociologist considers psychological features as socially produced and looks for the *social relationships* behind the actions, conducts, attitudes, and values of people. In the French context at least, this amounts to stating that the sociological point of view has to include structuralism.

The structuralist epistemology still seems to me a necessary stage for those who want to move from common sense to sociological thinking.[6] By inverting every assumption of the common sense discourse through which we like to represent ourselves as active people, conscious subjects of our actions, structuralism helps achieve the necessary break with naïve common sense. Take such statements as (to caricature): we do not act, but *are acted by*, social relationships; we do not talk, but *are talked by*, language; we do not think, but *are thought by* surrounding ideologies; we do not consume, but *are consumed by* the world of goods; once understood and assimilated, they tremendously facilitate moving away from the "psychologism"[7] latent in much of contemporary sociology and especially in empirical studies.

For instance, applying the structuralist point of view to the question of the logic underlying life trajectories, we have been led to the concept of *segmentation* of lives. We will explain it by an example: A bakery worker who, fed up with night work and long hours, quits his

6. The development of the structuralist epistemology for sociology and the argument that sociology, being the study of social relationships, must be structuralist have been best expressed by Pierre Bourdieu and Jean Claude Passeron in their various works. See especially Bourdieu, Chamboredon, and Passeron (1968) and, in English, the difficult but highly consistent paper by Bourdieu (1968). The irony is that this paper was written in May 1968, precisely when history was again on the move and seemed to make structuralism obsolete.

7. What we are referring to is the tendency to consider the ultimate determinations of societal life and daily life to be of a psychological nature—such as commonly shared values, attitudes, aspirations, and the like. Structuralism acknowledges their efficiency but considers them as *mediations*, mediating links that are themselves produced by social relationships.

job and becomes a street policeman feels a sense of progress and of continuity in his life. He is, after all, the same person. From the point of view of strictly structural relationships, however, he moved from an area organized by one social logic (production relationships in the artisanal bakery) to an area organized by a wholly different logic (the police as a state apparatus). Thus, from this point of view, he is not the same man anymore; for not only did he change roles, but if it is true that roles, and particularly work roles, penetrate the man himself and transform him, then it is the man himself who changed—or rather, was changed. We are thus led to consider any given life as made up of several *segments*, each one corresponding to a period embedded in a given system of social relationships (Bertaux, 1976).

This conception is useful on several grounds: It opens the door to a critique of *l'idéologie biographique*, that is, the common sense conception of a man's or woman's life as a whole, an unfolding totality having its uniqueness, its inner (if hidden) logic, its metaphysical meaning (Bertaux, 1976).

This conception of the individual is central to our Western culture. Its application not only to great historical figures like kings or saints but to everyone (or at least, to every *man*) is connected with the Renaissance humanism and with Protestantism, which itself is inseparable from the historical development of a class of merchants and entrepreneurs. Whatever its historical roots, it is now deeply encrusted in the ideological system of the West, regenerated everyday through all hero-centered cultural forms (novels, films, TV series, cults of political and theatrical stars). This individualistic ideology has now become an efficient *reality* in itself. It is the driving force that animates not only the dreams of many young people, but also the behavior of all career-oriented adults. It does *not*, however, shape all reality. Market forces and, ultimately, power relations act forcefully to actualize another logic, by which human beings are moved from one spot to another of the production system. Dreams are crushed, executives are fired, stars become has beens, factories and mines are closed down, peasants are pushed off the land, young men are enlisted in wars, and so on. Capital is on the move, and everybody is urged to follow; its network is worldwide and far beyond human, or rather political, control, and its accelerating pace is cutting more and more life courses into socially unconnected segments.

The discrepancy between the individualistic ideology, on one hand, and the actual reality of social relationships shaping lives, on the other, is at the root of many phenomena, like the famous identity crisis. The construction of "identity" in the individualistic sense of the term seems to require a social environment that is at the same time open enough to allow space for individual action (in philosophical terms, the exteriorization of interiority) *and* stable enough to allow for a projection of self in the future, a projection that is necessary if projects, plans, and elaborate strategies are to be developed. If the environment's changes are too swift and too unpredictable, the interiorization of exteriority threatens to destroy the fragile construction of our self-image. Mass unemployment, and the threats it contains for employed people are not psychological facts, but they have deep psychological consequences. The observable shift of self-definitions from work-centered to hobby-centered definitions is an interesting symptom.

There we are touching upon what Hareven has called, in her programmatic paper, "the phenomenology of the life course," that is, the "subjective" aspect of life as opposed to its "objective" aspect, which she refers to as behavioral. The two aspects are obviously related, as may be seen when sudden turns in a behavioral life course appear as consequences of an action resulting from a decision of the person. Seldom will the decision be wholly *of* the person; seldom will it be *only* an anticipation (and thus, interiorization) of external circumstances. Acts (actions, praxis) belong to both realms, the subjective and the objective, and constitute, in fact, the link between the two, while at the same time calling for an *Aufhebung* (the necessity to go beyond) of the objective–subjective conceptual dichotomy.

ATTEMPTING TO CHANGE ONE'S CLASS POSITION

In the bakery study, we found that most master bakers are in fact former bakery workers who succeeded in becomig self-employed by buying a goodwill from a retiring baker.[8] This does not mean that most bakery workers become self-employed. Although we have no means by which to give an accurate percentage, we are pretty certain that the proportion of bakery workers becoming self-employed is much less

---

8. We wondered about where these propertyless workers, coming invariably from poor families, could find the money necessary to buy the goodwill. The answer gave us a key to the understanding of a central mechanism in the reproduction of the artisanal form in the midst of developed capitalist economy. See below and Bertaux and Bertaux-Wiame (1981).

than the ratio of number of bakers to number of bakery workers—
45,000/70,000, or 64%—would indicate. As the demographic pyramid
of the profession shows, many young boys having entered apprenticeship at age 14 leave the trade during their 20s; at age 35 only half of
them are still there, either as bakers or as bakery workers.

Interviewing young bakers in their teens and early 20s, we found
out that most of them wanted to try to become a master baker. Adult
bakery workers, on the other hand, very seldom referred to any
youthful dreams of becoming self-employed. It could have been a
generation effect, an historical change in the social context; but the
opposite assumption, that is, that it is an age, or rather a life course
effect, a change in the life course of *any* cohort, seems to us more
plausible.

The crux of the matter is the question of becoming self-employed;
we soon discovered that in order to set up one's own bakery, a bakery
worker had to find *two* resources: money and a wife. Money was the
easiest to get (he, of course, had to reimburse it by working *very* hard
after becoming self-employed). But a wife who would enter gaily into
the dreary business of a full-time shopkeeper (and for a baker's wife,
full time means six full days a week, from 8 A.M. to 8 P.M. with a two- or
three-hour break at lunchtime, plus supplementary off-hour tasks)
and also do the full work of a housewife, a wife courageous enough to
go on smiling despite her exhaustion or bad mood, a wife clever
enough to understand immediately the logic of shopkeeping, which
means among other things that the money that falls into your cash
drawer is not yours until the various cycles of the business have been
completed, such a wife was difficult to find.

So we became interested in bakers' wives, about whom we had
heard very little up to this point, and also in bakery workers' wives.[9] By
listening to these women, by asking their husbands to tell us about
them (which they would not have done spontaneously, as shown by
our first round of life story interviews), we realized how crucial the
part of the woman was in a baker's couple. Not only is she responsible
for the success or failure (closing down) of the shop, she also has, as
the young wife of a bakery worker eager to be self-employed, the

---

9. Renée Colin conducted the first life story interviews, which rank among the best
that have been collected in this research. Interestingly enough, she did them for
herself, without expecting any money or degree (as an adult student she had attended
one of my exposés on this research), so she felt completely free to do them as she
wished.

power to crush the lifelong project of her husband by refusing to get involved in it.

We noticed a strange coincidence: Many of the successful self-made bakers had gotten married and become self-employed practically at the same time—in the same month, even the same week. One had an interesting slip of the tongue: When asked in which year he married, he answered, "*Je me suis installé, c'est-à-dire non, marié, en juillet 1965*" [I got self-employed, I mean *married*, in July 1965]. In fact he had done both things at the same time, as a carefully planned move.

We conducted a second round of interviews with a new group of sample adults and retired bakery workers, focusing not only on work life, but also on attempts to escape from the position of bakery worker, either by taking up some other job or by becoming self-employed. As, by definition, all of these assumed attempts had failed, it was understandable that in the first round of life story interviews, the men had not been too keen on mentioning them. In this second round we found indeed that such moves had been considered and often attempted. Several men stated that they had wanted to become self-employed; but each said that his wife refused to move along, either because she already had a job she liked, or because she was of fragile health, or simply because she thought it was not worth the very hard life it would be for several years. So these men remained workers all their life.[10]

Thus the attitude of the newly wed wife seemed to explain a lot; but being structuralists, we looked for something more, and found that in all these cases, the couple had been married at least one year before the opportunity came for finding a loan and becoming self-employed (both things go together, as it is usually the baker selling his goodwill who will take the huge risk of lending the money). During the first year of marriage to a bakery worker, the woman had had the time to *learn* what it meant to be a baker's wife and especially the wife of a self-made ("self-and-wife-made" would be more accurate) baker, which might explain why she refused to get into such a trap. All pretexts were good—fragile health, a good job, or the preservation of family life. Having found the money but having lost the wife (as a

10. In all cases but one, these statements were made in front of the wife, who agreed and gave details. In one case only, it is the wife who deplored, in front of her husband, his lack of ambition. It appeared later in a separate conversation that this man had for years said to his wife he was starting work at midnight, while he was, in fact, starting at 3 A.M., and that he had used this free time to live a very rich nightlife on his own.

future baker's wife), the candidates to self-employment had to leave behind their old dreams.

By contrast, the observed coincidence of marriage and *installation* (becoming self-employed) in the cases of successful self-made bakers took on a new meaning: These keen young men had been courting their fiancées while looking for the money and, as soon as they had found it, had jumped into marriage. For the young girl, the perspective of marrying not a worker but a future shopkeeper might have helped in reaching a positive decision; while, by tying her to him by the bond of marriage and not giving her the time to think it over, the young man had taken possession of the missing resource.

TIMING

Good timing, that is all there is to it, we could say. For, if the prospect of a loan helps to get the wife, the wife is *absolutely necessary* to get the loan. This is because of the very special nature of the goodwill itself: The value of a shop lies mostly in the number of customers that come every day to buy fresh bread. If there are, say, 300 such families (corresponding to about 1,000 persons), it means so many hundreds of kilograms of flour treated per month, the figure that is used to evaluate a goodwill; in this case, say, $40,000. Now, if the new bakers —the young couple—fail, which means, in fact, if the young *wife* fails in her role of *boulangère* (the skill of the man has been checked by whoever loans the money, and a bad worker—a rare case—will never get a loan), then the number of customers starts dropping, for there is always at least another bakery around the corner. After a few months, the number of daily visitors may have dropped by half, and the value of the goodwill will have followed. The young couple becomes unable to reimburse the trimestrial loans; they are kicked out; and the proprietors find themselves with a goodwill that is worth only $20,000. They have lost half of its value in a year's time.[11]

Thus the risk is great for the retiring couple who have no pension and rely on reimbursements for a happy retirement. They *must*, therefore, know as much as they can about the new wife—who is, most of the time, only a fiancée and has never worked as shopkeeper before.

In order to cope with this dilemma, the form of *gérance* has been invented, in which the young couple enters the goodwill not as proprie-

11. We have witnessed several such cases.

tor, but as a manager. But this is in itself a situation full of traps, which both partners try to avoid. The retiring couple know that the *gérants* will tend to repell customers in order later to be in a position to buy the goodwill at a lower price. For the young baker such an experience is even more dangerous than remaining a worker for some time after marriage because this time it is the real thing, but it is still not too late for his young wife to leave him and his heroic project.

So timing is the thing, and here again we meet with Hareven's program and her emphasis on the study of *timing* as related not to age but to the strategic necessities of life.

Praxis

Now that the distinction between the sociostructural and the ideological is defined, we must focus upon their relation. Here we find *praxis*, the unpredictable stream of conscious actions that continuously solves the contradictions between the wished and the possible, between wishes themselves, and between realistic possibilities themselves.

Praxis is not behavior. Behavior is action conceived as an answer to a given situation, and its original Pavlovian meaning may be extended to situations such as anticipations (i.e., goal-oriented behavior). The idea of praxis covers a much wider area that includes not only individual but also group and class actions; not only the acts by themselves but the thoughts orienting the action, thoughts that are subsequently modified by the experience gained through action; not only the modifications of the environment by the actor, but the modification of the actor itself by its own action.

The trouble with the praxis concept is, according to the academic sociologist, that it cannot be measured. This is true, and it explains why it is not sociologists, but philosophers, those oriented toward the analysis of the present as history (e.g., Sartre, Henri Lefebvre, Herbert Marcuse, and Jürgen Habermas) who have developed the idea of praxis. But if academic sociology cannot do anything with the concept of praxis, does that indicate a failure of the concept or a failure of this form of sociology? If sociology cannot take into account wars, social struggles, political battles, because their outcomes are unpredictable, what is to be questioned? Human history or sociology as social "science"? To find a way, not to explain but to *elucidate* such struggle processes which, after all, lie at the heart of history is the challenge for meaningful social research.

As the life courses we study have been shaped by history and, furthermore, as the actions of which they are the result have contributed to shape history itself—for history is not only made by visible, political forces, but also by the constant pressure of millions of invisible actions by individuals, families, small groups—sociology has to face the question of praxis and its relation to history.[12]

Anthroponomy or the Production of Human Beings Themselves

According to sociologists, people are not monads, that is, closed systems directed from within by a willful spirit, nor are they mere tools of the historicity of social forms, pure "carriers of structures" animated from outside by some impersonal process. They are actors playing roles, sometimes improvising, sometimes fighting each other; and they are, first, social products. "Society" does not confront "the individual" as an outside reality; rather, the inner self as a condensation of some social forms integrated over the years confronts in other selves other forms of social-historical condensation, usually within the framework of socially defined interaction where roles are largely prewritten.

But lest we be drawn toward a psychological analysis of people as social products, we should first focus on the process of production of people *as a whole*, not on the process of production of *one* person.

This is precisely where the concept of anthroponomy might prove useful. A neologism, it stands for the expression "production, distribution, and consumption of human energy"; it has been coined in obvious analogy to the term "economy," as taken to refer to the production, distribution, and consumption of goods (Bertaux, 1977).

We have been taught to conceive of the whole production of a given society as consisting merely of economic production. This reduction of social production to its economic aspect is erroneous. Any

12. On the conception of history as made also through people's pressure, see the British journal *History Workshop* (1976ff.); the last chapter of Paul Thompson's book *The Edwardians* (1976); and, on women, Isabelle Bertaux-Wiame (1978), in which the idea is developed that women, in their everyday lives, make history, for instance (but not only) by limiting their fecundity, which has far-reaching demographic and, ultimately, historical consequences.

society's production has two aspects: one is the production of goods, the other is the production of life itself or, to be more precise, the production of human energy, of the multiple forms of human energy.

This second aspect of production requires a huge amount of work, which is carried out within specific relations of production. In traditional societies, these relationships were kinship relationships. Most of the production of human energy, that is, preparing food; taking care of the babies, the sick, and the old; teaching children language and good manners; was attributed to women. This traditional way of fulfilling human-energy production or anthroponomic production persisted for a long time in industrial societies, which may explain why it also remained invisible for such a long time. Housework was not really considered as productive work, not only because of the sexism of theoreticians, but also because of their blindness to noneconomic forms of production. If, to begin with, we define production as the production of goods, it is no wonder that we become unable to conceive of activities that do not produce goods as productive activities.

Nowadays, however, more and more of the anthroponomic production is done within specific institutions, like the health system or the educational system, which draw a large share of societal resources. Thus the huge field of anthroponomic production is becoming visible at last. The concept of anthroponomy aims at accelerating this process of emergence and calls for the analysis of this specific area of social activity as a field in itself.

Anthroponomic theory, which so far exists only as a word, might eventually constitute one of the conceptual sets on which the analysis of life cycles and life trajectories could be grounded. For instance, life trajectories may be seen as outcomes of a massive process of *distribution* of people into social structure(s), and this process is closely related to that of the *production* of those same people. We have tried to develop this line of analysis elsewhere (Bertaux, 1977). Another example of the relevance of anthroponomic analysis is the obvious fact that the various stages of the family life cycle, as traditionally defined, correspond to the various stages of the production of children within the family. Families with children may be seen as units of production, and the necessities of the production of children have, so it seems to us, more explanatory power than the internalization of norms if we are to account for a whole range of family behavior, family strategies, and relationships within the family (here conceived as based upon necessary relationships of anthroponomic production).

But in order to convey the full meaning of the idea of "production of human energy," we will use a simple example, drawn again
from the bakery research. *Apprenticeship* is the process by which young
adolescents are transformed into future bakers. While this seems
obvious, a closer look at the inner workings of apprenticeship will
show that this process iṣ no mere "learning"; it is, in fact, a process of
deep restructuration of the mind and body of these young people, a
process that produces them into something new.

APPRENTICESHIP AS AN ANTHROPONOMIC PROCESS

A boy becomes an apprentice when, having reached his 15th
birthday, he is entrusted by his parents to a baker. A very short
contract form is filled out, by which the child agrees to work three
years for the baker and the baker agrees to teach him the trade. The
boy will live in the baker's house until the end of the apprenticeship.
The contract amounts to a total devolution of the *puissance paternelle*
(fatherly authority) (Bertaux-Wiame, 1976). The law makes it explicit
that the master baker has the *autorité parentale.* And no baker will forget
to say to the parents when bidding them goodbye, *"Nous le traiterons
comme un fils"* [We shall treat him as a son].

There are laws and regulations to protect workers from their
bosses; but no law protects children from their parents. Therefore, the
baker, who, in fact, stands in the relation of *patron/ouvrier* (boss/worker)
to the boy, will have full powers to enforce his will, which means
shouting, blows, punishments, and the like. Such is the framework of
apprenticeship.[13]

As most of our interviews about apprenticeship testify, apprenticeship in rural areas meant being awakened by the baker, often with
a pan of cold water in the face and on the pillow. "You want to sleep at
that age . . . ," said an old worker, recalling his youth. The apprentice
had to get down to the *fournil* after a quick bowl of coffee and begin a
long night of work that would end at noon. Often the boy would be
very sleepy on the job, his movements would get slower and slower,

---

13. A recent book, the autobiography of an Italian who as a child was a shepherd in
Sardinia for his father, describes very well this type of double relation between father
and son; the title of the book is *Padre Padrone (Father Boss).* (See Ledda, 1975.) It must be
added that we describe here the conditions of apprenticeship that have existed throughout the last 50 years (and probably longer) as they have been described to us by bakery
workers and bakers of all ages. A recent law (1974) tends to modify this situation by
having the apprentice spend one full week out of two in a technical school.

he would pause more and more often; hence, the constant shouting and punching by the master baker. The apprentice would also make unavoidable mistakes and receive memorable kicks in the bottom for it.

At last, lunchtime would come. Everybody would gather around the table, including the workers employed and the salesgirls, if any. The men would be tired, sometimes falling asleep "in their plate of soup," and would go to sleep right after lunch.

But the workday was not over yet. At 4 P.M. the baker would get up, wake up his apprentice, load loaves in the small truck, and start touring the countryside. When they came to a hamlet or a farm, the master baker would blow the horn. The women would come out, buy the huge loaves, and pay the baker who would remain at the wheel while the apprentice would unload the bread. Then off they would go to the next stop, be it rain or snow. When they came back to the shop it was around 7 P.M.; they would eat and go to sleep. And at midnight, the pan of cold water would strike again.

There were variations to this scenario. In towns, the apprentice's late afternoons were used to deliver bread, cakes, and pastries to restaurants, by bicycle. In some cases, for instance, if the apprentice was the baker's nephew (the worst situation, for if he tried to escape and go back to his family, he would be promptly brought back to the bakery), the baker's wife might ask him to do various tasks, like cleaning the shop, washing the car, or tilling the garden, whenever he seemed to be doing nothing.

Now, what is the meaning of this process of forceful pressure to work? To the sociologist it cannot be reduced to "teaching a skill." While apprenticeship lasts three years, it does not take more than a few months for a willful adult to learn the trade in its various aspects. We have met one baker who at age 14 with only six months of training replaced his master who had to go to war. Through very hard work the youth was able to run the *fournil* all by himself. Furthermore, apprenticeship used to last two years only up to the 1930s, when social laws started to be edicted to "protect" the apprentice.[14] Quite obviously, the

14. Before the 1930s, most "contracts" were purely oral. Bakers used to teach every-thing to the (unpaid) apprentice except one gesture, that is, putting the bread into the oven (the most difficult task). Apprentices had to break off *by themselves* the ever perduring situation of apprenticeship by deciding one day that it was enough. They walked away and hired themselves to another baker, as paid workers, pretending, of course, that they knew everything including *enfourner*. "If I had not walked out," said one retired bakery worker 50 years later, "I would still be there as an apprentice." As a particularly shy youngster he had stayed three-and-a-half years as unpaid apprentice. (See Bertaux-Wiame, 1976.)

length of apprenticeship as a process of skill learning is now grossly exaggerated. At first we interpreted this to be an extension of a situation of forceful exploitation that greatly benefitted the baker. Apprentice labor is unpaid labor (room and board was all they got until very recently); besides, the labor day is extended to its utmost limit, an extension that the baker imposes also on himself. This could not be done with a regular worker who is paid by the hour.

Our interpretation was obviously correct; but it might not tell the full story. As we realized later, apprenticeship as a learning process cannot be reduced to learning skills, recipes, and the unwritten rules of the social context. It is much more than that. Its main point, in fact, is to *transform the body*, to render it able not only to make and cook the dough, but to do it 12 hours in a row. The apprentice must not only learn the necessary skills, but he must also become able to execute the tasks very swiftly, while thinking about what comes next, and to do it by night, every night of the week but one (and before 1936, *every* night of the year).

The body wants to sleep at night, not in the afternoon; the apprenticeship means that the natural circadian rhythm of the body has to be overthrown and replaced by a very different one. The body wants to rest after a few hours of hard, compact work. It is necessary to make it much more resistant to fatigue not only in its muscles but, first, in its nerves and heart. The body wants to slow down the pace of work for a while; but the dough does not wait and neither will the customers, so that a *second souffle* has to be found. Given the life of a bakery worker and, even more, of a master baker, nobody can follow the pace of that life who has not been through the ordeal of apprenticeship, and at a sufficiently early age. A baker is like a long-distance runner running a marathon every night; and that takes training.

Artisanal relations of production do not produce bread and profit only; they also produce bakers. They reproduce them "daily" (nightly) in their grown-up age, but first, through apprenticeship. They produce them from scratch, through the shouting, punching, and kicking of the master baker on the soft dough of the apprentice.

From this example we may grasp what is meant by "process of anthroponomic production." The meaning of this expression cannot be reduced to that of "reproduction of labor power," a key concept in the Marxist literature. Anthroponomic production refers not only to the reproduction of labor power but also to its very *making* and to its deep *transformations*, which concern the whole being (the body *and* the mind, to use the old-fashioned dichotomy). Moreover, it encompasses all forms of human energy, whether this energy is sold or not as labor power. "Labor power" is the narrow window through which the economic mind looks at human energy, this strength that is equivalent with life.

Beyond Structuralism

The structuralist principle is built in the way we used life story interviews. We initially focused these interviews not upon opinions, attitudes, and values, but upon actions (which we rather call *des pratiques*); not upon the subjective meanings of the actions for the actors, but upon the *pratiques* themselves, their sequences and timing. As a result, our first interviews lacked human content. But we got what we wanted—practices, and by comparing the practical life courses of several bakery workers (and later, of bakers), we were able to get at the structural relationships that conditioned these practices. This part of the research was thus wholly oriented toward what Hareven calls the "behavioristic" side of the life courses; we were looking for the sociostructural relationships underlying observed behavior. To use life stories to get at the behavior and to move from observed patterns of behavior (over a number of cases) to the assumed structure of social relationships underlying them was our strategy.

It may be that it was successful only because we chose an homogeneous population to study, that is, people whose life courses were determined by one and the same set of sociostructural relationships. But even in this highly favorable content, the structuralist approach showed its limits. It allowed us to understand the *inner workings* of the artisanal bakery and how it shapes people's lives; but it could not explain why this artisanal form still exists in France.

We propose that it is the constant effort of all people in this artisanal branch that keeps it alive. To be sure, the sociostructural relations of the artisanal mode of production make this constant effort compulsory; with the high pace of work and life one either has to follow or drop altogether the life of a baker! But why do people not drop more often? Why are there so many people not only able but willing to keep up with this high rhythm? This is what a structuralist approach cannot understand.

With the conception of human beings as products of their young years, and here of apprenticeship, we came to understand why some people are still *able* to become artisanal bakers. This was already an important step forward. But why are they *willing* to do so? Why do they keep on fighting? Individually, it may be explained by the context of commercial competition: they must fight or fail. This is the rule of the artisanal game. But it is the very existence of this game that is problematic, an existance that structuralism has to take for granted. If tomorrow the artisanal bakery would disappear, we would certainly find a consistent explanation to this disappearance. In fact it would be easier to explain it than to explain its actual survival! But a theory that may explain at once one outcome and its contrary fails in explaining both. Focus on the life courses, hence on praxis, will eventually require that we move from functionalism and structuralism to something *beyond* structuralism—which will also mean beyond sociology as a *physique sociale*.

Structuralism focuses upon the way social relations embrace people who are seen as puppets enacted by the strings of socio-structural relationships. There is a softer version of this: It is Parsons's functionalism. For Parsons, as far as I understand his theory, it is in last resort the shared values of the consensus that breathe life into the human puppets. It sounds slightly more humanistic than French structuralism, but for the wrong reason. You may identify with the consensus (as Parsons did), and feel a quasireligious gratification for it, while it is utterly impossible to identify with sociostructural relationships, as they rob you first of your human identity. But whatever their differences, both conceptions stand together (as long as there is a firm social order) and fail together, as soon as some mass behavior arises that cannot be deduced positively from the established social order. Not only war, for instance, is beyond their explanatory power, but also the rebellion against war. As a global system, functionalism failed because the antiwar movement by its very existence broke the consensus and made everybody wonder for *whom* did the functions function. Structuralism fails, too, whenever some people appear to be literally stepping out of the "structures" and inventing their praxis, which may eventually end up in the creation of new structures.

One way to deepen the social-scientific approach is to extend structuralism to include the past as incorporated in the people of the present. People are not merely carrying contemporary structures, they are also carrying those parts of earlier structures that have made them what they are. People grow up in a changing world but retain at least some of their background. The more they do so, in fact, the more their behavior, being at odds with contemporary norms, appears *inner-directed*. On the other hand, the people who conform their behavior to contemporary norms (the *conformists* or the "other-directed," to use Riesman's [1950] expression) are the delights of structuralism and functionalism.

Each man and woman is the product of a given family, and through this particular family, a product of a given social group, of a social class, in a given society, at a given historical moment. Local sub-culture has made them what they are and will be, to a certain extent. By thinking in terms of production of human beings, we may better understand how past values and past patterns of behavior travel through time and reappear in latter generations.

But even this anthroponomic approach will not be enough to account for all the contradictions of reality as a sociohistorical process; and as the study of actual life courses follow closely these contra-dictions, we will eventually have to move to a more encompassing way of thinking. People are not mere products, although they are that, too. People, at least potentially, have their own praxis. As Sartre (1960) put it in one of his best works: "L'homme se caractérise avant tout par le dépassement d'une situation, par ce qu'il parvient à faire de ce qu'on a fait de lui" [What is characteristic of man is his capacity to transcend a given situation, to make something out of what has been made of him].

Here is, expressed in a nutshell, a fundamental philosophical question: Where history, social relationships, and praxis meet and merge, how do they interact to create new forms of human life?

REFERENCES

Bertaux, D. *Histories de vies—ou récits de pratiques? Méthodologie de l'approche biographique en sociologie* (unpublished report). Paris: Centre d'Etudes des Mouvements Sociaux, 1976.
Bertaux, D. *Destins personnels et structure de classe*. Paris: Presses Universitaires de France, 1977.
Bertaux, D. Ecrire la sociologie. *Social Science Information*, 1979, **XIX-1**, 7–25.
Bertaux, D. (Ed.). *Biography and society: The life history approach in the social sciences*. London: Sage Publications, 1981.
Bertaux, D., & Bertaux-Wiame, I. Artisanal bakery in France: How it lives and why it survives. In F. Bechhofer & B. Elliott (Eds.), *The petite bourgeoisie: Comparative studies of the uneasy stratum*. London: Macmillan, 1981.

Bertaux-Wiame, I. *L'apprentissage en boulangerie dans l'entre-deux-guerres: Une enquête d'histoire orale* (Master's thesis). Paris: Groupe de Sociologie du Travail, Université de Paris VII, 1976.

Bertaux-Wiame, I. *La participation des catégories dominées à l'action sociale* (research project). Paris: Centre National de la Recherche Scientifique, 1978.

Bourdieu, P., Chamboredon, J. C., & Passeron, J. C. *Le métier de sociologue*. Paris: Bordas, 1968.

Bourdieu, P. Structuralism and the theory of sociological knowledge. *Social Research*, 1968, **35** (4), 681–706.

Glaser, B., & Strauss, A. *The discovery of grounded theory*. Chicago: Aldine, 1967.

Hareven, T. K. The family life cycle in historical perspective. In J. Cuisenier & M. Segalen (Eds.), *The family life cycle in European societies*. The Hague: Mouton, 1977.

History Workshop: A Journal of Socialist Historians. Oxford: Oxford University Press, 1976ff.

Ledda, G. *Padre padrone: L'educazione di un pastore*. Milan: Feltrinelli, 1975.

Riesman, L. *The lonely crowd*. New York: Doubleday, 1950.

Sartre, J. P. *Questions de méthode*. Paris: Gallimard, 1960.

Thompson, P. *The Edwardians*. London: Weidenfeld & Nicholson, 1975.

7 Individual Time, Social Time, and Intellectual Aging[1]

GISELA LABOUVIE-VIEF

The fate of intellectual development in later life occupies a rather controversial status in the field of psychogerontology, and disagreement among researchers in this area is pronounced. This disagreement is not so much a function of a lack of consistent data, but rather has its basis in the motivation for studying intellectual changes per se. Interest in cognition has always been closely linked to the disciplines of philosophy and epistemology, and from this linkage researchers have, for a long time, derived a certain comfort in the belief of the objectivity of their conclusions. Yet, with the reformulations in philosophy of science and epistemology in this century, it has become obvious that such claims to objectivity are deceptive and that our conceptions of intellectual maturity often are complex rationalizations that result from, and serve to perpetuate, existing social systems with their particular distributions of resources along age, sex, and social class lines.

The present overview is not intented, therefore, to present a confusing summary of what is, in effect, a highly consistent data field. Rather, it will attempt to develop a twofold argument. First, it will point to certain historical changes in the definition of what constitutes efficient intellectual functioning. Second, it will demonstrate that these changes have an impact, in a rather profound way, on models of incremental or decremental transitions in intellectual functioning over the life span. Specifically, three model cases will be outlined: the growth–regression, contextual, and hierarchical life span views.

1. Preparation of this chapter was supported by a Research Career Development Award, NIA Grant 5 KO4 AG000 18, and by funds provided by the Institute of Gerontology at Wayne State University.

151

Universalistic Growth–Regression Models

Pioneers in the area of intellectual functioning have defined intelligence as our ability to adapt to changing environmental demands. In an attempt to construct concrete measurement methodologies, however, this definition has taken on rather specialized meanings in which the original rather broad connotations were lost under the pressures of operationism. In Boring's (1950) phraseology, intelligence came to be defined as that which intelligence tests measure.

As it happened, such tests arose in an intellectual climate that often served, if not to alienate the definition of intelligence from its intended meaning, at least to restrict it severely. From an historical perspective, the beginnings of research into intellectual aging coincided with an era of social Darwinism and logical positivism around the turn of the century (see Riegel, 1977, for an excellent historically oriented review). From this general orientation, the definition of intelligence derived both its content and its interpretive framework. Intelligence was seen within a model of biophysical reductionism according to which the mind could be dissected into basic elements that were presumed to reflect irreducible biological capacities: simple reactions, sensations, and perceptions.

These simple elements were seen to form the basic building blocks out of which more complex behaviors were seen to be synthesized in a more or less additive fashion. Thus a hierarchy of behaviors was conceived that was topped by the complex operations of formal logic, the apogee of mature cognitive behavior.

Such definitions were not conducive to incorporating the complexities of culturally and subculturally varying meanings of adaptability; and, indeed, a deliberate attempt was made to bracket culture and varied individual experience out of the definition of intelligence. Ebbinghaus's (1885/1913) approach to the study of memory is a telling example. Quite conscious of the complexities introduced by the historicity of subjects' memory, Ebbinghaus resolved to table the problem until learning and retention of very simple material (i.e., nonsense syllables) in rigidly controlled laboratory settings were better understood. This, he believed, offered "a possibility of indirectly approaching the problem . . . in a small and definitely limited sphere and, by means of keeping aloof for a while from any theory, perhaps of constructing one" (Ebbinghaus, 1885/1913, p. 65).

The view that we could approach a topic in such a theoretically aseptic manner was, of course, the theoretical stance of logical positivism. Equipped with this brand of naïve realism, then, this initial period set as its goal to uncover basic, biological dimensions of development and aging—dimensions that were presumed robust with regard to sociocultural variables (Labouvie-Vief, 1977; Labouvie-Vief & Chandler, 1978). The bias was toward uncovering stable, universal trends of growth and aging, and within this general framework empirical evidence was assimilated. Thus the growth of logical abilities up to adolescence was seen as primarily constrained by universal biological growth; and these logical structures themselves were seen to form the basis of universal moral and interpersonal skills. Similarly, initial evidence pointing to rather profound aging changes in psychomotor functioning, sensation, perception, reaction time, memory, and logical abilities all were seen to strengthen the case for a primary, universal biological aging decrement. And this primary aging component was seen to extend to such social behaviors as rigidity and social disengagement.

Yet such models left many phenomena unaccounted for. Ever since the first life span studies, research had shown a picture of both decrements and stability or even increments. In particular, deficits were lacking, or at least not pronounced, in tests that tapped culturally acquired knowledge, for example, vocabulary and general items of cultural information. This dualistic picture was integrated by proposing the differentiation between a form of intelligence that was thought primarily biological and culture free (i.e., fluid intelligence) and a second form that was presumed to be primarily culture bound (i.e., crystallized intelligence).

Thus the dualistic interplay of biology and culture was seen to produce this pattern of both growth and decline throughout adulthood:

> At first [fluid intelligence] and [crystallized intelligence] are indistinguishable. . . . The accumulation of Central Nervous System injuries is masked by rapid [neurological] development in childhood, but in adulthood the effects become more obvious. Fluid intelligence, based upon this, thus shows a decline as soon as the development of Central Nervous System structures is exceeded by the rate of Central Nervous System breakdown. Experience and learning accumulate throughout development. The influence of these is felt in the development of crystallized

intelligence, which increases throughout adulthood. It, too, will decline after the rate of loss of structure supporting intelligence behavior exceeds the rate of acquisition of new aids to compensate for limited änläge functions. (Horn, 1970, p. 466)

In essence, then, these models view growth and aging as a single-peaked function that parallels biological development. Metaphorically speaking, this is the view of a pyramid which, as its bottom erodes, becomes structurally weakened in a top-down fashion. Adulthood is not conceptualized as a developmental period per se, that is, a period that brings new and adaptive forms of change. At best, it achieves a compensatory stability masking rapid biological regression.

Contextual Models

Dualistic models of the fluid–crystallized type ultimately create an uneasy tension between the assertions that some skills are primarily biological and others are primarily cultural. To those who believe that, in ways still imperfectly understood, thought and behavior must map into biological structure, it is a polarization that cannot be legitimately maintained.

Still, this is a tension that ultimately rests in a metatheoretical assumption contained in growth–regression models—the assumption that on biological as well as physiological levels, developmental adaptability can be gauged by one single criterion. It is important to note that the polarization between biology and culture, much as it reflects the intellectual legacy of social scientists, is thought artificial by many biologists. The human brain by its very nature is designed for plasticity (e.g., Braitenberg, 1977; Jacobson, 1978) and, therefore, depends on cultural and social information to realize a particular adaptive repertoire. It is a consequence of this level of plasticity that adaptive repertoires will vary considerably from individual to individual and thus defy any one simplistic standard. Yet universalistic models have been highly static. Riegel has captured well the root of this static quality that in his view springs from time- and culture-bound models of social structure and economic realities:

> The main criterion for intellectual and personal excellence was the amount of information accumulated, just as the criterion for social respectability was the amount of wealth and property acquired. . . . It is not surprising [therefore] that the adult white

male engaged in manufacturing of trade appeared as the most successful competitor and became the standard for comparisons. None of the other individuals and groups—the young and the old, the delinquent and the deprived, the female and the colonial subject—were evaluated in their own terms but rather compared against this single yardstick. They were described in negative terms only, as deficient, deteriorated, retarded, or simply deviant. (Riegel, 1977, p. 7)

Specifically addressing aging, Kreps (1977) has similarly argued that notions of decrement in aging were strongly motivated by labor market needs and the pressures to create occupational opportunities for the young by moving the old out of the labor force. In this way, Kreps argues, a mythology of the deficient older worker was created to support an economic decision-making structure.

Such arguments, while they may not be definitely provable, nevertheless reflect a changing climate that has characterized developmental thinking in the past 20 or so years. It is a way of thinking that asserts that culture is part and parcel of our ways of organizing experience. It is a climate of pluralism that holds that deficit notions are quite relative to the standards by which they are assessed, which attempts to relate such standards to subcultural, cultural, and even historical changes in the adaptive demands placed on a collective of people and that asserts that the unilinear, unihierarchical models of developmental complexity are, in effect, the cause of many conceptual confounds and methodological artifacts. Here, specifically, we may cite three general areas of research that make an impact on this notion and render it one of enormous importance.

ONTOGENETIC/STABILITY VERSUS GENERATIONAL CHANGE

In the area of life span development and aging, the profound interpenetration between individual (ontogenetic) development and sociohistorical background remained a rather neglected topic until the early 1960s. To be sure, research reports demonstrating strong correlations between variables of intellectual competence and those of experiential backgrounds were available before. Thus Foster and Taylor (1920) already offered a detailed analysis of these issues. Even more pertinently, Tuddenham (1948) reported that of World War II recruits, the median intelligence test score corresponded to the 84th percentile of the World War I distribution. Such contributions failed, however, to make a significant impact on the field until more recently, when Schaie and his collaborators most vigorously put forward the notion that much of what would appear age-related variance can, in fact, be traced to sociohistorical change.

Schaie's starting point was the observation that ever since the first life span studies on intellectual development, researchers had reported striking discrepancies between cross-sectional and longitudinal studies (cf. Schaie, 1965): The former reported earlier and more dramatic losses than the latter. While such discrepancies were usually attributed to methodological factors such as the greater heterogeneity of cross-sectional samples and the high selectiveness of longitudinal ones, Schaie argued that more systematic factors were operating here, in particular, the changing cultural backgrounds of the age-cohort samples involved in cross-sectional research. To support this argument Schaie performed follow-up studies on different age-cohort groups, permitting a plotting in one grid of cross-sectional and longitudinal data. In general, this arrangement yielded a latticelike picture in which, on many of the subtests, each cohort occupied a rather stable trajectory for up to 14 years, while more recent (i.e., younger) cohorts tended to show systematically elevated positions (e.g., Nesselroade, Schaie, & Baltes, 1972; Schaie & Labouvie-Vief, 1974; Schaie & Strother, 1968). Thus it appeared that "most of the adult life span is characterized by an absence of decisive intellectual decrements. In times of rapid cultural and technological change it is primarily in relation to younger populations that the aged can be described as deficient, and it is erroneous to interpret such cross-sectional age differences as indicating autogenetic change patterns" (Schaie & Labouvie-Vief, 1974, p. 15).

This conclusion does not seem unreasonable as the cohort differences reported by Schaie and collaborators show close parallels with changes that have occurred during this century in both quality and quantity of education (Gonda, 1980). Still, not all of the age-group variance in adulthood may be accounted for by such educational changes only, and the cohort argument has been the focus of a rather animated debate (e.g., Baltes & Schaie, 1976; Horn & Donaldson, 1976). It should be noted that in Schaie's data, the cohort argument seems to hold much more forcefully for the younger and middle-aged cohorts; for those in their postretirement phase, longitudinal and cross-sectional gradients appeared to converge on nearly linear decline functions. To some (e.g., Botwinick, 1977; Horn, 1978) this has signaled the inevitability of biologically based deficits and suggested the conclusion that cohort-based analyses have not essentially changed the argument for regression. Others, in contrast, have pointed out that such an interpretation is not altogether inevitable. First, population decline functions may assess the increasing incidence of major diseases in the aging population rather than individual functions; in the absence of major disease (in particular, of the cardio- and cerebro-vascular type) such individual functions may show stability until a short period before death, thus forcing one to distinguish between a *gradual* population and a *precipitous* individual decline (see Baltes & Labouvie, 1973; Labouvie-Vief, 1977). Second, there is growing evidence that decline may often, in a feedback loop fashion, be built into the individual system according to the very mythologies (or age-grade norms) held up by a society, an argument to be taken up shortly again. But, third (as we will more fully argue in the next section of this chapter), it is also possible that many of the purported decrements of later life are part of a major reorganization of intellectual functions in adulthood.

CULTURAL BASES OF INTELLECTUAL FUNCTIONING

The cohort-based argument, with its implication that the attempt to decontextualize thinking is inherently mistaken, has served to remind adult developmental researchers that our analyses of adult intelligence must be closely allied with more ethnographic approaches in which a tie between the adaptive demands and opportunities (cultural settings) and the resulting intellectual repertoires of the individual are reintegrated. What has been missing thus far are more fine-grained qualitative analyses of exactly how cohort-oriented culture differences impact on purported deficits in the intellectual functioning of adults. Such analyses have, however, been attempted in an area that has shared the potential conceptual and methodological pitfalls of life span research—namely, that of cognitive anthropology. Here, similarly, unilinear models have raised the question of whether, by applying a specific standard developed in one culture, deficiencies are not virtually guaranteed to appear as we move to another culture.

As an example, take such relatively well-researched tasks as the classification of objects and the solution of formal syllogisms of the type used in Luria's (1976) study of schooled and unschooled people in Central Asia:

In the far north all bears are white. Novaya Zemlya is in the far north. What colors are the bears there?

As is true of older populations in Western cultures (Botwinick, 1978), uneducated people produce high error rates on such tasks. Within unilinear models, such errors have suggested a deficit in the integration and retention of logical relationships.

Upon closer examination, however, we usually encounter a number of rather consistent sources of such errors. As reported by Luria (1976) and elaborated by Scribner (1979), for example, uneducated people will often simply resist a solution to the task. They may assert, for example, that it is unanswerable in principle, as when replying "You should ask the people who have been there and seen them" or "We always speak of only what we see; we don't talk about what we haven't seen." Scribner (1979) refers to this stylistic tendency as a concrete bias and shows (as does Luria) that it is profoundly affected by formal education.

One might argue, of course, that this concrete bias reflects an inherent restriction on logical ability in the uneducated and/or old. Yet Scribner (1979) rejects such a notion. First, many subjects will occasionally adopt a primarily formal or theoretic approach to the problem, and, if they do, they *always* produce correct answers. Second, subjects often assimilate the information presented in the problem to their own ways of conceptualizing reality; they construct new (or their own) premises and correctly operate upon those. The following excerpt from Luria's study serves as a good example. Here three subjects were first shown a picture of a saw, an ax, and a hammer and were then asked if a "log" belonged to the same category (i.e., tools):

Experimenter (E): Would you say these things are tools?
All three subjects: Yes.
E: What about a log?
S-1: It also belongs with these. We make all sorts of things out of logs—handles, doors, and the handles of tools.
S-2: We say a log is a tool because it works with tools to make things.
E: But one man said a log isn't a tool since it can't saw or chop.
S-3: Yes you can—you can make handles out of it! . . .
E: Name all the tools used to produce things . . .
S-1: We have a saying: take a look in the fields and you'll see tools. (Luria, 1976, pp. 94–95)

If presented with the same task, city-educated subjects will almost inevitably exclude "log" from the category tools, and from this fact Luria (1976) argues that the uneducated display a deficit in classificatory behavior. Yet we also sense a different dimension; these Uzbekistan peasants appear engaged in a bantering argument about the proper definition of "tool," rejecting any one concrete definition and arguing for a more flexible and even creative stance. And indeed, while the experimenter attempts to guide the subjects toward a "correct" definition of tools, we are hard put to judge who is more rigid or concrete—the subjects or the experimenter!

The culturally relativist argument here espoused has been discussed more fully by other authors (see Cole & Scribner, 1974; Foss & Hakes, 1978; Glick, 1975). Similarly, it has been the focus of Labov's (1970) work on black English and his caution against jumping to conclusions about cognitive skills from a superficial look at speakers' surface language. More generally, it serves to warn us that conceptions of mature adult intellectuality are becoming more pluralistic and to call attention to the fact that growth and aging are directed by multiple standards that vary with social classes within cultures, between cultures, and across historical time (e.g., Buck-Morss, 1975; Cole & Scribner, 1974; Gregory, 1970; Neisser, 1976; Olson, 1976). Gregory has described this interplay particularly well:

> Until recently, men in all cultures handled rather similar objects and used them for similar ends. But with the development of technology, for large parts of the day one man may be concerned with queer properties of electronic circuits, another with magnetic fields and a third with zero gravity in which otherwise normal objects have inertial but not gravitational mass. These situations demand different skills: different ways of ordering, handling and seeing objects. As abstract and queer object properties become more important, we may expect languages to develop with deep structures to reflect the worlds which we discover and create: worlds which so far as we know are uniquely human. We are being cut off from the biological past which moulded the eyes and the brains and the speech of our ancestors. (Gregory, 1970, p. 166)

For the purposes of our present discussion, the important point is that, when evaluating notions of cognitive decrement, we must calibrate our standards according to the modes—often linguistic—a culture, subculture, or even individual has developed in order to deal with and to encode complex information. Hymes (1974) has referred to such modes as genres; Bartlett (1932) as schemata. The Soviet psychologist Leontiev (1977) has gone even further to suggest that such schemata create specific brain-based "functional organs" that serve to assimilate knowledge into preexisting modes of organization. In any case, the result of such concepts is a somewhat altered view of development in which the individual becomes socialized and specialized to deal with such genres. Conversely, a failure to comprehend or integrate information may not at all reflect a generalized decrement, but rather the individual's lack of familiarity with the genre used by the experimenter.

What is the evidence that such lack of calibration has contributed toward deficit notions? One method has been to look at history-related changes in the specific vocabulary content with which different cohorts are familiar. Lorge (1936) has shown that age comparisons between young and old adults could be manipulated to suggest increments or decrements depending on the specific words used. More recently, Gardner and Monge (1977) have demonstrated similar, systematic cohort differences in familiarity with specific vocabularies. Young adults, for example, have more expertise in vocabularies dealing with the usual school-based information. Older adults, conversely, may excel at information relating to modes of transportation, knowledge of finance management, categories of disease, and so on. Such cohort-based differences are bound to affect age differences in vocabulary retention. And indeed, Botwinick and Storandt (1974a, 1974b) reported reduction or even elimination of age-related differences on certain tests of mnemonic functioning when vocabularies were adjusted to deal with the specialized experience of young and old individuals.

At a level of more complex cognitive operations it must also be pointed out that the formalistic tasks used to assess logical integration are biased toward the young with their higher levels of education and, more specifically, toward those with science training. Such factors of professional specialization are bound to be important (see Botwinick, 1978), yet rarely controlled for. In a recent study, however, Sabatini and Labouvie-Vief (1979) found that differences between young and old adults on tasks of formal logic were *entirely* accounted for by professional specialization rather than age. Thus young and old scientists showed no age differences whatsoever, while scientists and teachers, either young or old, showed overriding differences.

If we adopt the view that intellectual performance is a response to the experiential settings of the adapting organism, then several ways that older cohorts differ from younger ones become very salient. Thus we may expect to find great differences between the environmental demands made upon adults and the aged in the community and students in school. We may speculate that these demands may produce differences in the way the subjects view the assessment situation. As was noted above, many tasks employed with the elderly were originally developed for use with children or young adults in educational institutions. The tasks have most frequently used materials devoid of meaning (i.e., have little functional utility). As suggested in the literature (Kogan, 1974; Labouvie-Vief, 1977; Labouvie-Vief & Chandler, 1978), the older adults may be partially disadvantaged with such tasks as they have a higher need for meaningfulness or relevance in tasks. In school, we are frequently assigned tasks for which the real-life relevance is obscure, and the materials are abstract to the point of being stripped of functional meaning. Students quickly find that success or failure depends upon an abstractness of thought applied to a broad range of tasks. Novelty alone may suffice to provide the motivation for such performances (Schaie, 1977). Most older adults, however, have been operating in a context with quite different contingencies.

In a world that makes a large number of demands upon our attention, strategies are necessary to limit information to a manageable proportion and even to limit those tasks upon which we will spend time. What may emerge is a pragmatism quite unacceptable in a school situation. Long years of attending to problems with a view to their pragmatic payoffs undoubtedly results in different motivating forces than those present in students. The latter, concerned with the acquisition of skills, may tackle a task, no matter how trivial, to develop and demonstrate such skills (Neisser, 1976; Schaie, 1977). The older adult may simply refuse to cooperate unless there is relevance and meaningfulness to the task (Labouvie-Vief & Chandler, 1978). Hulicka (1967), for example, found that elderly subjects improved dramatically in their performance on paired-associates tasks when the stimulus words were occupations and the responses were surnames rather than the more traditional nonsense materials. Similarly, Arenberg (1968) found meaningfulness an important dimension in problem solving in elderly subjects. When the problems in logic were changed from those involving color, form, and number to those involving food and people, the elderly performed significantly better. In some, then, it appears that purported deficits in the elderly often reflect, instead, their different stylistic and motivational needs that arise out of valid adaptive constraints.

AGE GRADING OF INTELLECTUAL COMPETENCE

Within the more sociological and ethnographic views discussed above doubts have been raised that universal intellectual losses are, in principle, a necessary concomitant of aging. It is true, nevertheless, that a considerable proportion of elderly individuals do experience deficits that may not be explained so easily by stylistic differences. As already mentioned, even in Schaie's research the cohort-based argument seemed to hold more strongly for young to middle-aged than for older adults. Thus some authors (e.g., Botwinick, 1977; Horn & Donaldson, 1976) have concluded that arguments of the type presented above may well displace the peak of intellectual performance into later adulthood; still, they may not qualitatively alter the view of age-related intellectual deterioration.

This conclusion may, however, present an overly conservative view, and it contrasts with a series of models that have more specifically addressed age-related *decline* (e.g., Baltes & Schaie, 1976; Rosenmayr & Rosenmayr, 1978; Labouvie-Vief, 1977). Maybe the best known prototype of such models is Bengtson and Kuuypers's "social breakdown model" (cf. Bengtson, 1973). In this conceptualization, the relationship between aging and intellectual functioning is to be viewed as a feedback loop through which social groups in marginal positions are actively induced into a role of social and intellectual incompetence. Once begun this induction initiates a cycle of self-fulfilling prophecies that is buttressed by mythologies and stereotypes surrounding socially held views of "normal" aging. As a result, a twofold socialization process is reinforced. First, many social institutions will actively discourage competent behaviors. Second, the target individuals themselves are subjected to a lifelong socialization process that leads them to internalize negative expectations. Rosenmayr (cf. Rosenmayr & Rosenmayr, 1978) has coined the poignant phrase of a "societally induced individual responsibility" to capture the implication that many elderly surrender to negative social stereotypes and thereby contribute toward their own decline.

Demonstrations for this cycle are to be found particularly in marginal groups of the elderly, such as those who are institutionalized. Often, the social expectation in such groups is one of irreversible decrement, and it is one that in interactions with patients is actively translated into a discouragement of competence-related behaviors by the staff (Baltes & Baltes, 1977; Macdonald & Butler, 1974). Yet often, relatively minor interventions into this breakdown cycle have resulted in dramatic effects. Schulz (1976) and Langer and Rodin (1976), for example, have shown that the patients' subjective control of events affects their cognitive, emotional, and even physical well-being. Such control may be heightened by simply involving the patient in decisions about everyday happenings, such as taking care of plants or knowing visitation schedules. Langer, Rodin, Beck, Weinman, and Spitzer (1979), in the same vein, have argued that memory deficits may result from institutional failures to make events memorable. Even more dramatically, the increased mortality often reported following institutional relocation was significantly alleviated when administrators implemented programs to familiarize and involve patients with the events and circumstances of the move (Schulz & Brenner, 1977).

Similar, intervention-oriented research has demonstrated beneficial effects in a wide arena of intellectual behaviors and with a wide arena of subject populations (for reviews, see Baltes & Baltes, 1977; Labouvie-Vief, 1977). In general, this growing body of research suggests that older people can, under appropriately designed conditions, learn to manipulate formal symbolic contents, decrease cognitive egocentricity, and, in general, display a much greater degree of intellectual plasticity than has been presumed possible.

Again, the argument emerging from this research is quite consistent: The routine cognitive performance of older individuals as it is assessed in many research settings may be an extremely poor indicator of what they could do, given proper supports. Age-related performance differentials, in contrast, often mirror the sociocultural milieu with the constraints and opportunities such milieus imply. And if attempts are made to take these milieus into account, it is often quite unjustifiable to consider adult intellectual development as a largely invariant, universal, and regressive–decremental sequence.

Hierarchical Developmental Models of Adulthood and Aging

Our own attention in the last few years has focused on a further theoretical issue. However pluralistic, contextual models have failed to view adulthood from the perspective of potential growth, and thus statements of regression are inherently relative to the standards of maturity, intellectual or otherwise, erected by current development models. This theoretical paradox has received much recent attention, and our own effort has been directed at reinterpreting purported deficits in the light of a more appropriately *adult*-focused view of the life course (Brent, 1978; Labouvie-Vief, 1980a, 1980b). In this view, then, properties of aging organisms must be derived from a general conception of systemic changes along the life span—changes that transform the system from stage to stage in a continuous fashion.

We might ask, at this juncture, why it should be desirable to return to an argument that favors a more general aging program— one that extends beyond arguing that aging can really be accounted for by the multitude of pluralistic pathways envisioned by contextual models. The reason is that contextual models by their pluralistic stance have had to take on a certain defensive posture in which the older adult, at best, can be seen to have maintained stability, pre-served his or her youth. Thus we discern an adherence to the notion that aging, per se, is a maladaptive process.

Yet there has been a recent interest in developing conceptualiza-tions that point out that such maladaptive features may arise, in part, from the anomalous situation that virtually all developmental models (save perhaps those of Erikson and Jung) have addressed themselves to youth rather than adulthood proper. This concern is well reflected in the instant popularity that works such as Sheehy's *Passages* (Sheehy, 1976) have achieved. It is also expressed, occasionally, by researchers into adult intellectual processes, as captured most poignantly in the following quote by two researchers in that field (Demming & Pressey, 1957):

> Most investigations of adult traits appear to involve this problem. For instance, the July 1956 issue of the *Journal of Gerontology* contains two excellent reports indicating decrease in problem solving in older years, as shown by an alphabet maze and a puzzle board. But should not problems and matter usual in adult life, rather than in childhood and school, be employed in such investigations? Might some of these adults have then be found

decidedly competent in dealing with problems in their world and of concern to them? Wechsler seems to have gone even further when he urged the probability that not only human abilities change with age, but that the significances of the abilities themselves are altered at different ages . . . and with different levels of functions at the same level. . . . It would seem that we ought to have special tests of intelligence for older individuals just as we now have them for young children. (p. 147)

The notion that aging brings adaptive forms of change does, however, face some conceptual challenges. Much evidence indicates that aging brings profound impairments in biological vigor and homeostatic capacity (Finch & Hayflick, 1977) as well as in sensory functioning and psychomotor alertness (Birren & Schaie, 1977). Still the question may be raised whether such changes do, of necessity, imply a generalized restriction of psychological adaptability.

Within the context of linear growth–regression models, with their implied pyramid metaphor, the answer to this question may appear to be an unqualified no. How is one to argue that a pyramid continues to grow on top when its bottom erodes away! Most models thus far have equated sensorimotor decline and the perceived difficulties with tasks of formal logic by fiat with reduced adaptability. Such a relationship is not necessary—at least, if we deal with adult organisms. It is important to distinguish here between behavioral systems that are in the process of development and those that have achieved a functionally efficient form. That is, while developmental psychologists usually claim that later systems are dependent on earlier ones (e.g., complex behavior in adulthood on more simple sensorimotor behavior in childhood), such a relationship may hold developmentally (i.e., over time) rather than at any given temporal interval. For example, the earlier mentioned interest in "simple" reactions usually led to a prediction that deficiencies at this simple level will produce even more marked deficiencies at more complex levels. The opposite is usually true, however: Once behavior is organized into complex sequences, it is actually more difficult to reconstruct the original units (Hayes-Roth, 1977).

We are really faced with two issues. The first relates to the fact that notions of simplicity or complexity take on meaning only in the context of the specific skills to which individuals, and even humans as a species, are adapted. Thus one must avoid the logical positivist fallacy somewhat flippantly captured by Jenkins (1974) who notes that without taking into account this phenomenological context, we might argue that riding a unicycle is a simpler, more basic skill than riding a bicycle and that mastering a tricycle is the most complex. The second issue relates to the problems that many models of cognition have implicitly assumed that cognition commences with a tape recorder like registration of objective events. Yet this model, which is predicated on the assumption of the organism as a perfect information processor, has been abandoned by modern cognitive psychology (Foss & Hakes; 1978). The Argentine writer Jorge Luis Borges has offered a particularly telling sample of the absurdity of this assumption in his short story *Funes the Memorious*. Funes one day took a fall from a horse, so the story tells, and thereafter forgot how to forget:

> On the falling from the horse, he lost consciousness; when he recovered it, the present was almost intolerable, it was so rich and bright. . . . He remembered the shapes of the clouds in the south at dawn on the 30th of April, 1882, and he could compare them in his recollection with the marbled grain in the design of a leather-bound book which he had seen only once. . . . He told me . . . "My memory, Sir, is like a garbage disposal." (Borges, 1962, p. 112)

Yet this perfection imprisoned him in a mindless, "stammering greatness":

> He was . . . almost incapable of general platonic ideas. It was not only difficult for him to understand that the generic term "dog" embraced so many unlike specimens of different sizes and forms; he was disturbed by the fact that a dog at three-fourteen (seen in profile) should have the same name as the dog at three-fifteen (seen from the front). . . . Without effort, he had learned English, French, Portuguese, Latin. I suspect, nevertheless, that he was not very capable of thought. To think is to forget a difference, to generalize, to abstract. (Borges, 1962, pp. 114–115)

On some level, however formidable in its brilliance, Funes's inability to "forget a difference" is highly reminiscent of the infant's inability to preserve the identity of an object through a series of temporal and spatial transformations. Piaget (Piaget & Inhelder, 1969) has traced the development of this object constancy concept in the first years of life and has shown that the integration of isolated visual images into an abstract concept that remains invariant through a series of transformations will eventually profoundly restructure the very perception of an object. Indeed, for the more mature child and adult it becomes almost unthinkable to revert back to this former unintegrated state. To quote Piaget,

> There is immediate perception as totality and sensations are now merely structured elements and no longer structuring. . . . The neurologist Weizsacker said . . . "When I perceive a house, I do not see an image which enters through the eye; on the contrary, I see a solid into which I can enter!" (Piaget, 1972, pp. 65–66; emphasis added)

The view expressed in this and Borges's example is one that is profoundly different from the view often held about development. Elsewhere (Labouvie-Vief, 1980a) we have called it the "nonlinear" view to capture the fact that, as we develop, we not only achieve integrations of a higher spatiotemporal order, but we also tend to give up those of lower order unless they can be integrated into higher-order concepts. Thus the pyramid metaphor is profoundly misleading in suggesting that throughout development, we become better and better information processors. In contrast, the nonlinear proposes a view of life course development in which different periods are characterized by dominant modes that supersede and replace earlier ones. The whole course of the life span thus can be conceptualized as a succession of single-peaked functions of different modes, each of which undergoes a period of growth, achievement of a functionally mature form, and then decline as it is superseded by a new mode.

This point is of significance since it forms, in our view, the cornerstone of any progressive theory of adult development. This is because it is no longer necessary, now, to adopt a defensive stance with respect to certain adult deficits—rather, it asserts that each stage entails both a progression and a destruction or dissolution.

Developmental researchers have rarely attended to the latter aspect—that of dissolution. Nevertheless, research examples demonstrating this aspect at earlier, preadult levels of development abound. Piaget (1972), in particular, has demonstrated that the accuracy of perceptual judgments may decrease after age 5 as the child acquires more complex projective notions of space. Thus for the younger child a perceptual configuration (e.g., two lines displaced in parallelogram fashion, e.g.,⸺) is two dimensional and unambiguous; for the older child and/or adult it is perceived as a projection of a three-dimensional array onto a plane, and thus estimations of length are entirely ambiguous! As a consequence, the relationship between developmental level and accuracy of response is disordinal: It will show an initial rise but then decreases as projective space comes to superordinate more simplistic (i.e., developmentally earlier) notions.

Piaget (1972) has heavily drawn on this principle of sub- and superordination in accounting for a number of developments in the area of perception. But the notion of suppression of developmentally earlier skills has been an important concept to several other developmental psychologists as well (Harlow, 1959; Leontiev, 1977; Luria, 1976; Vygotsky, 1962; White, 1965). In these various models, the concept has taken the shape of inhibitory mechanisms that characterize the development of cognitive control as previous automatic responses are interrupted (see Shiffrin & Schneider, 1977, for a similar but not developmentally oriented view). Upon developing a stable person schema, for instance, the infant may display a cessation of a ubiquitous social approach tendency when confronted with strangers (Kagan, 1972). Even more notable nonlinearities appear to mark the establishment of linguistic control over the motor behavior of young children (over an approximate interval of 4–7 years of age). The reader is referred to Luria (1976), Reese (1962), and White (1965) for extensive examples of such nonlinearities that are indexed, among others, by (1) a relative increase in the difficulty of using simple perceptual codes as more complex linguistic codes become available (Kendler & Kendler, 1962; Underwood, 1975) and (2) a concomitant relative decline in the efficiency of simple perceptual discrimination (Weir & Stevenson, 1959; Kendler & Kendler, 1962) and probability learning tasks presumably because of the interference of more complex hypotheses (Weir, 1964).

MEMORY

In the conception proposed here, it is no longer sufficient to ask if adulthood and aging are or are not characterized by mnemonic deficits. Instead, the question must be rephrased to examine which, if any, modes of mnemonic organization are characteristic of different stages of the life span.

We have already mentioned that most research thus far has examined memory changes with tasks that were fashioned after a view of memory as a passive event recorder. Thus, in examining the retention of verbal material, "accuracy" was scored by the ability to retain the verbatim content of such verbal messages as lists of words and, less frequently, sentences or paragraphs. The nonlinear view, however, rejects any single criterion of accuracy. Rather, it starts with the assumption that individuals may perform different kinds of transformation on the messages given. In sentence memory, for example, coding may be primarily in terms of verbatim content (e.g., "A rolling stone gathers no moss"), or it may be in terms of a meaning-preserving transformation such as a paraphrase (e.g., "Only a resting stone gathers moss"), or it may even be in a meaning-expanding transformation (e.g., "A restless soul remains rootless")— and the important point is that different criteria for accuracy may be partially *exclusive*.

Research on sentence meaning memory is still rather spotty. But what little evidence *is* available on such processes is entirely inconsistent with the notion that such processing is deficient in adulthood. Two studies, for example, dealt with the processing of sentence meaning rather than memorization of exact verbatim detail. One was a dissertation by Hurlbut (1976) and the second a study by Walsh and Baldwin (1977). Both used Bransford and Franks's (1971) paradigm, and no differences were found between young and old subjects in the integration of information across unit sentences. Yet younger (mean age 21.5) adults did recall more verbatim information than the elderly (mean age 71.9) (Hurlbut, 1976).

Is it possible to speculate, then, that adulthood brings qualitative changes in the processing of information? Could it be, for example, that the loss of specific, low-structure detail is a trade-off made while attending to higher units of meaning? And is it possible that this process continues throughout adulthood and becomes particularly pronounced at even higher levels of encoding, for example, the level of amalgamations of propositions in text material? The Soviet researcher Istomina and her associates (1967, in Loewe, 1977) advanced such an interpretation. Their study used isolated words and integrated texts as test items. When recall was in terms of isolated words, young subjects were much better than older subjects; but when recall was scored for higher order propositions and interferences, the old were better. Istomina *et al.* suggested on this basis that "with increasing age different aspects of memory change in different ways. While memory for immediate detail shows marked decline in later life, memory for logical relationships which are mediated by a process of active abstraction, not only fails to show any deficit, but does in fact improve" (cf. Loewe, 1977, p. 120; author's translation). More recently, Zelinski, Gilewski, and Thompson (1980) have also reported that elderly subjects tend to focus on such higher-order propositions.

Following up on this suggestion, we started pilot research on the processing of discourse. Our materials were short stories, and the age-related differences were striking: Younger subjects produced detailed, rather faithful summaries of the story; elderly subjects produced highly general summaries. Moreover, these summaries were often in a normative form such as a moral or a metaphor.

We have since followed up this finding more analytically. For instance, we are breaking down text structure into a number of hierarchical levels and are finding that older adults attend to higher-order propositions, younger adults to detail. At the same time, it appears that the elderly subjects attention to detail is qualitatively different from that of the younger subjects. First, they report they are disinterested in detail. Second, this lack of attention shows in their performance: When we build in foils at the level of detail (say, the story mentions a white crane sleeping), detail recall is systematically distorted in the direction of real-world interference (say, many elderly may recall a pink crane standing on one leg).

From this and similar evidence we have started to develop a working model that we are subjecting to test in a series of studies. It seems that in the study of aging and cognition, we must at once look at the integration of information at several levels. Thus we may find evidence of deficit when focusing on one level, only to find that when we go to another, deficit is made up. We might say, in other words, that it is possible, and certainly testable, to propose the following hypothesis: When we are dealing with stimuli of low structure, deficits in aging may appear pronounced. On the other hand, when we shift to stimuli of higher structure, we may be facing a kind of trade-off situation in which lack of detail processing is made up by meaning processing. And, indeed, it is not too far-fetched to conclude that this is an altogether adaptively useful strategy: The mature and older adult has experienced the limitations of his or her memory and has learned to attend to those codes that are less likely to be transitory, and thus are more permanent and stable.

This adaptive interpretation of the adult's attention to higher-order units of meaning, captured by Birren (1969) by the notion of an age-related "race between the bit and the chunk," receives support from several other empirical sources. First, it is known that if recall is followed for a prolonged period of time, lower-order information tends to decay rather rapidly while the recall of meaning-preserving kernel transformations displays more temporal stability (Bartlett, 1932; Dooling & Christiansen, 1977). Second, a few studies also have demonstrated that the elderly may have acquired more accurate knowledge of the functioning of their mnemonic system (Lachman & Lachman, 1979; Zelinski et al., 1980). Thus it is possible that they have learned to attend selectively to more informative units of meaning.

Again, it must be emphasized that this move toward stability, if supported by further research, involves both a gain and a loss. On the one hand, the lack of attention to lower-order, transitory units of meaning may imply that adult learning becomes relatively closed to new information intake. On the other hand, the adult may utilize structures already highly developed and specialized toward a continued structural recombination and stable reduction of experience— a process that may well capture the wisdom of the older organism (Seitelberger, 1978). Thus different periods of the life span again may display specialized but different modes of processing as captured in this statement by Schopenhauer:

> Life could be compared to an embroidery of which we see the right side during the first half of life, but the back in the latter half. This back side is less scintillating but more instructive: it reveals the interpatterning of the threads. (cf. Seitelberger, 1978, p. 215)

LOGIC AND SOCIAL PRAGMATICS

We have argued thus far that many reported changes in mnemonic functioning may in actuality reflect a developmental restructuring in adulthood. A similar argument may be applied to the area of logical development (Labouvie-Vief, 1980b), and from this perspective it is important to offer a satisfying interpretation of the adult's difficulty with cognitive tasks of the fluid type, that is, for his or her resistance to apply abstract modes of thought out of its concrete, day-to-day context.

It is significant to note, in this context, that most current measures of intellectual performance have been validated against criteria of academic success of young people involved in educational settings. Thus, although the picture of intellectual maturity derived from such tests may be particularly germane in that setting and at that stage of life, it may lack validity if applied to more mature adults and to new, nonacademic situations.

What is this youthful image of cognitive maturity? Adolescence, according to Piaget (1972), brings the movement from the concrete to the hypothetical, permitting the young person to operate in a world of possibility rather than just reality. The result is a high degree of flexibility; rather than being embedded in their own concrete viewpoint, youth are able to approach any subject matter from multiple perspectives. New possibilities and viewpoints alien to the youth's background cannot only be comprehended, they also can be generated by permutation; problems can be examined in a purely abstract, formal way for their logical cohesiveness while holding back judgments of personal likes and dislikes, and even pragmatic utility. As Piaget has pointed out, however, this new acquisition is only a necessary but not sufficient condition of adult life. This is in contrast to the view that states that logic can be understood merely from the aspect of their internal self-regulatory self-sufficiency. Rather, it states that logical equilibration is a matter of both internal and external regulation. Internally, logic permutes and recombines; it abstracts from the immediate given; it offers a hypothetical mechanism proliferating possible solutions to *changing* demands.

Still, being hypothetical, it does not entail an *internal* mechanism to distinguish between solutions that work and those that do not. It awaits, in other words, empirical validation. Without such pragmatic or empirical validation, no logical limits could be drawn between a brilliant scientific theory and a brilliant delusional system! As Piaget states,

> A formal logic makes possible a construction of forms of organization, ready to organize everything, *but from time to time organizing nothing, insofar as it becomes dissociated from its application!* (Piaget, 1967, p. 358; emphasis added)

It is possible, however, that this ability to engage in abstraction, *out of* the context of pragmatic considerations, is particularly adaptive in youth who are involved in exercising these newly acquired skills. As Schaie (1977) put it, this is an acquisition phase, a phase of taking in, a time of perfecting our skills while reserving judgment as to their concrete value or utility, a period in which foreclosure must be avoided in order to permit the development of mature commitments.

Much as the theme of youth is flexibility, however, that of adulthood is commitment. Careers must be started, intimacy bonds formed, children raised. Here, amidst a world of a multitude of possible alternatives, there is a need to adopt *one* course of action. This conscious commitment to one pathway and the concomitant disregard of others may indeed make the onset of adult cognitive maturity.

It is possible to suggest therefore, that the "pure" logic of the adolescent or youth that has served as the measurement standard of adults nevertheless is based on a mere budding but not yet equilibrated mode of thinking. And indeed this is just what Piaget suggests:

> With the advent of formal intelligence, thinking takes wings and it is not surprising that at first this unexpected power is both used and abused . . . each new mental ability starts off by incorporating the world in a process of egocentric assimilation. Adolescent egocentricity is manifested by a belief in the omnipotence of reflection, as though the world should submit itself to idealistic schemes rather than to systems of reality. (Piaget, 1967, pp. 63–64)

and

> True adaptation to society comes automatically when the adolescent reformer attempts to put his ideas to work. Just as experience reconciles formal thought with the reality of things, so does effective and enduring work, undertaking in concrete and well-defined situations, cure dreams. (Piaget, 1967, pp. 68–69)

Perry (1968) has addressed this issue in his empirical study of the intellectual and ethical development of college youth. Perry traces the conflicts and their eventual resolution experienced by college students as they move from the relatively closed, sheltered "logic" of their home environment to the pluralistic environment of a college community. Here, conflicts are created exactly by that feature of logic that Piaget calls the egocentricity of youth—a belief in the omnipotence of reflection. And this feature also creates, according to Perry, specific social and cognitive vulnerabilities: a search for absolute values, for authoritative statements, for ideological certainty. College life, however, may induce a slow erosion of this absolutism of adolescent logic:

> Reason reveals relations within any given context; it can also compare one context with another on the basis of metacontexts

established for this purpose. But there is a limit. In the end, reason itself remains reflexively relativistic, a property which turns reason back upon reason's own findings. In even its farthest reaches then reason will leave the thinker with several legitimate contexts and no way of choosing among them—no way at least that he can justify through reason alone. If he is still to honor reason he must now also transcend it; he must affirm his own position from within himself in full awareness that reason can never completely justify him or assure him. (Perry, 1968, pp. 135–136)

Thus for Perry, youth will eventually accept the inherent relativity of multiple intellectual perspectives. At the same time, however, this cognitive realization signals a new integration: we need to discontinue our search for logical certainty and accept the pragmatic constraints of adulthood. We need to give up absolutism and idealism for commitment and specialization.

Further empirical support of this position was recently presented by Gilligan and Murphy (1979) who applied Perry's theory to an ongoing longitudinal study of the moral reasoning of college students regarding their own life experiences. The study reinterviewed the students at the age of 27. Analysis by the Kohlberg standard method found two-thirds of the students moving from the highest principled moral stage at 22 years to a less advanced intermediate stage at 27 years. Using the Perry scheme, however, these moral philosophers confronted the "dilemma of the fact" and, finding in the experience of life's choices no single perspective to encompass the problems adequately, advanced to a dialectical understanding of the contradictions inherent in moral choice. This understanding arises from the empirical discovery of the consequences of choice and "embraces the problem of contradiction rather than expelling it from the cognitive domain" (Gilligan & Murphy, 1979). Thus, Gilligan and Murphy conclude:

> In our attempt to reconnect a cognitive stage theory of development with data on late adolescent and adult thinking about real problems of moral conflict and choice, we found it necessary to posit a different notion of maturity to account for the transformation in thinking that we observed. These transformations arise out of recognition of the paradoxical interdependence of self and society, which overrides the false simplicity of formal reason and replaces it with a more encompassing form of judgment. (Gilligan & Murphy, 1979, p. 33)

We may propose, then, two modes of cognition on adulthood that define the endpoints of a developmental continuum. At the one end, we see an individualized, relatively egocentric, formal, logical mode characteristic of youth. It is a mode that may be given to idealization and to a separation of thinking and affect (Neisser, 1976). At the other end, we may discern an awareness of complexity of social system embeddedness which creates new pressures toward syntheses. This hypothetical polarity is particularly well demonstrated in Birren's (1969) analysis of the decision making of successful career men and women of different ages. First, problems were defined differently by the two age groups. The younger ones defined them from the narrow individualistic (but, of course, stage-appropriate) perspective of their own career advancements. Thus they tended to seize upon an opportunity to demonstrate their competence to do a job single-handedly though at the cost of intellectual and work overload (and no doubt, occasional blunders). The older ones, in contrast, defined the problem as one maximizing benefits and minimizing risks for the system within which they operated. They had come to realize and admit their individual restriction in that endeavor and relied instead on the intercoordination of experts and advisors whose pooled resources might guarantee more stable payoffs.

It is important, at this juncture, to stress that each of those modes may have its own adaptive value. The younger adults, with their tendency to demonstrate their independence, may be able to develop highly specialized, often novel skills. The older adults, conversely, may feel overwhelmed by the demands of specialization; they may also, according to Birren, have developed a sharp awareness of their own limitations in dealing with information overload. Yet in so doing, they have also come to view decisions as embedded in a complex social matrix, and they have learned to utilize that matrix to optimize decisions. The critical issue is thus not whether one or the other mode is better in any absolute sense, but rather that effective social action may require the collaboration of both sets of resources. Brent (1978) has put forward this notion:

> The younger cohorts in any collective at any given time—i.e., those which most recently came into existence—seem to be specialized for providing the flexibility necessary for adapting to changes in existing environmental conditions and for expansion into new environmental niches, while the older cohorts appear

to be specialized for maintaining the existing organismic collective within the environmental niches to which they have already adapted—thus providing a secure base of operations from which the younger cohorts can venture out. (Brent, 1978, p. 25)

The above may strike some readers as an overly romanticized view of aging. It is certainly true that it may characterize the more exceptional older individual—the one who has survived earlier adaptive pressures successfully and integrated them into a stable, broad reference system. We do not wish, however, to deny that deviations from such an optimal standard are not frequent. Still, we also maintain that, if judging the older organism, we must rely on an age-appropriate standard rather than prematurely calling most manifestations of the older individual's behavior deficient, rigid, and so forth.

Ethologists, for example, have long pointed out that in any species that relies on the passing on of information from generation to generation the older organism brings adaptive assets. Sometimes the exploratory behavior of the young may serve the purpose of introducing innovative technology. Kawai's (1965) description of the acquisition of the potato-washing technique among Japanese macaques is a particularly striking example. While most monkeys clumsily attempted to clean sweet potatoes by wiping off the sand, a young monkey named Imo was first observed in 1953 to rinse potatoes in water. This efficient technique was quickly adopted by other monkeys. Significantly, however, it propagated along generational lines: It was first picked up by age peers and then spread more slowly to the older cohorts. Only two of the 11 older monkeys had adopted it 11 years later! Similar generational propagation has also been reported by Hinde (1974) and Jolly (1972).

The adaptive significance of such differential attraction to innovation is often attributed to the fact that the exploratory curiosity of the young can be detrimental to the troop as it may embrace adaptive and maladaptive techniques with undifferentiated, naïve enthusiasm. Thus the more "rigid" behavior of the older animals serves to select those innovations that are more likely to be adaptive. Rigidity may be too derogatory a term here, however; in actuality it may reflect a degree of accumulated wisdom that increases adaptive advantages for the troop. For example, older members of troops are often seen to serve as leaders by exerting control over exploratory behavior (Hinde, 1974; Kummer, 1971; Rowell, 1966), even though they may no longer be the strongest physically. As Kummer suggests,

There is little doubt that conservatism, too, is adaptive. The inflexible adults of the Koshima troop form a safety reservoir of the previous behavioral variant, which will survive the invention for at least ten years. If the new behavior should turn out to be harmful, say because of parasitic infection, they would survive. In spreading new behaviors, adult rigidity has the same function as low mutation rates in evolution. (Kummer, 1971, p. 129)

Feuer (1974) has presented a similar analysis in his discussion of the innovations introduced by 20th-century physicists, and Brent (1978) has argued, even more generally, that the collective of younger and older cohorts brings the combined advantage of providing both flexibility and stable security.

Yet it would be premature to conclude that creative ingenuity and cautious resistance to it are perfectly correlated with age. Kawai's (1965) report once again offers a suggestive example. Two years after inventing the potato-washing technique, Imo invented the much more complex technique of separating wheat from sand by throwing them into the water and waiting for the sand to sink and the wheat to float. Again the habit propagated along generational lines, however, with a significant difference. Potato washing had been most readily adopted by the 1- to 2½-year-old monkeys. In contrast, the complicated wheat trick was adopted only by the 2- to 4-year-olds. Kummer suggests that this pattern may involve the additional element of stage-related behavioral maturity:

> The possibility of a behavioral innovation depends in part on the genetically determined range of potential modifications, and . . . different behavioral modifications are related to different stages of individual maturation in which they are realized most easily. (Kummer, 1971, p. 123)

This suggestion is significant here because it throws a new light on life span studies that have reported similarly age-lagged relationships in creative contributions of adults of different professional specializations: Mathematicians often are found to make their contributions earliest, followed in approximate order by natural scientists, artists, philosophers, and historians (Dennis, 1966). The usually advanced interpretation relies on an early decline of complex logical abilities. Yet is it not pertinent to suggest, along with Piaget's earlier cited statements, that mathematics requires *less* complex skills than those demanded of empirical sciences as it starts with pure deduction but zero content? Or is it pertinent to suggest that the age pattern of creative contributions thus suggests a systematic progression in which the likelihood to be creative depends upon the degree to which creativity requires the integration of empirical data beyond pure deduction?

Concluding Note

In sum, we have argued that interpretations of purported deficits are altogether relative to the particular theoretical model within which they are assimilated. Within the universalistic, biologically oriented regression model, the case for regression has appeared to be open and shut; contextual models have argued for a more pluralistic stance; but hierarchical models, finally, have shown that in spite of certain adaptive losses, aging brings new adaptive gains.

It remains to be pointed out, however, that the hierarchical argument does not simply raise the universalistic argument to a higher level of generality. Rather it is seen here to offer an integration of more contextualistic stances as well. Gutmann (1977), for example, has carefully documented that throughout many cultures the elderly are considered as more meditative and integrative. Yet only in some cultures have these qualities accrued prestige to the older individual and helped reinforce a degree of gerontocracy:

> Thus, extremes of climate appear to reduce gerontocracy, as does impermanency of residence. Conversely, male gerontocracy increases as society becomes more stable and more complex. In organized folk settings, the usefulness and prestige of the aged depends on their wisdom, their experience, their acquired property rights, and their ritual powers. (Gutmann, 1977, p. 312)

Concomitantly, the loss of traditional culture associated with modernization has often brought a loss of status and enforced disengagement with all the detrimental consequences these conditions imply for the elderly person. In fact, we may surmise that the popularity of regression-oriented views and aging is exactly a consequence of similar historical changes. In turn, as our age structure is changing, and with it the likelihood that many more individuals will live to a fairly old age with fairly high levels of education and health, we hope that the pendulum may swing back and permit us a view of aging that is dictated by a concept of the normality of aging rather than the superiority of youth.

REFERENCES

Arenberg, D. Input modality and short-term retention in old and aging adults. *Journal of Gerontology*, 1968, **23**, 462–465.

Baltes, M. M., & Baltes, P. B. The ecopsychological relativity and plasticity of psychological aging: Convergent perspectives of cohort effects and operant psychology. *Zeitschrift für Experimentelle und Angewandte Psychologie*, 1977, **24**, 179–197.

Baltes, P. B., & Labouvie, G. V. Adult development of intellectual performance: Description, explanation, and modification. In C. Eisdorfer & M. P. Lawton (Eds.), *The psychology of adult development and aging*. Washington, D.C.: American Psychological Association, 1973.

Baltes, P. B., & Schaie, K. W. On the plasticity of adult and gerontological intelligence: Where Horn and Donaldson fail. *American Psychologist*, 1976, **31**, 720–725.

Bartlett, F. C. *Remembering*. Cambridge, England: University Press, 1932.

Bengtson, V. L. *The social psychology of aging*. New York: Bobbs-Merrill, 1973.

Birren, J. E. Age and decision strategies. In A. T. Welford & J. E. Birren (Eds.), *Interdisciplinary topics in gerontology* (Vol. 4). Basel: Karger, 1979.

Birren, J. E., & Schaie, K. W. (Eds.). *Handbook of the psychology of aging*. New York: Van Nostrand Reinhold, 1977.

Borges, J. L. *Ficciones*. New York: Grove Press, 1962.

Boring, E. G. *A history of experimental psychology* (2nd ed.). New York: Appleton-Century-Crofts, 1950.

Botwinick, J. Intellectual abilities. In J. E. Birren & K. W. Schaie (Eds.), *Handbook of the psychology of aging*. New York: Van Nostrand Reinhold, 1977.

Botwinick, J. *Aging and behavior* (2nd ed.). New York: Springer, 1978.

Botwinick, J., & Storandt, M. *Memory, related functions and age*. Springfield, Ill.: Charles C. Thomas, 1974. (a)

Botwinick, J., & Storandt, M. Vocabulary ability in later life. *Journal of Genetic Psychology*, 1974, **125**, 303–308. (b)

Braitenberg, V. *On the texture of brains*. New York: Springer, 1977.

Bransford, J. D., & Franks, J. J. The abstraction of linguistic ideas. *Cognitive Psychology*, 1971, **2**, 331–350.

Brent, S. B. Individual specialization, collective adaptation and rate of environmental change. *Human Development*, 1978, **2**, 21–33.

Buck-Morss, S. Socioeconomic bias in Piaget's theory and its implication for cross-culture studies. *Human Development*, 1975, **18**, 35–49.

Cole, M., & Scribner, S. *Culture and thought: A psychological introduction*. New York: Wiley, 1974.

Demming, J. A., & Pressey, S. L. Tests "indigenous" to the adult and older years. *Journal of Counseling Psychology*, 1957, **4**, 144–148.

Dennis, W. Creative productivity between ages of 20 to 80 years. *Journal of Gerontology*, 1966, **21**, 1–8.

Dooling, J. D., & Christiansen, R. E. Levels of encoding and retention of prose. In G. H. Bower (Ed.), *The psychology of learning and memory* (Vol. 11). New York: Academic Press, 1977.

Ebbinghaus, H. *Memory*. New York: Teachers College Press, 1913. (Originally published, 1885.)

Feuer, L. *Einstein and the generations of science*. New York: Basic Books, 1974.

Finch, C. E., & Hayflick, L. (Eds.). *Handbook of the biology of aging*. New York: Van Nostrand Reinhold, 1977.

Foss, D. J., & Hakes, D. T. *Psycholinguistics*. Englewood Cliffs, N. J.: Prentice-Hall, 1978.

Foster, J. C., & Taylor, G. A. The application of mental tests to persons over 50. *Journal of Applied Psychology*, 1920, **4**, 29–58.

Gardner, E. F., & Monge, R. H. Adult age differences in cognitive abilities and educational background. *Experimental Aging Research*, 1977, **3**, 337–383.

Gilligan, C., & Murphy, J. M. Development from adolescence to adulthood: The philosopher and the dilemma of the fact. In D. Kuhn (Ed.), *Intellectual development beyond childhood*. New York: Jossey-Bass, 1979.

Glick, J. Cognitive development in cross-cultural perspective. In F. D. Horowitz (Ed.), *Review of child development research* (Vol. 4). Chicago: University of Chicago Press, 1975.

Gonda, J. The relationship between formal education and cognitive functioning: A historical perspective. *Educational Gerontology*, 1981, in press.

Gregory, R. L. *The intelligent eye*. New York: McGraw-Hill, 1970.

Gutmann, D. The cross-cultural perspective: Notes toward a comparative psychology of aging. In J. E. Birren & K. W. Schaie (Eds.), *Handbook of the psychology of aging*. New York: Van Nostrand Reinhold, 1977.

Harlow, H. F. Learning set and error factor theory. In S. Koch (Ed.), *Psychology: A study of a science* (Vol. 2). New York: McGraw-Hill, 1959.

Hayes-Roth, B. Evolution of cognitive structures and processes. *Psychological Review*, 1977, **84**, 260–278.

Hinde, R. A. *Biological bases of human social behavior*. New York: McGraw-Hill, 1974.

Horn, J. L. Organization of data on life-span development of human abilities. In L. R. Goulet & P. B. Baltes (Eds.), *Life-span developmental psychology*. New York: Academic Press, 1970.

Horn, J. L. Human ability systems. In P. B. Baltes (Ed.), *Life-span development and behavior* (Vol. 1). New York: Academic Press, 1978.

Horn, J. L., & Donaldson, G. On the myth of intellectual decline in adulthood. *American Psychologist*, 1976, **31**, 701–709.

Hulicka, I. M., & Grossman, J. L. Age-group comparisons or use of mediators in paired-associate learning. *Journal of Gerontology*, 1967, **22**, 46–51.

Hurlbut, N. L. *Adult age differences in sentence memory*. Unpublished doctoral dissertation, University of Wisconsin, 1976.

Hymes, D. Ways of speaking. In R. Bauman & J. Scherzer (Eds.), *Exploration in the ethnography of speaking*. London: Cambridge University Press, 1974.

Jacobson, M. *Developmental neurobiology* (2nd ed.). New York: Plenum Press, 1978.

Jenkins, J. J. Discussant's comments. In R. L. Solso (Ed.), *Theories in cognitive psychology: The Loyola Symposium*. Potomac, Md.: Erlbaum, 1974.

Jolly, A. *The evolution of primate behavior*. New York: Macmillan, 1972.

Kagan, J. A. A conception of early adolescence. In J. Kagan & R. Coles (Eds.), *Twelve to sixteen: Early adolescence*. New York: Norton, 1972.

Kawai, M. Newly acquired precultural behavior of the natural troop of Japanese monkeys on Koshima Island. *Primates*, 1965, **6**, 1–30.

Kendler, H. H., & Kendler, T. S. Vertical and horizontal processes in human problem solving. *Psychological Review*, 1962, **69**, 1–18.

Kogan, N. Categorizing and conceptualizing styles in younger and older adults. *Human Development*, 1974, **17**, 218–230.

Kreps, J. Age, work, and income. *Southern Economic Journal*, 1977, **April**, 1423–1437.

Kummer, H. *Primate societies: Group techniques of ecological adaptation*. Chicago: Aldine, 1971.

Labouvie-Vief, G. Adult cognitive development: In search of alternative interpretations. *Merrill–Palmer Quarterly*, 1977, **23**, 227–263.

Labouvie-Vief, G. Adaptive dimensions of cognitive aging. In N. Datan & N. Lohman (Eds.), *Transitions of aging*. New York: Academic Press, 1980. (a)

Labouvie-Vief, G. Beyond formal operations: Uses and limits of pure logic in life-span development. *Human Development*, 1980, **23**, 141–161. (b)

Labouvie-Vief, G., & Chandler, M. J. Cognitive development and life-span developmental theory: Idealistic versus contextual perspectives. In P. B. Baltes (Ed.), *Life-span development and behavior*. New York: Academic Press, 1978.

Labov, W. The logic of nonstandard English. In F. Williams (Ed.), *Language and poverty: Perspectives on a theme*. Chicago: Markham, 1970.

Lachman, J. L., & Lachman, R. Age and the actualization of world knowledge. In L. W. Poon, J. L. Fozard, L. Cermak, D. Arenberg, & L. Thompson (Eds.), *New directions in memory and aging: Proceedings of the George Talland Memorial Conference*. Hillsdale, N.J.: Erlbaum, 1980.

Langer, E., & Rodin, J. The effects of choice and enhanced personal responsibility: A field experiment in an institutional setting. *Journal of Personality and Social Psychology*, 1976, **34**, 191–198.

Langer, E., Rodin, J., Beck, P., Weinman, C., & Spitzer, L. Environmental determinants of memory improvement in late adulthood. *Journal of Personality and Social Psychology*, 1979, **37**, 2003–2013.

Leontiev, A. N. *Probleme der Entwicklung des Psychischen* (2nd ed.). West Germany: Fischer, 1977.

Loewe, H. *Lernpsychologie: Einfuehrung in die Lernpsychologie des Erwachsenenalters*. Berlin: Deutscher Verlag der Wissenschaften, 1977.

Lorge, I. The inference of the test upon the nature of mental decline as a function of age. *Journal of Educational Psychology*, 1936, **27**, 100–110.

Luria, A. R. *Cognitive development: Its cultural and social foundations*. Cambridge, Mass.: Harvard University Press, 1976.

Macdonald, M. L., & Butler, A. K. Reversal of helplessness: Producing walking behavior in nursing home wheelchair residents using behavior modification procedures. *Journal of Gerontology*, 1974, **29**, 97–101.

Neisser, V. *Cognition and reality*. San Francisco: W. A. Freeman, 1976.

Nesselroade, J. R., Schaie, K. W., & Baltes, P. B. Ontogenetic and generational components of structural and quantitative change in adult cognitive behavior. *Journal of Gerontology*, 1972, **27**, 222–228.

Olson, D. R. Culture, technology, and intellect. In L. B. Resnick (Ed.), *The nature of intelligence*. New York: Wiley, 1976.

Perry, W. I. *Forms of intellectual and ethical development in the college years*. New York: Holt, Rinehart & Winston, 1968.

Piaget, J. *Six psychological studies*. New York: Random House, 1967.

Piaget, J. Intellectual evolution from adolescence to adulthood. *Human Development*, 1972, **16**, 1–12.

Piaget, J., & Inhelder, B. *The psychology of the child*. New York: Basic Books, 1969.

Reese, H. W. Verbal mediation as a function of age level. *Psychological Bulletin*, 1962, **59**, 502–509.

Riegel, K. F. History of psychological gerontology. In J. E. Birren & K. W. Schaie (Eds.), *Handbook of the psychology of aging*. New York: Van Nostrand Reinhold, 1977.

Rosenmayr, L., & Rosenmayr, H. (Eds.). *Der alte Mensch in der Gesellschaft*. Reinbek, West Germany: Rowohlt, 1978.

Rowell, T. Forest living baboons in Uganda. *Journal of Zoology*, 1966, **147**, 344–364.

Sabatini, P., & Labouvie-Vief, G. *Age and professional specialization in formal reasoning*. Paper presented at the 1979 Annual Meeting of the American Gerontological Society, Washington, D.C., November 1979.

Schaie, K. W. A general model for the study of developmental problems. *Psychological Bulletin*, 1965, **64**, 92–107.

Schaie, K. W. Toward a stage theory of adult development. *International Journal of Aging and Human Development*, 1977, **8**, 129–138.

Schaie, K. W. External validity in the assessment of intellectual development in adulthood. *Journal of Gerontology*, 1978, **33**, 695–701.

Schaie, K. W., & Labouvie-Vief, G. Generational versus ontogenetic components of change in adult cognitive behavior. A fourteen-year cross-sequential study. *Developmental Psychology*, 1974, **10**, 305–320.

Schaie, K. W., & Strother, C. R. A cross-sectional study of age changes in cognitive behavior. *Psychological Bulletin*, 1968, **70**, 671–680.

Scribner, S. Modes of thinking and ways of speaking: Culture and logic reconsidered. In R. O. Freedle (Ed.), *New directions in discourse processing* (Vol. 2). Norwood, N.J.: Ablex, 1979.

Schulz, R. Aging and control. In J. S. Carroll & J. W. Payne (Eds.), *Cognition and social behavior*. New York: John Wiley, 1976.

Schulz, R., & Brenner, G. Relocation of the aged: A review and theoretical analysis. *Journal of Gerontology*, 1977, **32**, 323–333.

Seitelberger, F. Lebensstadien des Gehirns—Strukturelle und funktionale Aspekte. In L. Rosenmayr (Ed.), *Die menschlichen Lebensalter*. Munich: Piper, 1978.

Sheehy, G. *Passages: Predictable crises of adult life*. New York: E. P. Dutton, 1976.

Shiffrin, R. M., & Schneider, W. Controlled and automatic human information processing: II. Perceptual learning, automatic attending, and a general theory. *Psychological Review*, 1977, **84**, 127–190.

Tuddenham, R. D. Soldier intelligence in World Wars I and II. *American Psychologist*, 1948, **3**, 149–159.

Underwood, B. J. Individual differences as a crucible in theory construction. *American Psychologist*, 1975, **30**, 128–134.

Vygotsky, L. *Thought and language*. Cambridge, Mass.: MIT Press, 1962.

Walsh, D. A., & Baldwin, M. Age differences in integrated semantic memory. *Developmental Psychology*, 1977, **13**, 509–514.

Weir, M. W. Developmental changes in problem-solving strategies. *Psychological Review*, 1964, **71**, 473–490.

Weir, M. W., & Stevenson, H. W. The effect of verbalization in children's learning as a function of chronological age. *Child Development*, 1959, **30**, 143–149.

White, S. Evidence for a hierarchical arrangement of learning processes. In L. P. Lipsitt & C. C. Spiker (Eds.), *Advances in child development and behavior* (Vol. 2). New York: Academic Press, 1965.

Zelinski, E. M., Gilewski, M. J., & Thompson, L. W. Do laboratory tests relate to self-assessment of memory ability in the young and the old? In L. W. Poon, J. L. Fozard, L. Cermak, D. Arenberg, & L. Thompson (Eds.), *New directions in memory and aging: Proceedings of the George Talland Memorial Conference*. Hillsdale, N.J.: Erlbaum, 1980.

8 Gerontology in a Dynamic Society

LARS TORNSTAM

Elements of a Framework

This chapter focuses on attitudes and aging within a dynamic society. The first part gives a brief description of the basic framework in which I find it fruitful to work on gerontological problems. The second part discusses the application of the frames of reference described in the first part.[1]

WHAT IS GERONTOLOGICAL KNOWLEDGE?

Gerontology is the scientific study of the aging process, in its biological, psychological, and social aspects. Many of the results stemming from the research within these areas have direct consequences for our way of perceiving a growing social problem as well as for the various ways society might solve these problems. My first statement is that our scientific way of defining and restricting gerontological concepts has direct consequences for people's way of per-

1. Since spring 1977 the Swedish committee for future-oriented research has been supporting a research project, "Elderly Persons in Society—Yesterday, Today, and Tomorrow." This project is part of a broader project in the social theory sector aimed at achieving a closer understanding of human relations and forms of behavior. An interdisciplinary steering group is responsible for coordinating the project, and it has been my task to consider some paradigmatic problems related to the project. With this approach the steering group is aiming toward the formulation of some common frames of reference for the practical work in the various research programs within the larger project. It is with such a background that the first part of this chapter should be read.

ceiving the "problems of aging." In our way of defining gerontological problems, we are responsible for the creation of a gerontological reality. We can define it as a process with continuous economic, psychological, and other *losses*, causing an increased degree of individual *dependence*. But it can also be regarded as a process, whereby experience and knowledge in life are accumulated and where the opportunities for a liberation of intellectual and other resources continuously increases. Perceptions of the aging process also guide the solving of problems of aging. So far, gerontological research has stressed the view of increased dependence in old age more often than it has of liberation. For future research, it would be important to view dependence and liberation as balancing each other.

The stress on the concept of liberation, and the *liberation of bound resources*, is very much in consonance with a modern way of discussing the *quality of life*. The concept of "quality of life" in earlier research very often has been formulated in negative ways. Quality of life has often been synonymous with preventing disease, preventing social isolation, and the like. But nowadays research has started to posit more positive definitions, where individual liberation, intellectual liberation, and feedback of knowledge are central concepts. These notions of liberation can be defined in terms of welfare and well-being, meaning individuals' access to resources and the disposition of such resources in order to control their living conditions. This connotation of the quality of life is grounded in a normative definition of human beings and society, where the goal is for people to govern their own lives by means of their relations to other people, nature, and society.

The factors influencing individual actions at any moment are:

1. the situation; the structure of possibilities
   a. restrictions of the environment
   b. individual resources
2. perception of reality
   a. the individual's perception of the situation
   b. the individual's perception of self, in relation to the environment
3. the individual's value system

In this perspective, the liberation of bound resources has several different meanings. One possible meaning is that environmental restrictions are transformed to resources. A large river might constitute an environmental restriction for the population living by the riverside, but by the use of other resources, the river can be transformed to a new resource for irrigation or for transportation. The question is: Which kind of intervention resources leads to the transformation of environmental restrictions into new kinds of resources?

Another meaning of the liberation of bound resources refers to change in an individual's definition of the situation and of self in relation to the environment. This transformation of restrictions to resources assumes that the individual in many cases is not clearly aware of factual or potential resources and that one way of liberation is through awareness of their existence.

A third meaning of the liberation of resources notes that many elderly might be unable to use their factual resources of various kinds because their own value systems interfere. For example, many elderly people deliberately do not use their skills as resources in the labor market because they do not want to take jobs away from the younger generation.

Similar to the first, a fourth connotation of the concept of liberation of resources refers to a more traditional way of fighting environmental restrictions, which tend to be resource binding. Much of the preventive geriatrics and also much of the intervention in elderly persons' dwellings where the aim is to prevent emergencies or social isolation should be seen with this perception.

Related to the concept of the liberation of resources is also the paradigm of exchanges in resources and in power as formulated by Emerson (1976), Blau (1964), and others. Many gerontologists, among them Hudson (1976) and Rosenmayr (Rosenmayr & Rosenmayr, 1978), consider exchange theory to be one of the better theoretical approaches for gerontology. Exchange can be analyzed on an individual level or between age groups such as the elderly, the middle aged, and the youth in society. These age categories are relative of course. As Ariès (1962) has shown, the borderlines between these categories were culturally and historically defined. The categories of both children and the elderly are rather new concepts. It was with the creation of a school for children that we first found a separate and distinguishable category of "school children"; it was when the social reforms of retirement were carried through that we found a new and distinguishable category, "retirees." Future research on exchange relationships between the various age categories in society will have to take into consideration the fact that the category "elderly" cannot be given any absolute connotation but rather has to be related to the various definitions of aging in different time periods. Nor could the elderly be defined as a homogeneous group, nor even as a group in the sociological sense. The category "elderly" does not show the distinguishing features for a sociological group; they lack the feeling of a group identity and do not interact primarily as an age group.

DEFINING SOCIAL PROBLEMS

According to Rubington and Weinberg (1971), a social problem can be defined in at least five different ways, and at the same time each of these implies ways of solving the problems. One way of perceiving a social problem is in terms of *social pathology*. In this perspective on the "problems of aging," people no longer remain "normal" in regard to bodily movements, social networks, demands for community services, and so on. Whether the absence of normality refers to a statistical pattern, a clinical standard in medicine or psychology, or an ideal people hold in terms of certain moral codes, the social pathological perspective focuses interest on the single individual. This way of defining problems of aging also views individuals as the targets of various kinds of interventions. If a social network that is breaking down or social isolation are perceived as problems of aging, we will automatically within the perspective of social pathology find the solution of the problem on the individual level, rather than on the sociostructural level.

In another perspective, the focus is moved from the single individual to the social organization (Rubington & Weinberg, 1971). We can, according to Rubington and Weinberg, regard social problems as the result of *social disorganization*. By the processes of industrialization and urbanization, which characterize all Western countries, society has been growing so fast that its various parts do not fit together any longer. The old tales about the elderly as knowing best are no longer in consonance with a society characterized by a dramatic technological and intellectual development. The process of urbanization moves younger people into towns, while the elderly remain in the old locations. With this way of perceiving the problems of aging, quite different solutions follow. What has to be done concerns more general and sociostructural corrections, rather than interventions for single individuals.

In a third perspective, social problems are viewed as latent and manifest *value conflicts*. In such a perspective criminality is a result of an inherent conflict between different groups in society and their different ways of defining justice. From this point of view, the problems of aging might be regarded as a continuous and unavoidable conflict between the industrial market's need for young, competent, and highly productive manpower, on the one hand, and the aging individual's need for self-actualization by productive work, on the other hand. The earlier and earlier absence of the elderly from the labor market is within this perspective the result of such an unavoidable conflict situation.

In a fourth perspective Rubington and Weinberg (1971) look at social problems through *deviant* behavior. The stress is on the fact that certain individuals in society do not correspond to the social norms and that much of deviant behavior is created in a learning process. Passive and withdrawn behavior among retired people would be regarded as a result of a learning process.

Finally, Rubington and Weinberg (1971) describe the possibilities of perceiving social problems in terms of *social labeling*. It is through the reactions of people around us that we are labeled as criminals or elderly.

Gerontologists sometimes take their points of departure from one or the other of the above mentioned perspectives. The remarkable fact is that rather few researchers seem conscious of their choice of paradigm. Since different paradigms also imply quite different ways of solving the problems of aging, it might be advisable that gerontologists make themselves more paradigm conscious in these respects.

In addition to these different ways of perceiving the problems of aging, there are within gerontology other theoretical approaches, or paradigms, that are often used arbitrarily, namely, a life cycle or life perspective as described by Neugarten and Berkowitz (1964), Riegel (1978), and Lowenthal (1976); an activity theory, Havighurst (1963); a disengagement theory, Cumming and Henry (1961); a theory of symbolic interactionism, Rose (1965); a theory of minority groups, Barron (1953) and Streib (1965); a theory of subcultures, Rose (1962); and a theory of pressure groups, Trela (1971) and Pratt (1974).

THE CROSS-DISCIPLINARY PERSPECTIVE

Irrespective of the kind of paradigm to be used, the problems under study are of such a character that to a large degree they cross traditional academic lines. The scientific study of a phenomenon such as aging can be done in many ways and within various disciplines.

Aging can be studied on a level where the primary interest is in the single individual, what happens to him or her biologically or psychologically when he or she is aging, as in the social pathological perspective.

This theoretical level, shown in Figure 8-1, is called the individual level or the microlevel. When we are trying to describe how the inner organs of the body are changing with age or investigating how the intellectual capacity is changing, we are working on this level. It is to be noted that the research on the microlevel is subdivided into one medical and one psychological part, but there are, of course, no absolute barriers between the individual's mind and body. All psychosomatic diseases are examples of how the mind is influencing the body. We all know how psychological stresses can result in ulcers or heart pains. The reverse is also true, that the bodily health is influencing the mind even if these influences have shown up to be far more complicated than what was thought from the beginning. In Figure 8-1, arrow 7 illustrates how the mind and body constantly affect each other.

Next is the mezzolevel. The focus is no longer on the human being as an individual but as a group member. Within this theoretical level social psychology is to be found: how people affect each other through sex and age roles. People in our environment expect us to act differently depending on whether we are men or women, if we are young or old. Aging implies drastic changes in the dynamics on the so-

Figure 8-1. Theoretical levels in gerontology.

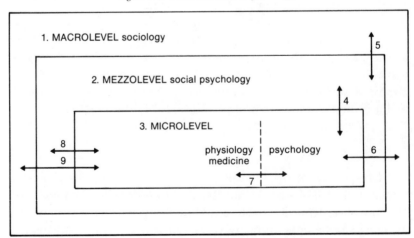

cial psychological level that affect the individual level, the microlevel. Many modern stress diseases can be explained in terms of features within the human setting, and intellectual capacity can also be influenced by the social psychological climate. A setting that is characterized by hostility and rivalry is regarded as a cause of psychological and medical problems for the individual. Also, the group climate is influenced by single individuals and their various psychological and physiological appearances. An individual with special psychological problems as well as an individual with specific physical handicaps colors the group climate. The continuous interdependence between the group level and the individual level is illustrated by arrows 4 and 8 in Figure 8-1.

Despite the fact that the microlevel and the mezzolevel are intimately interrelated, most of the research within these different fields is carried out in different institutions and within different faculties. The physiological research within the individual level is carried out within the faculty of medicine, while inquiry into individual psychology is carried out within psychological institutions. The mezzolevel constitutes a traditional field for sociologists, but psychologists are also very much interested in this theoretical level. Within our research program there is an effort to transcend these traditional boundaries, and a subprogram focuses on health and illness in the aging process. It is stimulating to notice how researchers within this subprogram are broadening their scope to understand individual health and sickness in a social psychological or psychological perspective and within the framework of the macrolevel, which in Figure 8-1 is symbolized by the outermost frame.

SOCIOSTRUCTURAL BASES

The individual's health or sickness during the process of aging occurs within a continuously changing society. This awareness can be systematically handled by reference to continuously changing bases in the social structure on a specific theoretical level, the societal level, or the macrolevel. The influence of this level on the other theoretical levels can be the target for special attention. Within this macrotheoretical level the interest is focused on such phenomena as the means of production in a society, the type of family patterns, the religion, the dwelling patterns, the distribution of economic and political resources, the welfare patterns, the distribution of knowledge, and the rate of technological change.

These macrotheoretical factors are interrelated. The distribution of knowledge is, for example, in part dependent on the rapidity of technological changes. In a society with a traditional youth-oriented school, a rapid technological change causes the distribution of knowledge to automatically be uneven—to the disadvantage of the elderly. The skills learned by youth in school are going to be less and less valuable as time passes. The consequence is that as we grow older, the knowledge we have becomes less valuable. The macroreality, however, also governs the reality on the other theoretical levels. The social psychological invariances are, for example, operating in a slightly different way in a society with uneven distribution of knowledge in comparison with a society with evenly distributed knowledge. In a society where the young people have the most valuable knowledge, the status order within groups is affected in favor of the young people. In very much the same way, group processes are affected in different religious systems where elderly are looked upon in different ways. In the Hebrew tradition the elderly are honored, which also is reflected in the everyday life. In Figure 8-1 arrow 5 illustrates this relationship. This arrow also reflects an influence in the opposite direction, where the continuously ongoing group processes in the society are gradually changing the reality on the macrotheoretical level. This is rather self-evident. It is within the interactions of everyday life that people change their society.

This self-evident fact is, however, *not* reflected in gerontological research. To the extent that gerontologists study sociostructural phenomena and their changes in the processes of aging, they concentrate on the possible effects on the individual level or on the social psychological level.

Gerontologists have to consider that single individuals, groups of individuals, and social institutions participate in a continuously ongoing dialectic process, where social institutions are as much affected by the ongoing group processes in society as vice versa. In praxis this implies that gerontological research can concentrate not only on studying effects of part-time pensioning systems, modernized old-age care, and so on, but it can, to the same extent, focus on how old people in society—as individuals or groups, as pressure groups, or by their numbers—are affecting or changing society and its institutions. In which ways are the growing Grey Panther movements affecting the political decision making at the community or governmental level? Are there causal relationships between the number of the elderly in society and their modes of organization and the modes of decision making in county councils? This is a new type of question that has to be raised together with the more traditional ones, which are looking for the effects of various sociopolitical interventions. This dialectical interdependence between group processes in society and the social structure has to be analyzed with great care.

The reality on the macrolevel is also governing the reality on the microlevel. A society that on the macrolevel is characterized by a rather strong future orientation and an ethic where the members of society are valued according to their productional capacity, must have different effects on the individual psychological level than a society that stresses the past and has a humanistic ethic. Western society is a future-oriented society. In every movement our attention is toward the future, and for most of our time we are planning what to do later. For the elderly, who have most of their lives behind them, such a future-orientation implies a psychological stress, which eventually can be the cause of psychological problems. We have a functional ethic, which implies people are highly valued if they are productive but devalued if they are unproductive. Individuals who by age or handicap are unable to reach the goals of productivity are hereby exposed to psychological stresses. Arrow 6 in Figure 8-1 illustrates this case. This arrow also symbolizes a process that has an opposite direction, which can be illustrated by the individual psychology of various politicians who have been of utmost importance for change in society. This is an influence from the individual level, the micro-level, to the society level, the macrolevel, which have a dialectic relationship.

Also the biological aspects on the microlevel have to be explained and understood within the frame of a macrotheoretical perspective. Specifically, many diseases in industrial countries have to be understood within a macrotheoretical framework. In an industrial country, most of the coronary diseases, which today are major medical problems, can be explained in terms of the special character of an industrial society. In very much the same way the norms within the teenage culture are behind the fact that young girls from time to time underfeed themselves in such a way that doctors have to treat them for malnutrition. As arrow 9 in Figure 8-1 shows, the patterns of the society level, on the macrolevel, also influence the individual's physiological and medical reality.

From what has been said above, it should be clear that to a much larger extent gerontological research should pay attention to the dialectic interdependences among the theoretical levels described in

Figure 8-1. There is already a rather well-established tradition from which to benefit, but this tradition has rarely been used within gerontology. Early social theory as formulated by Durkheim, Tönnis, and Weber, and by Park, Burgess, McKenzie, Wirth, Redfield, Mannheim, and others describes the consequences of changes in population, its number density and heterogeneity. On the individual level, from their view, the interaction between groups and institutions in society becomes segmented, utilitarian, and of subordinate importance for the individual, rather than integrated and of prime importance. The personality tends to be changed from a relatively rigid type, molded by the traditional society, to a more flexible type, which has been necessary in our pluralistic and variable society. Back (1976) describes how low and decreasing natality is going to produce a widening of the generation gap and an increase in the number of individuals with living parents, grandparents, children, and grandchildren. On the other hand, Shanas and Hauser (1975) as well as Back (1974) describe how the decreasing natality lends to a larger and larger number of individuals who find themselves with no relatives at all. Because of these changes the institution of the family is supposed to be less important in comparing the situation today with that in earlier times. The importance of age groups is supposed to be increasing in comparison with the importance of the family group. Also, in such discussions the demographic situation is connected with personality development in later life. This is the case because the content of later life in part depends on the social situation we expect to be in at that time, which in its turn is dependent on the demographic development.

These discussions are mainly hypotheses, but they stimulate the linkage of the macrotheoretical level with the levels which in Figure 8-1 are termed micro- and mezzolevels. *This connection of theoretical levels is fundamental if gerontology is to be developed in a dynamic developmental perspective.* If we neglect this connection of theoretical levels, and especially if we neglect to realize the very great importance of the macrotheoretical level on all the other levels, we must accept the fact that gerontology is going to be *static.* In the long run this also implies rather uninteresting research. Such research becomes unusable for showing future alternatives for action.

One example of this is the following: Several empirical investigations have shown how geographical distribution creates problems of isolation for the elderly. Approximate age is one type of status similarity that quite a lot of research has shown to be of importance for the formation of friendship relationships. This phenomenon has been documented by Lazarsfeld and Merton (1954), Heider (1946, 1958), Festinger (1957), and Newcomb (1961). Even if such predictions also have an empirical support (see Rosow, 1967; Riley, 1972; Tornstam, 1975) the reasoning tends to be static because it presupposes that the society level remains unchanged. The discussion becomes more fruitful if we start to explore the dependences between the society level and the social psychological level. We might start by asking under which macrosociological preconditions this phenomenon would cease to occur. Which sociostructural variables should be changed in order to extinguish the rule that elderly need elderly in order to form new relationships?

It must be fully understood that these types of questions rest on a fundamental difference between the so-called pure sciences—mathematics, physics, chemistry, and so on—and the social sciences. Different from the natural sciences, the behavioral and social sciences have possibilities to affect and change the invariances that are regulating and governing reality. The technician can hardly change the law of gravitation, but the sociologist is able to suggest means of changing social psychological "laws." The social sciences can, and should, not only try to find invariances or laws, but also try to suggest how such laws could be extinguished. According to the Norwegian sociologist Galtung (1974), the social sciences are not only invariance seeking but also have an invariance-breaking possibility.

Another reason for broadening the theoretical scope is that gerontological research has a tendency to be led by dogmas. From time to time researchers use their data very uncritically. Often this practice can be seen as a conflict between a scientific approach and the humanitarian motives stimulating researchers to participate in gerontological research.

THE PROCESS APPROACH

Besides the importance of a broadened theoretical scope, gerontological research has to put more stress on individual and societal processes of change. In the perspective of a dynamic society, the problems of aging have to be studied in three different time perspectives: (1) the individual aging process, (2) the process of new generations being born, living, and dying, and (3) the process of the histori-cal development. The concepts of cohort, cohort analysis, life cycle, and life cycle analysis are the tools for this awareness.

Riley (1972) argues that we always have to consider two parallel time dimensions. One can be expressed by chronological age, as a rough indicator of the individual's place within his or her life cycle, and the other relates the individual's life cycle to the history of society. In the contemporary gerontological research much interest has been directed to the cohort analysis. As Rosenmayr and Eder (1978) say, there is, however, a risk involved in this approach if researchers concentrate *too* much on such cohort differences. It might become impossible to interpret cohort differences if they are not analyzed, at the same time, in the perspective of the microlevel and the individual's personal development. I think Rosenmayr and Eder's argument is that a kind of neo-Freudian reasoning is rather important in these matters. Events early in the individual's life are of great importance in later life, but these earlier life events also have to be put into historical perspective. Having grown up in the "happy '60s" produces quite another life cycle in comparison with having grown up in the years of depression. Should the processual studies be designed as comparisons between conditions at different points in time, as a trend analysis, or should the concentration be on compari-son between longer historical periods—either within the frame of the individual life cycle or in the historical perspective.

Another approach is to focus the interest on various kinds of transitions. Foner (1978), for example, discusses such transitions within the individual life cycle and concentrates on various passages between different periods in the individual's life. Transitions, such as retirement, are different in different cohorts because every cohort exists under unique historical conditions. Hammarström (1975) and several others have also argued that an emphasis on transitions is fruitful in the historical and cultural perspective. It has been shown how, under such cultural transitions, certain problems of aging are identified. They can also be studied in relation to the individual life cycle perspective by investigating which changes appear in normal life cycle patterns.

Recent research on the life course has emphasized the need to look at such transitions not strictly as individual moves but also in synchronization with collective family moves (Hareven, 1978). The retirement period is a rather new phenomenon and yet even within it at least two distinguishable subperiods have appeared: one period under which the old person is rather healthy and active and a later one, when health decreases dramatically. According to a newly undertaken Swedish investigation (Pensionär-75, 1977) the first period lasts until about the age 80.

To sum up, in the dynamic perspective we have to realize that the specific life periods we see today are the result of an ongoing social process. To some small extent this process of change is predictable, but in other ways it is completely dependent on the kind of sociopolitical decisions made by our elected representatives. An important gerontological task in the borderland between gerontology and political science is to study and to foresee the consequences of different types of political decision making for old people.

POSTINDUSTRIAL SOCIETY AND PROBLEMS OF AGING

The single historical and cultural transition, which has been singled out as the most important concerning problems of aging, is without doubt the transition into the industrial society. According to Bell (1974) this transition is characterized by (1) the substitution of human power in the industry with mechanical power, (2) a dramatic increase in agricultural production, which also implies technological development that liberates people and capital for the needs of the industry, (3) a shift from agriculture to industry, (4) an accelerating degree of urbanization, (5) a differentiation of states, industrialized and developing, (6) a change to more materialistic and secularized values.

Within gerontology these changes have been assumed to create new problems for the elderly in society. A closer analysis has shown how many of these "facts" have not been any more than assumptions that historians found to be false. It is of utmost importance that historical research help us clarify the assumptions on which our current inquiries are based.

Now Western societies are on their way into a new period, the postindustrial society. Bell (1974) points to some fundamental changes to come in the postindustrial society: (1) The fossil energy, which now is the dominating energy source, is replaced by nuclear energy or energy sources such as sun energy or wind energy. (2) A continuous automatization within industry will reduce the need for human manpower. As a consequence of this and of a changing need structure among people, the need for staff in various service sectors will increase. (3) With more advanced industry and technique, the need for highly educated staff is going to increase. (4) There is going to be a geographic separation between industrial areas, commercial centers, and dwelling areas. (5) As basic materialistic values, which have been predominant during the first phases of industrialization, are more and more met, the strongly work-oriented ethic is going to diminish. It will be replaced by an ethic where questions about quality of life come into the foreground, a process that already has started. This tendency is increased by a larger and larger proportion of the population outside the direct labor market.

The basic values fundamental in the industrialized world, values such as justice, freedom, and integrity, also have to be seen in a dynamic perspective. The value patterns that are going to be fundamental for the perceptions of the problems of aging, will quite probably be different in 50 years. It follows that it is not only important to connect the perceptions of problems of aging with the norm and value systems, but also to study the changes of the value and norm systems.

The transition into the postindustrial society is assumed to imply several changes in the perception of the problems of aging. Lakoff (1976) describes how the combination of fewer physical demands within jobs and the decreasing degree of the population working in direct production are going to affect our attitudes toward the elderly. The incompleteness of such discussions must, however, be noted. They disregard coming conflicts over scarce resources, and these predictions are nothing more than hypotheses to be tested.

MYTHS AND DOGMAS

If gerontological research is going to be useful for the planning of the future society, it must be based on sound assumptions on the past and the present and the processes that have led from past to present. Without going into detail in these matters I would like to mention three important myths, which need to be explored further.

1. The transition from preindustrial to industrial society has been described as one from an ideal situation to a bad one. Such a before–after approach is very much simplified, however, in part because the proportion of elderly people never has been of any importance before the industrial period (Laslett, 1976). There is no

simple way to compare the conditions for people 65–75 years of age today with conditions for people of corresponding ages 100 years ago. It becomes quite necessary, as stated above, to introduce a concept of variable age categories, in which case the befores and afters become incomparable.

According to a traditional assumption, the processes of industrialization and urbanization had a very important influence on the family patterns and the interaction between the generations. According to this assumption, the family patterns in the old agrarian society were dominated by the extended family, which was composed of several generations who lived within the same household. Within this setting, it is assumed that everybody had meaningful tasks.

With the transition from home production to industrial production, it is also assumed that the dwellings for younger people and the elderly were separated, whereby the traditional extended family pattern was broken down. In the preindustrial era the elderly were supposed to have power and authority within the family. They were respected for knowledge and experience, and most of the properties were controlled by them. With industrialization, it was assumed that the nuclear family pattern, which includes only parents and their unmarried children, is supposed to have become more and more common. An impressive number of researchers (Messer, 1968, is one of them) regard these nuclear family patterns as the major source of the lost status and authority of the elderly today. The elderly lack a position in the nuclear family; they have a family, but they do not belong to any family.

Many authors believe this postulated transition from the extended multigenerational family to the nuclear family to be the cause of the changed relations between family members; and for the elderly these changes have been in a negative direction. Well-known authors like Durkheim, Simmel, and Tönnis have emphasized the isolation of the nuclear family, as have Linton (1959) and Parsons (1943, 1959).

This conception of the extended multigenerational family as the dominant family pattern in the agrarian societies, however, has been disputed over the past decade. Sjoberg (1960) argues that the extended multigenerational family has been possible only among wealthy elites in feudal areas. Several others state, especially concerning the United States, that the conception of the "happy three-generational family" in the 17th, 18th, and 19th centuries is nothing but a myth. This family form had probably not been very

numerous nor especially happy (Goode, 1963; Hareven, 1976). In
Sweden there was a system in which elderly people without resources had to go begging in a systematic and predecided manner or
were auctioned away as *utackorderingshjon* to the farmer or the peasant
who bid the lowest. Also among peasants with farms there was a rule
that with the help of a registered contract they handed the farm over
to the children. This was a pattern that in reality implied rather poor
material conditions. Gaunt (1978) has, in a study of the conditions in
northern Finland, shown that these contracts had sources of conflicts
built in between the generations. These and other findings by historians provide more and more reason to believe that the classicial
family in the Western "nostalgia," as Goode (1963) puts it, is a stereotype. Besides these revisions, it must be remembered that the structural changes in industrial society have caused a geographical separation of the generations. Younger people in the labor market have
moved to the cities where there are jobs, while the elderly have
remained in the old dwellings. The future consequences of these
changes will be interesting.

   2. It has been generally assumed that as a result of industrialization and urbanization the elderly in today's society have come to be
lonely and isolated. This assumption in much of gerontological research has been used as a base for future research. This description
fits badly with the social reality. Instead, empirical investigations, in
particular in Sweden, show quite another picture in which elderly
people tend to be rather well integrated in today's society. Elderly
people have good relations with their children, and feelings of loneliness are predominant only for a minority (Babchuk & Beates, 1963;
Hess, 1972; Olsen, Trampe, & Hansen, 1976; Pensionär-75, 1977;
Roos, 1975; Tornstam, 1978).

   It is of utmost importance to continue the research in these
matters. The fact that the processes of industrialization and urbanization do not appear to have caused the kind of isolation, as was
believed, could suggest that these processes have not yet been fully
consummated. Hareven (1978) seems to have the opinion that the
rather good social integration of today's elderly has to be regarded
as a result of the sociostructural conditions of an earlier period. In
other words, this is a case of cultural lag. The effects of urbanization
and industrialization are to be seen in the future cohorts.

   Another frequent assumption on the transition from preindustrial to industrial society is related to the individual level. The tradi-

tional description is that the transitions between different periods in life took place smoothly and without problems for the individual in the preindustrial society, while the transitions between different phases in life have come to be discontinuous and connected with severe transitional problems during the industrial phase. This kind of description is now being questioned, too. Foner (1978) has, by analyzing ethnographical material, concluded that preliterate societies and modern Western society show the same degree of stress in connection with transitions between different periods in life. The difference is rather that the types of stresses are different in today's society from preliterate society. If role discontinuity is considered most crucial at the transition into retirement in today's society, one could argue that the transition to adulthood was the most discontinuous event in the preliterate society.

3. One of the fundamental reasons why the "problems of aging" have attracted so much attention is that the proportion of individuals in the upper half of the age scale has dramatically increased in all industrial societies. In many discussions this has been explained by the "facts" that people live longer and by the efforts of modern medicine. Even if it is true that people's mean life expectancy in industrial society has increased, this is not primarily so because people grow older but because more people have survived to adulthood and are growing old. Furthermore, the one single factor most responsible for the increase in the proportion of the elderly is the decline in the natality. These are just examples of how basic demographic changes affect not only separate individuals and their life cycles but the whole society and its way of functioning. This also points to the necessity of continuous efforts within gerontology where demographic projections are connected with various other gerontological problem areas.

Attitudes and Aging within a Dynamic Society

As mentioned in the introduction to this chapter the purpose of the first part has been to express some aspects of the basic framework in which I find it fruitful to work with gerontological problems. In the second part of this chapter I discuss the concept of attitudes, attitudinal change, bases of attitudes, and so on, within the framework created in the first part.

In gerontological research the studies of attitudes have a rather long tradition. Kogan (1977) dates this history back to more than a quarter of a century ago when Tuckman and Lorge (1953) initiated a series of empirical studies on the attitudes toward elderly people. Despite the honorable early approach within this area, the studies of Tuckman and Lorge have deficiencies that many of the following researchers have inherited. Kogan (1977) shows how Tuckman and Lorge, as many of the ancestors, had used the concept of attitudes without keeping apart emotional aspects and cognitive components. The following are some sample statements, taken from a rather late Swedish attitudinal investigation, which exemplifies the problem:

- Elderly prefer to be by themselves.
- Most elderly are in bad health.
- Elderly feel very lonely.

The answers given to such questions include a mixture of knowledge about the elderly and their conditions and feelings about the elderly. The following two items are from the same questionnaire:

- It is a ridiculous sight seeing elderly wearing shorts.
- Elderly are entitled to receive the help they need.

The answers express more of an emotional attitudinal component. It is a striking fact that many attitudinal investigations have come to mix knowledge and feelings about the elderly. This has been noticed by several researchers, for example, Kogan (1961a, 1961b), who tries to construct attitudinal scales for the measurement of feelings only. Others, such as Kilty and Feld (1976) and Rosencrantz and McNevin (1969), have questioned the unidimensionality of attitude. These types of questions make it necessary to introduce into every discussion of attitudes and aging an analysis of the very concept of attitudes.

ATTITUDES: DOMAIN OF THE CONCEPT

By the examples given above it has been shown that the attitudinal concept includes both a component of feelings and a component of knowledge. To this we also have to add a component of behavior. In the more traditional attitude literature it is customary to distinguish an emotive component from a behavioral component. An attitude is defined as a predisposition to (1) feel and (2) act in a certain way when confronted with an attitudinal object, which in our case is constituted by the social category "elderly." Since this disposition to feel or act in a certain way in relation to the elderly can be based on various degrees of knowledge about the elderly and their conditions, it is clear that we have to distinguish three fundamental components in the concept, namely, (1) the emotive component, (2) the cognitive component (the knowledge), and (3) the behavioral component.

When we distinguish the three components in the attitudinal concept, it is easy to presume that the patterns of feelings, knowledge, and behavior regard single individuals. It is single individuals, we believe, who on the basis of a certain degree of (or lack of) knowledge about the elderly, feel in a positive or negative way and behave, or do not behave, in a special way. But these three fundamental components in the concept of attitudes can also be studied in a manner where groups of individuals are the focus of interest. Rather than the feelings of separate individuals, it is then a question of how groups are expressing feelings of pro and con in relation to other groups. Finally, the three basic components of the attitudinal concept can also be studied in a manner where the more general goals for the society are spelled out.

Three different ways in which the three components of attitudes can be studied directly correspond to the three different theoretical levels, which were mentioned in the first part of this chapter. These levels were (1) the microlevel, or the individual level, (2) the mezzolevel, or the group level, and (3) the macrolevel, or the society level. The combination of these theoretical levels with the three basic attitudinal components constitutes the domain or property space of the attitudinal concept, as shown in Figure 8-2. In this figure the positions in the property space, as created by the two dimensions, are

Figure 8-2. The domain of attitudes.

	Emotions	Cognitions	Behavior
Macrolevel Society level	Social ideals Basic goals Morals	Surveys Investigations Newspapers	Constitutions Laws Statutes
Mezzolevel Group level	In and out groups Group pressure	Facts Stereotypes Prejudices	Solidarity Mobbing Customs Social sanctions
Microlevel Individual level	Love, hate Sympathy Antipathy	Facts Stereotypes Prejudices	Individual behavior

of more importance than the terms or concepts I have used to describe the various positions. The figure implies an enlargement of the concept of attitudes, or rather an awareness of what normally is excluded when discussing attitudes.

The domain of the attitudinal concept, as described in Figure 8-1, can be used to articulate certain problems, solved or unsolved, in relation to attitudes and aging. Some of these problems—love or hate, sympathy or antipathy, positive or negative feelings—which we have in relation to the elderly can be based on various degrees of knowledge about the elderly, and the step from feeling to behavior can be of various length.

The relations between the attitudinal emotions and cognitions can be rather complicated. When people have poor knowledge about the elderly and their conditions but still make statements about the elderly, we term stereotypes, prejudices, or categorizings. A stereotype can, however, be connected with positive as well as negative feelings toward the elderly.

In a large American investigation Harris (1975) studied how younger people perceived the problems of the elderly in relation to how the elderly themselves perceived their problems. The respondents had to express whether they believed the elderly to perceive criminality in society, bad health, bad economy, loneliness, bad education, and so on. Two main results are outstanding in this study. One is that the younger people systematically tended to believe the elderly have more problems in comparison to what the elderly themselves said. The other is that the rank orders among the different kinds of problems are different for the elderly and for the younger, who were asked what the ranking list for the elderly would be. At the time of the preparation of this chapter, the Sociological Institute in Uppsala was undertaking a replication of this study. Very preliminary results show a trend similar to the results described for the study in the United States. One of the most remarkable findings in the Swedish study will probably be an enormous discrepancy between the degree of elderly people feeling lonely and the degree to which they are believed to have such a problem. More than 90% of a random sample population believe the elderly to have problems with loneliness, while less than 10% of the elderly themselves express problems of that kind. This is only one small example of many such remarkable discrepancies.

STEREOTYPES

We have just been discussing the relations between the cognitive and emotive components of an attitude, without considering various probable reasons for wrong or stereotype conceptions. When, in everyday language, we are using the stereotype concept, we refer to a tendency to describe such categories as elderly, criminals, and immigrants with only the linguistic label as point of departure.

Such a stereotypic description of the elderly could be that they are in bad health, lonely, rigid, and dull. For most elderly people this stereotypic description is false. Other stereotypic descriptions of the elderly could be these: Most of them have vascular diseases; the lung capacity tends to decrease when growing old; suicide is more common among the elderly than among younger people; the elderly usually need more time to learn. The last set of statements are true for the elderly as a category, but, of course, they do not need to be so for separate individuals. This shows how a stereotype can be more or less false or more or less true. One interesting issue is the relation we can find between stereotype and the emotive component of the attitude on the one hand, and the real truth on the other.

The stereotype is a part of a wider concept—the concept of categorization. To systematize and categorize the reality around us, categorization is a necessity. As human beings we have a rather limited possibility of perceiving and registering the almost infinite variety of stimuli in our environment. It would hardly be possible to perceive any order or any structure in our environment if we could not create an order by different categorizing processes. It would be impossible to find any order among the thousands of different animals in nature if we could not categorize them into groups like insects or mammals. In the same way, it would be impossible to understand anything of the social structure if we did not group together people or situations with similarities. We distinguish between men and women, workers and employers, rich and poor, because the social reality is so organized that it is meaningful and rational to categorize people in this way. On the other hand, if a social analysis distinguishes between brown-eyed people and people with other eye colors, this would be nonsense since nothing in society in any way is organized around this categorization. Is it more rational to distinguish between younger people and the elderly than between brown-eyed and people with other eye colors? In several aspects it is, since quite a lot of the social reality is related to people's age. Very important is the fact that the structure of the labor market is related to these categorizations. Even if it can be said to be rational and meaningful to distinguish between separate age categories, this does not mean that the stereotyping itself is rational. Stereotyping is characterized by so many attributes that we could hardly find a single individual within the category on which all these attributes would fit.

The problem can be clarified by going back to Figure 8-1. On the macrolevel the cognitive elements of the attitudes are expressed as basic knowledge from surveys, investigations, and so on. Even if such investigations show that about 50% of the elderly do not have their own teeth, that half of the elderly have vascular diseases, that the lung capacity of the elderly tends to go down, that suicide is more common among the elderly than among younger people, that old people usually need longer time for learning something new, this knowledge becomes transformed into a stereotype when you try to describe a single elderly man or woman in terms of these findings. While the findings just mentioned have the character of probability statements, or percentages of the elderly with this or that attribute, they tend to receive an absolute and qualitative meaning in the stereotype. In this way you can say, according to Kogan (1977), that stereotyping is not necessarily a total misconception of reality, but rather a part of the human categorizing process. The probabilistic character of reality, however, has been lost and replaced by deterministic or categorical statements.

As mentioned earlier, there is also another type of stereotype, that which lacks even a small reality base. It is not yet known how these two different types of stereotypes and the emotive attitudinal component are intermixed. It is suggested that in situations of danger or threat it often becomes necessary for a group to strengthen their internal solidarity, and this often takes place by the indication of psychological, and other, distances to groups. So-called in and out groups are formed. Under such processes it is probable that non-reality-based stereotypes will be formed. Swedish workers feeling their jobs threatened by Syrian immigrants are strengthening their own in-group solidarity by the description of the threat in stereotype and non-reality-based terms. Might it also be that the preconditions for non-reality-based stereotype conceptions about the elderly are supported in economic depressions, when people in the labor market feel a threat to their well-being, a threat from those nonproducers in society?

THE MULTIDIMENSIONALITY OF ATTITUDES

When discussing attitudes, we must not only distinguish among emotions, cognitions, and behaviors. Each of these factors are in themselves multidimensional. We have, for example, illustrated the emotional part of the attitudes with words like love, hate, sympathy, dislike, for, against, positive, and negative. This at the same time illustrates how the emotional part of an attitude is multidimensional in different ways. One way refers to the fact that the emotive component can include different kinds of feelings. For example, the feeling of hate is something different from the feeling of dislike. In this way, the feelings in relation to the elderly can constitute a mixture of fear, dislike, love, and so on.

Another aspect of the multidimensionality is expressed in a study by Kilty and Feld (1976), who found younger people's attitudes toward the elderly and their position in society grouped around four major attitudinal dimensions. The first has to do with the general entitlements for older persons, the second is related to societal rejection of older people, the third is related to entitlement to remain in the community, and the fourth is concerned with the reciprocity between the elderly and the community. This is only one example of how the multidimensionality comes into expression in the attitudinal research.

By realizing the multidimensionality of attitudes, we can also analyze contradictory attitudes toward the elderly. Within a single individual this might be expressed by feelings of positive emotions toward parents, together with a negative irritation toward their powerlessness and nonproductivity. Again referring to Figure 8-1, it can be seen that on the macrolevel the emotive component has to do with the political ideals and the ethics in the society. For several reasons, we should increase our focus on the attitudinal components on the societal level. As we are going to see in the pages ahead, there might be a risk that the political ideas and the ethics in society to an increasing extent are deviating from the everyday reality in which elderly people live and in which different kinds of staff who are working with the elderly live. There can also be a contradiction between the ideals spelled out by the politicians and the nonoutspoken feelings that in reality govern behavior.

The discussion hitherto has shown the attitudinal concept to be complex and embracing several subcomponents. Implicitly this discussion also points to a question of a more general nature. What part does the attitudinal concept have in a wider theoretical framework? The discussion so far has shown that there is no simple relationship between the emotive cognitive and behavioral components of the attitude. In any case it is much too simple to say that the emotive and behavioral aspects of the attitude are a direct result of the cognitive aspect. On the contrary, research shows how information campaigns to cut down stereotypes do not easily bring about changes in the emotive component of attitudes or in behavior. The cognitive component to quite a high degree is dependent upon the emotive component. Human beings are looking for knowledge that is congruent with their feelings. Some attitudinal researchers, like Krech and Crutchfield (1948), by definition include such a tendency in their attitudinal concept. This tendency to perceive reality in a certain way, to search for knowledge selectively, is of course closely related to the cognitive attitudinal component. If we feel negatively toward immigrants, it is probable that we will seek such information that is going to support our negative feelings. This tendency to look for information that is congruent with our feelings can also be explained in terms of Festinger's (1957) theory of cognitive dissonance.

Even if, in this way, we can more clearly see patterns in feelings, knowledge, and behavior, the question of how these patterns were formed is left without an answer. The attitudinal concept in itself no longer becomes the most central and most interesting one, but rather the more fundamental factor behind attitudes becomes the more important concept. This more basic factor is, in my opinion, the *values*, or the value structure in the society. Like Rokeach (1973), I would like to see the concept of values and value structures as the more general one, and the attitudes as the consequences of the former.

An important difference between the concepts of values and attitudes is that attitudes are always centered around a special attitudinal object or a special situation. To illustrate this, let us suppose productivity and effectivity to be two of the basic values in our society. We are all indoctrinated to be productive and effective. These values as such are not related to any special person, any special object, or any special situation. On the other hand, these basic values can easily be transformed into attitudes by feeling or acting negatively toward people who are unproductive and ineffective. Our tendency to look down on the elderly and others who are not living up to our ideals of productivity and effectivity may be examples of this. Maybe we also select such information that confirms these negative feelings, and maybe we even behave in consonance with this.

Another difference between the basic values and the attitudes is that attitudes often are very complex and multidimensional, while basic values are unidimensional. A third difference as mentioned by Rokeach (1973) is that basic values are relatively few, while the number of attitudes, built upon these values, can be as many as the numbers of specific attitudinal objects or situations.

THE VALUE STRUCTURE. In his discussion of the value concept, Rokeach (1973) points to some attributes that help us to see the value concept in relation to the attitudinal concept. As a result of very early indoctrination of basic values in connection with the early personality development, basic values are characterized by a much greater stability than attitudes. Those who since early childhood have been taught that productivity and effectivity are important values probably have to deal with these values as parts of their personality during the major part of the life cycle. The individual value structure is changing, but stability is apparent, especially in comparison with more easily changed aspects of attitudes.

Both examples of values just discussed—productivity and effectivity—are instrumental values in comparison with the terminal value of living a comfortable and materially wealthy life. Among terminal values, Rokeach distinguishes between personal and social values. Values like a wealthy life, salvation, and self-respect are examples of personal terminal values. While values like a world at peace, national security, and a beautiful world are examples of social terminal values. In a corresponding way Rokeach distinguishes between two types of instrumental values—moral and competence. Intellectuality is an example of competence values, while forgiving and obedience are examples of moral values. Not living up to the instrumental competence of values results in feelings of personal inadequacy, while trespassing on instrumental moral values results in feelings of guilt. This conceptual framework is important and interesting because above all the elderly fail in regard to the instrumental competence values. This kind of failure, or feeling of failure, is important to consider in relation to attitudes toward elderly. Rosenmayr (Rosenmayr & Rosenmayr, 1978) argues that to a very large extent it is the ideal of capability within work life that is infiltrating the whole society as a common basic value, and that there is a marginalization and disintegration of all those who do not fulfill this ideal.

Rokeach (1973) reduces 36 terminal and instrumental values to seven more fundamental value dimensions. These are:

1. immediate versus delayed gratification
2. competence versus religious morality
3. self-constriction versus self-expansion
4. social versus personal orientation
5. societal versus family security
6. respect versus love
7. inner versus other directed

For the future studies of attitudes and their value bases, it might be fruitful to use an approach of the kind described by Rokeach. This would make it possible to connect specific attitudes with the basic value structure and, thereby, create a mean for analyzing the relations between value structure, negative emotions in relation to elderly, bad knowledge about elderly, and various dispositions for behavior in relation to elderly. As a starting point for such a study, let us formulate the hypothesis that negative emotions in relation to elderly are based on a value structure stressing immediate gratifications, competence, self-constriction, personal orientation, family security, respect, and other directedness.

As we now can see, questions about attitudes and aging cannot be answered by concentrating only on the emotive, cognitive, and behavioral aspects of attitudes. The discussion has to be brought back to more fundamental values, which are the bases of the attitudes. Rosow (1962) argues that many well-intentioned programs, like information campaigns, integration programs, and charity actions, are scratches on the surface as long as we do not bring the discussion back to the more fundamental causal factors. Thiberg (1976) has an argument of the same kind in a discussion about the possibilities of reaching an understanding between different generations. A related thought was formulated by Slater (1970) to point out that Western societies are trying to "solve" a lot of social problems by getting them out of sight, making them invisible. Instead of attacking the real bases of social problems, there is a tendency to treat only the symptoms. The discussion has now brought us to a point where the basic values have to be regarded as more fundamental. But, from where are our basic values coming? We are now going to turn to this question, with the aim relating attitudes, values, and their most basic causes to each other.

THE ORIGINS OF VALUES. Lenzer (1961), like many other gerontologists, has observed how aging seems to be very different in different sociocultural systems. It has been noted how the Hebrew tradition in the Bible prescribes that you should honor your father and mother. It has been observed that the situation in old Greece was contradictory. In Greece, the elderly were idealized in novels and tales, while the ancient Greek society in reality was youth oriented and hated old age. To grow old in ancient Greece was regarded as a destiny worse than death. An early liberating death was regarded as a gift from heaven. Patterns in the militaristic Roman empire were very much the same. As an ideal, aging was good; but in reality aging was bad. Even if scholars have observed variations in attitudes toward elderly in different sociocultural settings, they have seldom been able to uncover the basic components in this sociocultural variation.

Using the old Hebrew tradition, the Roman and the Greek empires, and some contemporary societies, two basic factors can be pointed out. With some simplification we can argue that in the Hebrew tradition, where the elderly to a larger extent were honored, such ideas are a significant part of the cultural pattern. In the more materialistic Greek and Roman cultures, the elderly were in reality less honored. Both the Roman and the Greek empires built their wealth on what in today's terminology would be called an antagonistic imperialism.

Our argument is that two different bases for an existing value structure are to be found. One of these factors is the material and sociostructural bases of the culture, the other factor is the spiritual basis. Without going into detail in a discussion of various cultural evolution theories, it can be mentioned that Sorokin (1937) in his cyclic theory describes an oscillation between cultures with a very materialistic attitude and cultures with a spiritual attitude, where ideas and ideals have greater importance than material wealth. Further on we are going to return to a discussion of how Western society is changing in these respects.

THE SPIRITUAL BASIS. The spiritual basis of a value structure can be both of an internal and an external kind. The external spiritual basis refers to phenomena like the dominant belief system, which affects the functioning of the society and at certain times has a high priority over material values. Internal spiritual basis refers to spiritual phenomena that are more directly related to human nature itself. The individual's insight into his or her own limited life, the perception of bodily breakdown, and changes preceding unavoidable death, can in themselves be fundamental bases to some terminal as well as instrumental values. Anthropological studies have given us reason to believe that besides the well-known cultural relativity, there are some common patterns found in every culture that result from commonalities among human beings.

It cannot be said that internal spiritual bases are internal in any absolute and final way. Physical decline, which is experienced as frightening and threatening, is not only a biological process but a biological process perceived through cultural sentiments. Our fear of death is not only caused by the fact that our life is going to end but also from the way this knowledge is handled in various cultures. In this way it can be said that the external and internal spiritual bases are related to each other, but for analytical purposes it might be a good idea to distinguish between them. There is an observed tendency particularly among people working with the elderly to deny negative feelings in relation to aging and death. The distinction between external and internal spiritual bases helps these people working with the elderly to recognize a spiritual base in themselves.

In the same way that the internal and external spiritual bases are not independent of each other, the material and spiritual bases are not independent of each other. The hypothesis is rather that the material bases to a certain degree affect the spiritual ones. Another way of expressing this is that our way of perceiving the questions of aging, life, and death in their religious and psychological senses is connected with our culture in its material and sociostructural senses.

THE MATERIAL AND SOCIOSTRUCTURAL BASES. The material and sociostructural bases refer to conditions necessary for the development and survival of the human culture as well as the means of using and distributing fundamental material factors. With such a view the physical environment with its resources is to be regarded as the most fundamental material basis. The access to land for agricultural purposes, water, minerals, and manpower are examples of such basic material components. The ways to make use of these bases and to organize society for these purposes make up the sociostructural basis. A historical analysis can show how the presence or absence of material resources is crucial for the way a culture develops. Because of changes in access to pasturage and animals, ancient nomads and hunters were forced to live a mobile life, which also left its mark on value patterns and modes of behavior in relation to elderly and disabled people. It was necessary for the nomads to undertake continuous resettlement under primitive conditions, which made a so-called humane care of elderly impossible. There are several descriptions of how elderly were deserted, left behind, or killed when they could no longer follow in the raids. When the material conditions admitted a permanent settling and production gave a surplus, the basic preconditions for changes in the value system existed and, thereby, the preconditions for a primitive old-age care.

FUNCTIONALITY IN SOCIETY IS MOST IMPORTANT

Rosenmayr (Rosenmayr & Rosenmayr, 1978) has analyzed the position of the elderly in society and concluded that their positions have always been decided by their functions in society. The division of labor seems to be especially important in regard to the development of value patterns and attitudes toward the elderly. The production of goods needed by, or believed to be needed by, society is one of the most central material bases, and this fact also patterns the value structure in society. The ways in which people are used in production influences our ways of evaluating ourselves and others. In today's society the production of goods is carried out within a highly effective and highly productive industry, which at the same time is stratifying people according to their productivity and effectivity. In societies where production to a large extent is based on physical manpower and physical strength, stratification according to age is important. Bodily strength decreases with age, and the contribution to production thereby diminishes.

The description above is complicated by the fact that elderly people have another potential function—bringing knowledge and skills to succeeding generations when society is stable. Rosenmayr

(Rosenmayr & Rosenmayr, 1978) attacks the common idea that elderly people automatically had this function in traditional agrarian society. We must at least, Rosenmayr says, differentiate between peasants and craftsmen. It was only the older craftsmen who in reality had this function. The vast majority of the elderly within the traditional agrarian society were not craftsmen, but rather were poor farming workers who for a limited time offered their bodily strength for sale. Added to this are the processes of land reforms within agriculture, which meant that the old way of farming no longer was applicable. The potential function of the elderly as those who brought over knowledge and skills from one generation to another was thereby reduced.

Contrary to opinion, it is probably that industrialization did not have that extraordinary importance for the position of the elderly in society. The more fundamental material and sociostructural bases of today's values and attitudes toward the elderly probably have to be sought in times much further back than the period of industrialization during the nineteenth century. When we, like Rosenmayr, state that the status and the prestige of the elderly to a large degree can be associated with their functions in society, this almost inevitably leads to exchange theory in which goods, power, and control over resources are central concepts. Blau (1964) uses such a perspective in which sources of power are key words. Emerson (1976) is another of the theorists in this area. Many recent gerontologists, including Rosenmayr (Rosenmayr & Rosenmayr, 1978), have stated that this approach is fruitful. Hammarström (1975) in a cross-cultural study shows how the disposition and control over land and other resources are crucial for the status and prestige of the elderly in society. Descriptions of the exchange situations of the elderly suggest increasing disadvantage for them.

Even within an unbalanced power situation there might be a norm of reciprocity, as described by Gouldner (1960). The still un-answered question is under what conditions this norm of reciprocity operates. Rosenmayr (Rosenmayr & Rosenmayr, 1978) discusses this problem in terms of the need for an overbalancing of the exchange, but the issue is rather to study the various forms of exchange rules, among which overbalancing is one, and find the conditions under which they are working. For example, how much time can elapse between "gift" and "return" before the norm of reciprocity ceases to be valid? Is this time dependent on the speed of social change in society? The hypothesis behind these two questions is: In a stable society with almost no cultural change, there is a lifelong duration of the norm of reciprocity, but the faster society changes, the shorter the time the norm of reciprocity is valid. Eventually it will be replaced by some other norm of exchange.

Drawing on Hudson and Binstock (1976) and others, it is with a power perspective that the problems of aging should be viewed. Our social structure forces the elderly to pay a much higher price in terms of unemployment than any other age group. At the same time unemployment and nonproductivity are negative values in our culture. A counterargument to this is that our contemporary retirement system has not been imposed on people against their will but rather as the result of a deliberate struggle by the labor unions. The evolution of a welfare system, however, has to be analyzed in a comparative way. The development must be understood in terms of political processes, technological development, and humanitarian ideals. Historical, cultural, and ideological forces have to be analyzed in their interaction with the development of contemporary welfare systems that have followed very different pathlines in different societies. Many observers believe the strongly liberal traditions of England and the United States to have been ideological breaks in this respect. Heclo (1974) has found important differences in the welfare systems of England and Sweden. In some cases the development of social welfare systems has taken place with the aim of preventing political opposition. The early social welfare system in Germany has often been described in this way. As a working hypothesis in a Swedish research project the historian Olsson (1978) argues that the early Swedish retirement system from 1913 can be regarded in part as an adaptation of social policy to changes in industry. Elderly workers were to an increasing degree regarded as unproductive and ineffective, and the retirement system was an easy way to get rid of old workers. This was more true because it was likely that workers themselves would support these new reforms, which in reality meant turning over the burden of a retirement system from industry and society to workers themselves. According to this view, the development of the early retirement system in Sweden was characterized by a rather odd consonance between labor unions and the socialist parties struggling for retirement reform and industries wanting to get rid of ineffective and unproductive elderly workers. Rubenstein (1978) describes the German concentration camps in terms of means to get rid of unnecessary manpower and supplies us with a rather frightening perspective for the future where preretirement systems and euthanasia are going to be used as means for the same purpose.

Against the material and sociostructural background described, it is interesting to go back to Figure 8-1 for a moment. On the macrolevel the emotive components of the attitudes are described in terms of societal ideals, and the behavioral component in terms of laws and statutes. We have to be aware of the possibility of a very basic difference between expressed ideals and realities, as in laws and statutes. When politicians are prepared to develop a retirement system where everybody from age 60 should be able to retire in order to develop his or her own interests and enjoy life in a joyful leisure life style, the *real* ideal might in fact be to adapt the social policy to productivity within industry. At the same time, increased time in basic and secondary school results in shorter and shorter periods of participation in labor markets. Looking at Figure 8-1, we can foresee the risk of a discrepancy between outspoken ideals and the reality created by laws and statutes.

In his famous book on the American dilemma, Gunnar Myrdal (1962) noted an increasing distance between ideals and reality in the American society. Especially for black people the ideals of freedom, equality, and self-fulfillment became impossible to reach within the American social structure. According to Comfort (1978) black people and the elderly are comparable in these respects. While we are praising ideals such as equality, independence, productivity, and self-fulfillment, the social structure to an increasing degree is making it more and more difficult for elderly to reach these ideals. Compulsory unemployment, which retirement in reality is, contradicts a variety of important instrumental competence values in contemporary society.

Within the labor structure some bases can be found for new attitudes toward the elderly and other people not participating in the direct labor market. Lakoff (1976) describes how the combination of the decreased demand of physical strength and the decreasing percentages of population participating in production will cause the devaluation of the elderly in industrial society to be replaced by a much more positive picture in the future. The ongoing automatization in industry is decreasing the need for human manpower. With changes in people's need structures, the demand for manpower within various service jobs is going to increase. It will no longer be possible to retain the strongly work-oriented ethics when an increasing degree of the population no longer works within the direct production. Instead this ethic is going to be replaced by another one in which questions about quality of life are placed in the foreground—a process that already has started.

Another consequence of the changes in the labor market is that the future will probably offer a much larger proportion of jobs suitable for elderly people. Eisdorfer (1978) believes that the future labor-market situation will make it necessary to redefine drastically today's definitions of aging and retirement. It is quite possible, according to Eisdorfer, that the future will bring with it radical redistribution of jobs and unemployment, in comparison with today's situation. Maybe, Eisdorfer says, today's dominant one-career pattern is going to be abandoned and replaced by a pattern where most people have several job careers during a life cycle. Maybe we will also have a pattern in which compulsory sabbatical periods are intermixed with work and continuous education. In a similar way Neugarten (1978) believes that our work orientation in the future is going to be changed to a life pattern including various combinations of work and leisure. Shanas (1975) also believes these changes will help extinguish the stratification of people according to age.

NEW VALUES

In both a theoretically and empirically interesting study, Inglehart (1977) describes how Western society is slowly changing its basic value pattern. Inglehart takes his point of departure from the personality developmental theory formulated by Maslow (1954). The various needs of the individual, Maslow proposes, are arranged in a need hierarchy. When the more fundamental needs are met, new needs are introduced; and when these needs have been met, further new needs are introduced. In this way the human need structure is escalated from elementary needs of food, shelter, and sexual outlet, via security, belongingness, and appreciation to the need of self-

fulfillment. With his cross-cultural study, Inglehart shows how nations who have reached different positions in such a need hierarchy
also show a different value structure. A society with lack of basic
material resources is going to stress material values to a much larger
degree than a society where the basic material needs have been met.
Nations that have undergone a rapid material development in the
same way are characterized by significant differences in value structure between generations. Since the need and value structure is
primarily developed during childhood and youth, and only changes to
a limited degree during life, differences in value patterns between
young and old are created.

Inglehart's study provides an awareness of new bases for attitudes toward the elderly. In the future postmaterial values rather
than material ones are going to constitute important bases for attitudes toward the elderly. Inglehart also points to the fact that individual satisfaction or dissatisfaction in the future is going to be more dependent on the subjective perception of reality, rather than on an
objective material situation. When basic material needs are increasingly met, the subjective perception of need will increase in importance. Vickers (1970) states that all human freedoms and rights are
social artifacts that have been created and preserved by the existing
social and political patterns. Vickers believes that the ties of general
humanity are going to be very strained in the future in national and
international arenas.

Attitudinal Change

It is with the discussion on the previous pages in mind that questions
about attitudinal change should be considered. It is now possible to
realize that these questions cannot be discussed in any simple way. Do
we want to change the emotive component? If so, is it the emotive
component for separate individuals, groups, or is it rather a question
of ideals for the whole society? To what degree do we want to change
the cognitive component? To what degree is it behavior itself we
want to change? Could it be that questions about attitudinal change
should concentrate to a decreasing degree on information or educational campaigns concerning the elderly and to an increasing degree
on the values and the material basis behind the attitudes? It is my
opinion that these questions should be answered affirmatively. By

neglecting the material basis and the value structure behind the attitudes, we are at risk of hiding the real problems. In contemporary studies, as well as in historical ones, the fruitful approach should be to reveal the relationships between the material basis, the value patterns, and specific and concrete attitudes toward the elderly.

REFERENCES

Ariès, P. *Centuries of childhood*. New York: Knopf, 1962.

Babchuk, N., & Beates, A. P. The primary relations of middle-class couples: A study in male dominance. *American Sociological Review*, 1963, 377–384.

Back, K. W. Personal characteristics and social behavior: Theory and method. In R. H. Binstock & E. Shanas (Eds.), *Handbook of aging and the social sciences*. New York: Van Nostrand, 1976.

Barron, M. Minority group characteristics of the aged in American society. *Journal of Gerontology*, 1953, **8**, 477–482.

Bell, D. *The coming of post-industrial society: A venture in social forecasting*. London: Heinemann, 1974.

Blau, P. M. *Exchange and power in social life*. New York: John Wiley & Sons, 1964.

Comfort, A. A biologist laments and exhorts. In L. F. Jarvik (Ed.), *Aging into the 21st century: Middle-agers today*. New York: Gardner Press, John Wiley & Sons, 1978.

Cumming, E., & Henry, W. E. *Growing old: The process of disengagement*. New York: Basic Books, 1961.

Eisdorfer, C. Societal response to aging: Some possible consequences. In L. F. Jarvik (Ed.), *Aging into the 21st century: Middle-agers today*. New York: Gardner Press, John Wiley & Sons, 1978.

Emerson, R. M. Social exchange theory. *Annual Review of Sociology*, 1976, 335–362.

Festinger, L. *A theory of cognitive dissonance*. New York: Evanston, 1957.

Foner, A., & Kertzer, D. Transitions over the life course: Lessons from age-set societies. *American Journal of Sociology*, 1978, **83** (5), 1081–1104.

Galtung, J. Science as invariance-seeking and invariance-breaking activity. *Sociologisk Forskning*, 1974, **No. 4-5**, 64–85.

Gaunt, D. Unpublished manuscript presented at the Ninth International Congress of Sociology, Uppsala, August 1978.

Goode, W. J. *World revolution and family patterns*. New York: The Free Press, 1963.

Gouldner, A. W. The norm of reciprocity: A preliminary statement. *American Sociological Review*, 1960, **25 (2)**, 161–178.

Hammarström, G. *Det sociala åldrandet: Ett tvärkulturellt perspektiv*. Uppsala: Akademisk Avhandling, 1975.

Hareven, T. *Historical changes in the life course and the family: Policy implications for the aged*. Paper presented before the Select Committee on Aging, U.S. House of Representatives, and the Select Committee on Population, U.S. House of Representatives, May 24, 1978.

Harris, L. *The myth and reality of aging in America*. Washington, D.C.: National Council on the Aging, Inc., 1975.

Havighurst, R. J. Successful aging. In R. H. Williams (Ed.), *Process of aging* (Vol. I). New York: Atherton Press, 1963.

Heclo, H. *Modern social politics in Britain and Sweden: From relief to income maintenance*. New Haven, Conn.: Yale University Press, 1974.

Heider, F. Attitudes and cognitive organizations. *Journal of Psychology*, 1946, 107–112.

Heider, F. *The psychology of interpersonal relations.* New York: John Wiley & Sons, 1958.

Hess, B. Friendship. In M. W. Riley *et al.* (Eds.), *Aging and society* (Vol. III). New York: Russell Sage Foundation, 1972.

Hudson, R. B., & Binstock, R. H. Political systems and aging. In R. H. Binstock & E. Shanas (Eds.), *Handbook of aging and the social sciences.* New York: Van Nostrand, 1976.

Ingelhart, R. *The silent revolution: Changing values and political styles among Western publics.* Princeton, N.J.: Princeton University Press, 1977.

Kilty, K. M., & Feld, A. Attitudes toward aging and toward the needs of older people. *Journal of Gerontology,* **1976**, 586–594.

Kogan, N. Attitudes toward old people: The development of a scale and an examination of correlates. *Journal of Abnormal and Social Psychology,* 1961, 44–54. (a)

Kogan, N. Attitudes toward old people in an older sample. *Journal of Abnormal and Social Psychology,* 1961, 616–622. (b)

Kogan, N. *Beliefs, attitudes, and stereotypes about old people: A new look at some old issues.* Paper presented at the 30th Annual Scientific Meeting of the Gerontological Society, San Francisco, 1977.

Krech, D., & Crutchfield, R. S. *Theory and problems of social psychology.* New York: Knopf, 1948.

Lakoff, S. A. The future of social intervention. In R. H. Binstock & E. Shanas (Eds.), *Handbook of aging and the social sciences.* New York: Van Nostrand, 1976.

Laslett, P. Societal development and aging. In R. H. Binstock & E. Shanas (Eds.), *Handbook of aging and the social sciences.* New York: Van Nostrand, 1976.

Lazarsfeld, P. F., & Merton, R. K. Friendship as a social process: A substantive and methodological analysis. In M. Berger, T. Abel, & C. H. Paye (Eds.), *Freedom and control in modern society.* Princeton, N.J.: 1954.

Lenzer, A. Sociocultural influences on adjustment to aging. *Geriatrics,* 1961, 631–640.

Linton, R. The natural history of the family. In R. N. Anshen (Ed.), *The family: Its functions and destiny.* New York: Harper & Row, 1959.

Lowenthal, M. F., & Robinson, B. Social networks and isolation. In R. H. Binstock & E. Shanas (Eds.), *Handbook of aging and the social sciences.* New York: Van Nostrand, 1976.

Maslow, A. H. *Motivation and personality.* New York: Harper & Row, 1954.

Messer, M. Age grouping and the family status of the elderly. *Sociology and Social Research,* 1968, **52**, 271–279.

Myrdal, G. *An American dilemma: The Negro problem and modern democracy.* New York: Harper & Row, 1962.

Neugarten, B. L. The future of the young-old. In L. F. Jarvik (Ed.), *Aging into the 21st century: Middle-agers today.* New York: Gardner Press, John Wiley & Sons, 1978.

Neugarten, B. L., & Berkowitz, L. *Personality in middle and late life.* New York: Atherton Press, 1964.

Newcomb, T. M. *The acquaintance process.* New York: Holt, Rinehart & Winston, 1961.

Olsen, H., Trampe, J. P., & Hansen, G. *Familjekontakter i den tidige alderdom* (Report No. 1, fra forløbundersøgelsen af de aeldre). Institute for Social Research Publication No. 74, Köpenhamn, 1976.

Olsson, L. *Industrialiseringen, de äldre arbetstagarna och pensioneringen.* Research plan, Depart-of History, University of Lund, Sweden, 1978 (mimeo.).

Parsons, T. The kinship system of the contemporary United States. *American Anthropologist,* 1943, **45**, 22–38.

Parsons, T. The social structure of the family. In R. Anshen (Ed.), *The family: Its functions and destiny.* New York: Harper & Row, 1959.

Pensionär–75. *Pensionärsutredningen SOU 1977:98.* Stockholm: Liber, 1977.

Pratt, H. J. *Old age association in national politics. Annals*, 1974, 106–119.

Riegel, L. The influence of economic and political ideology upon the development of developmental psychology. *Psychological Bulletin*, 1978, 129–141.

Riley, M. W. *Aging and society* (Vol. III): *A sociology of age stratification*. New York: Russell Sage Foundation, 1972.

Rokeach, M. R. *The nature of human values*. New York: The Free Press, 1973.

Roos, K. *Aktivitet och åldrande: Socialpsykologiska studier kring aktivitet och åldrande*. Uppsala: Akademisk Avhandling, 1975.

Rose, A. M. The sub-culture of aging: A topic for sociological research. *Gerontologist*, 1962, **2**, 123–127.

Rose, A. M. A current theoretical issue in social gerontology. In A. M. Rose & W. A. Peterson (Eds.), *Older people and their social world*. Philadelphia: F. A. Davis, 1965.

Rosencrantz, M. A., & McNevin, T. E. A factor analysis of attitudes toward the aged. *Gerontologist*, 1969, 55–59.

Rosenmayr, L. *The many faces of the family.* Paper delivered at the 10th International Congress of Gerontology, Jerusalem, 1975.

Rosenmayr, L., & Eder, A. *Family and future: Reflections on intergenerational relations and social change.* Paper presented at the 11th International Congress of Gerontology, Tokyo, August 1978.

Rosenmayr, L., & Rosenmayr, H. (Eds.). *Der alte Mensch in der Gesellschaft*. Munich: Rowohlt, 1978.

Rosow, I. Old age: One moral dilemma of an affluent society. *Gerontologist*, 1962, 182–192.

Rosow, I. *Social integration of the aged*. New York: The Free Press, 1967.

Rubenstein, R. L. *The cunning of history*. New York: Harper & Row, 1978.

Rubington, E., & Weinberg, M. S. *The study of social problems: Five perspectives*. New York: Oxford University Press, 1971.

Shanas, E., & Hauser, P. M. Zero population growth and the family life of old people. *Journal of Social Issues*, 1975, **30 (4)**.

Sjoberg, G. *The preindustrial society*. New York: The Free Press, 1960.

Skoglund, J. *Aging and retirement: Studies of attitudes toward the elderly in Sweden*. Uppsala: Akademisk Avhandling, 1977.

Slater, P. *The pursuit of loneliness: American culture at the breaking point*. Boston: Beacon Press, 1970.

Sorokin, P. A. *Social and cultural dynamics* (Vol. I). New York: American Book Company, 1937.

Stearns, P. N. *Old age in European society: The case of France*. London: Croom Helm, 1977.

Streib, G. F. Are the aged a minority group? In A. Gouldner & S. M. Miller (Eds.), *Applied sociology*. New York: The Free Press, 1965.

Thiberg, S. *Generationernas möte—i den fysiska miljön?* Unpublished paper presented at the Norsam Conference, Marienlyst, Helsingör, October 1976.

Tornstam, L. De äldres behov från socialgerontologisk synpunkt. In C. Ström & Y. Zotterman (Eds.), *Boendeformer för pensionärer*. Stockholm: Liber, 1975.

Tornstam, L. *Åldrandets socialpsykologi*. Stockholm: Rabén & Sjögren, 1978.

Trela, J. Some political consequences of senior center and other old age group membership. *Gerontologist*, 1971, **11** (2), Part II, 118–123.

Tuckman, J., & Lorge, I. Attitudes toward old people. *Journal of Social Psychology*, 1953, 249–260.

Vickers, G. *Freedom in a rocking boat: Changing values in an unstable society*. London: Allen Lane, The Penguin Press, 1970.

Zitomersky, J. *Toward coherent research: A review of the memoranda submitted*. Department of History, University of Lund, Sweden, 1978 (mimeo.).

9 Old Age, Retirement, and the Social Class Structure: Toward an Analysis of the Structural Dynamics of the Latter Stage of Life

During the last decades, in most of the industrialized countries, old age has begun to emerge as a social problem. The growing awareness of this issue has been accompanied by a pressing need for research and further reflection on the question. This need has given rise to the development of a new area of study: gerontology. The greatest headway in this new discipline has undoubtedly been made in the United States, where it exerts the most widespread influence today.

In the branch of study with which we are concerned—sociology— the studies carried out on old age have yielded a sizable body of information on the living conditions and the behavior of the elderly and have contributed toward advancing our knowledge of these questions. Nevertheless, the theoretical standpoint most widely adopted in sociological studies of old age appears to contain certain limitations that we will discuss. Many of the studies on old age have caused the topic to become self-confining because they have attached so much weight to age grading and to the individual's role and status in an age-graded system. They have disregarded what old age owed to the general social mechanisms for the distribution of power and riches, as they function in our society. Thus the analysis of old age promoted is more fatalistic than critical.

The aim of this chapter is to propose a different theoretical approach to the study of the latter stage of life, an approach that might go beyond the limits mentioned. We also hope to show, by offering certain empirical results, what might be the heuristic effect of such an approach.

In the theoretical perspective proposed here, old age is regarded as an expression of society's fundamental social relations.[1] It is suggested that the contours of old age are shaped by the system of social positions established by the state of social relations of production in a given society and, more specifically, by the process of reproduction of this system of positions and of the social agents within these positions, a process that develops throughout the life cycle.

We have described this perspective as an "analysis of the structural dynamics of the latter stage of life." By using the term "structural," we are attempting to express two things. First, old age is a structured not a homogeneous state because it reflects the structure of the social relations peculiar to the society under study. Second, social relations structure and determine the content of old age and they generate "old age."

Our approach, then, is an attempt to meet the question of the social production of old age. It is less concerned with studying the characteristic of old age than with examining the production of these characteristics by the social system.

The "dynamic" approach underlying this study suggests that old age must be investigated in the context of the entire life course. This is not a new approach. It has already been followed by Neugarten (1964, 1976), Riley and Abeles (1977), Bengston (1973), and Chudacoff and Hareven (1979). These authors have stressed the need to examine the influence of events and conditions of life that dominated during the earlier stages and of the historical circumstances shaping the experience of different cohorts on old age and retirement. In our opinion, however, the "developmental" approach has not as yet examined the consequences and the effect of the positions held in social relations on old age. Certain studies along these lines have concentrated on generational factors. They have attempted to compare the models of the life course specific to different cohorts and to investigate their implications for the latter stage of the life course.

---

1. "Social relations" is used here in the sense given it in the Marxist conceptualizations.

There have been no studies that have endeavored to pursue such an analysis in terms of class positions rather than of generations.

The analysis of the structural dynamics of the latter stage of life regards retirement and old age as expressions of the terminal point in the general process of the reproduction of social relations. This process presupposes not only the distribution of the social agents within a system of social places but also their requalification for these places throughout their passage through the different ages. At its final point of development, this process directly molds old age, shaping its contours and its content within a given society.

The Limitations of an Approach toward Old Age
in Terms of Role and Status

The analysis of most sociological studies on old age and retirement is based on the classical concepts of role and status. In a given society, each position on the age grading correlates with a specific role and status system. From this perspective, the study of old age leads to an attempt to answer two fundamental questions: (1) What transformations occur in the role and status system when the social subjects move on from mature adulthood to old age? (2) In what ways do these changes affect the behavior of aging people?

Sociological research into old age has largely revolved around these two principal questions. Nevertheless, although researchers have adopted common theoretical principles, they have not all provided the same answers to the questions. Clearcut divergences have emerged: Authors have variously considered the entry into old age as corresponding to a process of isolation (Parsons, 1942), of disengagement (Cumming & Henry, 1961), or reinvolvement in family life (Litwak, 1965; Sussman, 1965, 1968; Townsend, 1963), or, finally, of striking a new balance in social activity, one that is determined by the subject's personal predisposition, role flexibility, and the opportunities offered by the environment (Havighurst, 1954, 1965; Pollack, 1948).

It is worth noting that the authors diverge mainly over the second of the two questions raised: They are not in agreement as to the effect on the subject's behavior of the changes in the role and status system. By contrast, they are unanimous in holding that in our society the transition from late adulthood to old age is matched by a decline in social standing and by a shrinking of the role system, even though the loss of certain roles may be "partially compensated" by the assumption of other new roles.

The above observation may help us to describe more accurately the inherent limitations of a theoretical approach to old age based essentially on functionalist concepts of role and status in which the analysis is focused on the subject's position on the age grading. The adoption of such an approach, in fact, results in the study of old age being restricted to the confines of the existing state of affairs. As soon as old age is effectively defined by the specific way in which the social organization molds the role and status of the elderly in relation to the other age groups, it is no longer permissible to call into question the distribution of role and status governed by this organization. In such an approach, the marginality and social devaluation that have been so powerfully attested to among the elderly are in danger of becoming settled as fixed characteristics peculiar to that age group. Consequently, from the outset any questioning of the social mechanisms that determine the molding of this stage of life is excluded. This approach, then, tends to introduce a "naturalist" concept of age, insofar as it relies on an interpretation of old age through a "nature," that is, a substance and its characteristics. From this standpoint, old age is considered a homogeneous entity that can be isolated and whose substance can be extracted by analysis. The main theories of old age mentioned above are supported by the same naturalist philosophy that leads us to seek a single model for aging, whether it be isolation, disengagement, or activism. These theories represent the different attempts to get down to the essence of old age. Ultimately, in these theories, age is considered as a natural condition with its own peculiar effectiveness independent of the social and historical contexts. The danger here is that we risk attributing to old age, as innate and original characteristics, those properties that it, in fact, derives from the social system in which it is incorporated.

This kind of approach isolates the problems of old age from the general social mechanisms with which it is involved and, in particular, from the process of the social distribution of power and riches operating in our society.

Analyzed apart from that which governs the functioning of the social system, old age can no longer be related to any but individual factors. Sociological literature on old age has given a preponderant place in its analysis to the psychosociological factors. It has concentrated mainly on exploring the individual characteristics of personality or of situation that will allow for responses that are best adjusted to a social and personal condition undergoing rapid transformation.

This approach never enables us to establish how old age and its characteristic features are produced by the social system.

A fresh examination of the issues involved in old age must be undertaken, and new approaches to the overall problem must be devised. In what follows, we indicate some openings that might lead to advancement in this direction.

Old Age, Retirement, and the Individual's Position in Social Relations

In order to establish how old age is affected by the social system of which it is part, we must reveal its connections with the structure of social relations upon which society is based. Once this has been done, the behavior of the elderly will no longer be analyzed in terms of psychosociological reactions to a situation defined by the individual's position on the age grading. It will instead be analyzed in terms of social practices, that is, as an expression of the structure of social relations.

Although in simple societies age and sex represented two of the chief elements of social differentiation (Balandier, 1974), in our present social systems membership in a particular age group no longer suffices as a means of defining the place held by the individual in social relations. Each age group finds its members distributed within a system of places defined by the existing state of social relations in the society concerned. This distribution of social subjects at each point on the age scale is incorporated into the general process of the reproduction of class relations. The maintenance of the social order established by a social system presupposes both the repro-duction of the class system and the reproduction of the social agents in these class positions. The study of old age from this perspective amounts to an investigation of the extent to which old age is affected by the distribution of social agents in a system of social places and in particular to a discovery of how much it is influenced by the ways in which the agents have throughout their life course been requalified by the interplay of social determinants for the positions they are to occupy and to what extent they are subjected to these positions.

This approach would lead us toward a novel appreciation of the issue, as may be seen from a specific example. In the classical analyses of old age, isolation was often described as one of the attributes of the process of aging, as an inherent characteristic of a particular stage of life that was defined by retirement from professional life and by the decline of the parental functions. In the new perspective, isolation appears as the product of certain class positions and of the repeated, cumulative processes of requalification in these positions, which the individuals holding them have constantly undergone throughout their life course. Isolation, then, emerges as the effect of certain positions within social relations that have prevented the establishment and continuation of a framework of sociability to accompany the individual's advance in age. What used to be attributed, in classical analyses only, to position on the age grading would from now on be interpreted as the effect of the division of labor and of the distribution of resources, power, and influence among the social groups. Old age can no longer be regarded as the locus of specific mechanisms peculiar to a particular stage in life and endowed with a nature of their own; it is to be seen, instead, as the focal point of general social mechanisms, the cumulative effect of which is to produce concomitantly social exclusion, marginality, and isolation. The source of isolation will then have been established, thus revealing the logic of the cumulative patterns.

The structural approach to old age outlined above interprets old age not as a breakaway but as a process: It is an approach that assumes a "life course perspective." The contours or characteristics of old age are interpreted via the specific life trajectory corresponding to each of the places defined within social relations. Corresponding to each social position there is, in fact, a typical life trajectory, a specific life course that is made up of a succession of original patterns of events occurring in accordance with a particular timing. In studying the influence of the state of social relations upon old age in a given society we need to tabulate the great diversity of the social practices of old age and reconstitute each of the life courses that objectively opens, in the last stage of life, onto these different forms of typical behavior. The position held by individuals within social relations has a profound effect on their life trajectory because it exercises concurrently direct effects and indirect effects through a set of factors that act as mediators and relay and multiply the initial impact of the position.

For example, the way in which the family is made up, the manner in which family exchanges take place, and the course followed in professional life are all largely determined by class position. The size of the family and its manner of functioning have a predefining effect on the forms that the maintenance of the family structure may take as the members advance in age, just as they also determine the possibility of its disintegration. The entry into professional life and the place held by the individual within the process of production merely entrench more firmly the effects of upbringing in the family already sanctioned by the school grade. But, once produced, these factors—together with their correlatives (economic resources, leisure opportunities, degree of biological aging, and morbidity rate)—will shape the further destiny of the agents holding these positions. In particular, the cumulative effect of these different elements is such that there is a strong risk of premature professional decline in certain social positions.

The social practices of the elderly are an expression of this long chain of social determinants that shaped progressively their conditions in old age. It will be the aim of the analysis to reconstruct the dynamics of the complex causal structure by which the system of positions held in the social relations of production—with its numerous retranslations and induced effects—shapes the latter stage of life.

Social Class and Socioeconomic Status[2]

The theoretical perspective offered here excludes a conceptual definition of the system of social place that would allow only for a simple interpretation of the differences among groups holding differentiated positions. In this approach, it is necessary that the analysis of the differences is associated with the analysis of their production by the social system, and this presupposes a definition of social structure in terms of social classes and not of socioeconomic status.

The concept of social stratification, as opposed to that of social class, differentiates among groups without clearly positing the prin-

2. As it is not our intention to contribute further to the discussion on the theory of social classes, we restrict ourselves to a few brief remarks on this concept that occupies an important place in the approach toward old age that we are proposing. Readers who wish to enter more deeply into this question might consult the work of fundamental importance carried out by Poulantzas (1975) and the extensions suggested by Wright (1976).

ciple and the logic of their differences. Occupational status and income, taken either separately or together, are not sufficient as a definition of social class. Furthermore, they allow for a subdivision of the population into upper-, middle-, and lower-class strata: The groups thus formed represent mere aggregates. It is possible to analyze the characteristics of these groups differentially, but we can hardly go beyond the ascertainment of regularity between the individual's belonging to a particular social stratum and the conditions and the way of life of those in old age. By characterizing the groups only in terms of their relative positions on a continuous scale of stratification, we exclude the possibility of going back to a study of the constituent social processes of the heterogeneity established. By contrast, the concept of social class puts forward the idea of a genetic definition of class positions that links them directly to the social mechanisms by which they are generated. To return to the definitions suggested by Poulantzas (1975), social classes represent the overall effect—in the field of social relations—of all the structures of the mode of production. They reflect the social relations of production within a particular society. Since the mode of production combines the economic, political, and ideological structures, social classes cannot be reduced to the levels of occupational qualification. Social classes are defined not only by their place in the process of production, and by their position within the technical division of labor, but also by their position within political and ideological structures. Consequently, the traditional Marxist definition, which analyzes the class structure of the capitalist mode of production by basically contrasting the two antagonistic classes—capitalist and proletarian—must be upheld. Within each of these antagonistic positions, we must distinguish class fractions and class strata. These distinctions can be made both in terms of the economic, political, and ideological roles played by these different subgroups in the process of capitalist appropriation of labor surplus, and also in terms of the role played by these subgroups in the process of organizing and controlling production.

Toward an Empirical Analysis of the Structural Dynamics
of the Latter Stage of Life:
Presentation and Discussion of Some Results

An empirical study carried out on a sample of 1,000 French pensioners, formerly wage earners, and representing a cross section of different levels of occupational qualification has enabled us to test the heuristic effectiveness of the structural theoretical perspective elaborated above.

The survey was carried out through a questionnaire (240 questions) and a time budget. Information was gathered on the subjects' past lives—education, professional, and family background—leisure activities, and living conditions, behavior, and attitudes at the time of the study. The retrospective nature of the data collected made it possible to reveal the complex causal system through which a set of past and present situations, reflecting the numerous redefinitions of class position, combined to produce specific retirement practices. Although the transversal nature of the study does not enable us to follow the dynamics of the production of social practices up until the latter stage of life, it does permit us to outline the long chain of social determinants through which the characteristic contours of old age are shaped by the position formerly held by the subject in the division of labor and in political and ideological relations.

We shall mention certain results from the study that we carried out in 1970, the results of which have been exhaustively analyzed elsewhere and published (Guillemard, 1972, 1974), that strike us as particularly significant with regard to the theoretical approach developed in this chapter. First, we shall outline the different forms of typical retirement behavior that we consider most pertinent; second, we shall shed light on the most powerful social determinants of this behavior; and, finally, for certain class positions, we shall reconstruct the processes by which retirement practices are shaped throughout the individual's life course.

THE TYPOLOGY OF SOCIAL PRACTICES
IN THE RETIREMENT SITUATION

A theoretical typology of retirement practices has been developed in terms of the general social orientations that are given priority expression in retirement behavior.

This typology enables us to distinguish five types of retirement practices that have been empirically constructed from indicators drawn from the time budget. These are briefly described below.

1. Retirement may involve the subject's social withdrawal (disinsertion). This is a practice we have described as *withdrawal retirement*: It is accompanied by extreme reduction of the subject's social activity and of his or her social relationships network. The rhythm of the day

is broken only by actions performed in order to ensure biological survival (eating, sleeping, and caring for the body); these activities are separated by long dead periods of waiting to perform the subsequent biological function. In this practice, everything takes place as though, with the arrival of retirement and the removal of all the demands associated with work, time ceased to be structured by any but the biological needs. The term "social death" describes this practice, which is seen as biological survival dissociated from any social meaning.

2. The life of retirement may become focused on reinsertion into the social organization. This may take the form either of the pursuit of a creative activity that acts as a substitute for professional activity or of the stepping up of consumer activities once the individual's role as a producer has fallen away. The first form of reinsertion is described as *third-age retirement*[3]: It actually represents a new stage in life, in which professional demands give way to freely chosen creative activities (artistic creation, hobbies, etc.) that have the same structuring power over the individual. *Leisure retirement* corresponds to the second form of reinsertion into the social organization. It represents reinsertion through consumption. The time freed by retirement is devoted to cultural improvement or leisure activities (holiday journeys, exhibitions, theatre shows, etc.). The typical time budget for this practice may be characterized by the diversity of the activities involved and the multiplicity of the social contacts. The daily rhythm is determined by activities outside the home, and the time devoted to biological activities is extremely restricted.

3. Life in retirement may be concentrated on political dimension rather than on reinsertion into the social organization. It may acquire its meaning from opposition versus acceptance of the place assigned by the social system to the aged person.

Protest retirement centers around a militantism for the protection of the interests of the retired. This practice is characterized by the considerable amount of time devoted to associations of the elderly or to the assumption of responsibilities within such organizations.

Acceptance retirement is reflected by hyperintegrational behavior by which the retired endeavor to show that they have accepted the social status assigned to them. This form of retirement is typified by

3. The term "third age" is used commonly in France. Life, it implies, has three stages—childhood, adulthood, and "third age." With each stage a new positive phase of living may begin.

overabsorption of the socially sanctioned cultural values that are given priority status by the mass media. In this practice, the time budget characteristically involves lengthy periods of daily exposure to the media of mass communication.

The operationalization of this typology has led to the construction of five empirically independent ordinal scales on which each subject has been individually rated.

THE SYSTEM OF DETERMINING RETIREMENT PRACTICES

The use of different techniques of the empirical analysis of causality has enabled us to establish the set of situations underlying each of the typical forms of behavior. Analysis has shown that the practices followed in retirement are directly determined by the level and the nature of the resources that the individual was able to build up "during his or her past life." By resources, we mean all of the intellectual, social, biological, and material assets or acquisitions available to the retired person. In speaking of these resources, we must distinguish between "assets" and "potentialities."

Assets are the elements immediately available to the actor for the maintenance of his or her social position and biological situation. Three indicators have been used for assessing the state of these goods: individuals' financial resources, biological situation, and capital of social relations.

Potentialities cover all the actor's skills and abilities that might be invested in order to obtain goods indirectly. They are measured by the level of education, the position held in the process of production, and the extraprofessional skills acquired by subjects during their active nonworking lives. We shall briefly mention again the main links observed in this study between the level and the nature of the individuals' resources and the forms of their social activities.

If, on reaching the threshold of retirement, subjects had been unable to preserve a certain level of resources, social activity becomes paralyzed from the moment they cease working. *Withdrawal retirement* is determined by a situation of resource lack and resourcelessness. By contrast, the preservation of resources ensures the maintenance of a certain pattern of social activity that is a reflection of the exact conversion of the available resources.

The availability of accumulated resources determines the actor's reinsertion into the social organization. If resources consist mainly of

potentialities, the conversion of these resources leads to the enjoyment of creative retirement, that is, *third-age retirement*. If, on the other
hand, resources consist chiefly of assets, the employment of these
resources corresponds to a development of consumer activities that
consequently determines the emergence of *leisure retirement*.

If there is a contradiction of levels in the actor's resources,
characterized either by a high—positive—level of assets counter-
weighted by negative potentialities or by the reverse, the social actor
is led to adopt practices pertaining to the political sphere. These
practices challenge the social order when the contribution expressed
by the subject's level of potentialities exceeds the level of his or her
social retribution that can be globally measured by the level of assets
possessed. These practices become incorporated in a gratifying situation when the circumstances are reversed, that is, when the assets
possessed attain a high level while the potentialities remain at a very
low level.

Two techniques of causal analysis have been used jointly to
reveal the complex underlying causal structures of each of the types
of social practice. After a multivariate analysis carried out in accordance with the patterns established by Lazarsfeld (1955), a regression
analysis was undertaken in order to make it possible to establish a
hierarchization of the causes and assess the amount of variance
explained by the whole of the causal model proposed.

Space does not permit us to elaborate on all of the results
obtained from the application of the two analytical techniques outlined above. We shall restrict ourselves to the presentation of two
determining models leading to two clearly contrasted practices: the
withdrawal retirement and the leisure retirement.

THE DETERMINATION OF WITHDRAWAL RETIREMENT. The place formerly held by the subject within the social relations of production
plays a crucial role in the system by which withdrawal retirement is
determined. The exercise of a professional activity that involved
mere execution without permitting any control over the means and
organization of work and without offering any security against instability or stagnation in professional life (e.g., by providing a career
structure) emerges as one of the most influential factors in the
shaping of a withdrawal retirement practice.

Multivariate analysis, as is shown by Table 9-1, enables us to
establish the following:

1. The place formerly held within the social relations of production discriminates most powerfully with respect to withdrawal re-

Table 9-1. *Main Results from the Multivariate Analysis Concerning the Withdrawal Retirement Practice*

	Resources[a]													
	Potentialities								Assets					
	W		E		NWA		I		H		BA		SR	
	−	+	−	+	−	+	−	+	−	+	−	+	−	+
High score on the scale of withdrawal retirement practice[b] Total subjects	48%	26%	40%	31%	42%	30%	41%	30%	45%	24%	39%	19%	39%	26%
Mean test Correlation coefficient	n = 706 χ² = 26.55 (p<.001) Q = .39		n = 703 χ² = 6.16 (p<.02) Q = .21		n = 707 χ² = 9.87 (p<.01) Q = .26		n = 606 χ² = 8.06 (p<.01) Q = .24		n = 692 χ² = 33.92 (p<.001) Q = .45		n = 599 χ² = 29.95 (p<.001) Q = .47		n = 707 χ² = 12.30 (p<.001) Q = .29	
Consistency of the relation according to the following control variables	I H BA SR NWA E				H				E NWA W I SR		E W NWA I SR H		E NWA W I	
Specification of the relation according to the following control variables			W NWA I H BA SR		W E I BA SR		H BA E W NWA SR		BA				H	
Fallacious character of the relation													BA	

[a]Explanation of abbreviations: W, position formerly held within the social relations of production; E, level of education; NWA, frequency of past nonwork activities; I, present income; H, state of health; BA, biological age; SR, social relations capital.

[b]The percentages given in the first line indicate the frequency of the high degree of withdrawal retirement in accordance with the modalities of each of the explanatory variables. These percentages are calculated, on each occasion, for the entire body of subjects corresponding to each of the modalities of the explanatory variables used.

tirement. Thus it will be observed (Table 9-1) that 48% of those who had held purely executant positions within social relations of production very roughly the working class in its nonskilled components adopted a retirement practice for which a very high score was obtained on the index of withdrawal retirement. By contrast, only 26% of those who had held different positions in productive social relations figured comparably on the same index.

2. This relation is one of the most consistent because it remains unchanged regardless of the control variables introduced. Furthermore, the regression analysis indicates that the variable "executant position in the production process" comes out at the top of the hierarchy of causes. The coefficient ratio of partial regression (r), estimated by means of the coefficient phi, is equivalent to .22. The factor "poor health" follows immediately afterward in the hierarchy of causes $(r = .16)$. Poor education is a less powerful factor $(r = .10)$. With respect to this practice, low income level plays a far less important role $(r = .02)$ than is generally attributed to it.

The coefficient of multiple correlation (R), the significance of which has been tested by the F of Snedecor, is equivalent to .48 for the causal model of withdrawal retirement and is significant at the .01 level. A considerable part of the variance in this practice is explained by the model proposed.

THE DETERMINATION OF LEISURE RETIREMENT. The practice of leisure retirement is adopted when a certain capital has been conserved by the time the threshold of retirement is reached and when this capital is composed of what we have described above as "assets." Two factors play a basic role in the system of determining leisure retirement: the possession of a high level of resources and the enjoyment of sound health measured by objective state of wealth and biological age. The analysis of regression enables us to establish that these factors exert a comparable influence in the causality system. The value of r is .29 for the biological state and .21 for income. The other factors included in the causal model play a less important role (social relations capital, position held within the social relations of production, and educational background). R is equivalent to .42. The set of independent variables is significantly linked (F being significant at the .01 level) to the dependent variable.

Multivariate analysis confirms the great discriminating power of the factors of income and biological state over leisure retirement (cf. Table 9-2). This analysis also establishes the consistency of the relations linking these factors to retirement practice. Likewise, it brings

Table 9-2. *Main Results from the Multivariate Analysis Concerning the Leisure Retirement Practice*

		Potentialities						Assets							
		W		E		NWA		I		H		BA		SR	
		+	−	+	−	+	−	+	−	+	−	+	−	+	−
High score on the scale of withdrawal retirement practice[b]	39%	59%	39%	45%	39%	47%	38%	49%	35%	55%	31%	55%	40%	50%	39%
Total subjects		$n = 706$		$n = 703$		$n = 707$		$n = 606$		$n = 692$		$n = 599$		$n = 707$	
Mean test		$\chi^2 = 19.33$		$\chi^2 = 2.76 \ (p<.10)$		$\chi^2 = 5.22 \ (p<.02)$		$\chi^2 = 14.84 \ (p<.001)$		$\chi^2 = 38.75 \ (p<.001)$		$\chi^2 = 13.94$		$\chi^2 = 9.4 \ (p<.01)$	
Correlation coefficient		$Q = .39$		$Q = .13$		$Q = .17$		$Q = .30$		$Q = .45$		$Q = .30$		$Q = .23$	
Consistency of the relation according to the following control variables								E W NWA		E W NWA		E W NWA		E W NWA	
Specification of the relation according to the following control variables		I BA H													
Fallacious character of the relation				I BA SR		BA SR									

[a]For explanation of abbreviations, see Table 9-1.

[b]The percentages given in the first line indicate the frequency of the high degree of leisure retirement in accordance with the modalities of each of the explanatory variables. These percentages are calculated, on each occasion, for the entire body of subjects corresponding to each of the modalities of the explanatory variables used.

out the intermediary role of the position formerly held with social relations of production in the process of shaping this retirement practice. The fact of having been formerly engaged in an activity involving control over the organization of our own work, a high level of personal initiative, and a position of power in a firm's hierarchy (the role of supervision), acts favorably toward the accumulation of assets. Consequently, the overwhelming majority of those who achieve leisure retirement are persons who have held decision-making and supervisory positions in process of production and who today, moreover, possess a relatively fairly high level of resources. Of the retired persons in this category, 63% adopt leisure retirement. By contrast, only 44% of those who have financial resources but who did not occupy positions of authority and control over the production process actually adopt a leisure retirement practice.

PREPARATORY STEPS TOWARD AN ANALYSIS OF THE DYNAMICS OF THE PRODUCTION OF RETIREMENT PRACTICES

The study, of which we have outlined some of the results here, confirms the existence of causal links between the situations of resources, which themselves reflect the position formerly held in social relations and the history of this position, and the social practices of retirement. On the basis of the information provided by this study, we are able to establish a schematic reconstruction of the dynamics by which the position held in social relations—with all its multiple redefinitions and implications—progressively shapes the contours that may be taken by social practice in the latter stage of life.

We will now discuss the reconstruction of the processes. We will be indicating certain preparatory steps toward an analysis that can be systematically developed only from longitudinal-type studies. Here we will limit ourselves to the consideration of two antagonistic positions in social relations. For each, we will outline the long chain of social determinants through which these positions lead to the production of opposing models of retirement.

There are two ways in which the position held in social relations governs the amount of the resources that may be accumulated. On the one hand, it controls the amount of social riches distributed to the agents who occupy these positions and who are also required for such positions. On the other hand, it governs the capacity to maintain and renew the stock of social resources that the individual may possess.

Individuals whose position in the social relations of production has been one of exploitation and in political and ideological relations one of subordination receive a correspondingly poor share in the distribution of social riches. This share is limited to the amount necessary just for the reproduction of labor strength. The effect of this unequal distribution is redoubled by the differential capacity of the agents to combat the process by which their acquisitions and possessions are devalued.

The distributed share devalues even more swiftly if one is placed in a dominated position in which one is rendered unable either to maintain or to renew one's stock of goods and skills. In old age, at the culminating point of the evolution, those who on account of their exploited position have received few resources and have seen them drop rapidly in value find themselves in a situation radically opposed to that of those who within social relations held a position that not only placed riches at their disposal but also gave them the means of reproducing these resources.

For the former this means social death, while for the others it means having the opportunity of remaining socially inserted in a situation—retirement—which is actually characterized by the absence of a role to fulfill and by the nonrequirement of any form of social cooperation whatsoever.

We shall mention just some of the interconnections between the concrete social mechanisms by means of which the social agents are distributed, then reproduced in their respective positions of exploitation and domination, throughout their entire life course and up until old age. We shall see in what way the forms of the distribution of resources to which these positions accord the right, and the degree of exposure to the process of devaluation that is characteristic of these places, force the agents into their places as they gradually advance in age by preventing them from qualifying for other places.

We begin with an analysis of the working-class situation. The working class has a purely executant role on two counts: It has no ownership of the means of production, and it is deprived of any control over these means. Consequently, this class finds itself subjected to a precisely defined organization of labor under the authority, supervision, and instruction of the managerial staff. Their situation as executants has direct effect on the stock of skills they are able to accumulate or renew while performing their professional activity.

The working-class workers perform a professional activity that prevents them from implementing decision-making capacities and personal autonomy and which undermines the general technical qualifications that the school system may have provided. With advancing age, their abilities will therefore rapidly decline. It is now known that the process of aging is differential and that it primarily affects the skills least often used.

In the premature devaluation of the working class's labor force we can see one of the effects of the inability of the working class to retain and sustain its acquisitions with the encroachment of age. The premature decline of the value of the working class's labor force can be apprehended at two levels: professional regression and the risk of unemployment. A sizable proportion of the working class experiences downclassing with advancing age, while the best qualified among the occupational categories, between the ages of 50 and 65, are given professional promotion and regular salary increases. The aging members of the working class are also affected earlier and more strongly than the other occupational categories by unemployment, the average duration of which is longer for them.

Consequently, the activity of production not only has the effect of distributing the agents within the system of social places, it also progressively qualifies individuals for these places and subjects them to these positions. And if the agents are not already prequalified for an exploited position by schools and family background, they are of necessity reduced to this status by the firm. This is because, on the one hand (as we have just seen), the technical division of labor as organized in our society does not allow for the continuation of autonomy nor for the reproduction of the cultural capital they may have formerly possessed. And, on the other hand, because this division of labor governs the distribution of social riches and thus determines the relatively weak capacity for consumption of the class occupying the dominated position within the social relations of production.

On account of its position in the social division of labor, the working class receives in exchange for its labor no more than is necessary for the reproduction of its labor force. The weakness of the economic means at its disposal—the effects of which are doubly increased by the subordinate position of this class in political and ideological relations—has a consequential effect on the level and standard of living of this class and also on the workers' capacity to cultivate and maintain their skills in their extraprofessional life.

The objective conditions of labor (demanding work conditions, length of the working day) determine the deterioration of free time (Friedmann, 1960). Leisure time is most often a time for recuperation. Moreover, the objective conditions of the working-class existence are such that the workers' free time is eaten away by obligations and all kinds of external situations (the lack of cultural and social facilities in their residential area, housing difficulties that serve to accentuate family constraints, the length of time spent in commuting from work to home). Quite apart from the objective conditions that alienate the workers both at work and in their nonworking lives, there are also numerous ideological side effects that cause individuals who hold a subordinate position in social relations to find themselves deprived of a whole system of leisure time amenities (submission to the dominant model of consumer leisure), which are, on the other hand, readily available to the dominant classes (dilettante relationship toward time and cultural products).

The cumulative result of these different factors is that the working class reaches the threshold of retirement less well equipped than the other classes for converting free time into leisure. Now, retirement is characterized precisely by the access it offers to socially nonrestricted time. Retired persons from the working class are, therefore, the least well armed for controlling and organizing their free time in retirement according to their own inclinations; this free time then becomes empty time.

Lastly, the living conditions of the working class combined with their working conditions are such that the workers are unable to maintain their health. This situation primarily affects the longevity of workers, whose lives are shorter on the average than those of the other occupational categories.[4] Out of 1,000 workers taken at the age of 35, only 498 survive to the age of 70; while out of 1,000 people in high executive posts, 719 are still alive at the age of 70 (Desplanques, 1973). Second, it also affects the workers' state of health. In each age group, the surviving members of the working class are, on the

4. The poor survival rate of the working class does not only affect the length of their objective future. It also has repercussions on their chances of preserving—with the onset of old age—the network of social relations in which the members, who are recruited from among peers in age and social class, have the same life expectancy.

average, in poorer health than those in the other occupational categories. An extremely detailed longitudinal study carried out in France demonstrated that the working class had a senescence ratio considerably higher than that of the other occupational categories. It was established that in terms of biological age, a working-class worker aged 53 was 4½ years older than a high-ranking executive of the same age (Aillaud, 1970). The working class is, therefore, the least well placed for acquiring goods and skills all along the life cycle and for maintaining them.

A position within social relations that is defined by the individual's executant role in the process of production and by his or her subordinate role in political and ideological relations offers poor expectations of a social life in the latter stage of life. Such a position does not, in fact, enable individuals to build up throughout the life span the resources necessary to maintain their social insertions in the latter stage of life. For agents who have held such positions, retirement will mean withdrawal from all social life. As a result of the regular social mechanisms, some aspects of which have been mentioned above, the working class is driven toward social marginality and isolation in later life.

Let us now turn to the dynamics of the production of retirement practices in the case of persons who held a position in social relations at the opposite pole to the position held by the working class. One may characterize this position by the system of places held by higher executives.

Unlike the members of the working class, the higher executives find that functions are conferred upon them—in both the technical and the social division of labor—all of which tend toward easing the acquisition, preservation, and renewal of the tangible benefits derived from the school and family background.

In the process of work, these people find that they are granted power in ratio with their knowledge and that they are entrusted with the organization of production, which is nevertheless implemented in accordance with capital demands. In their work, they enjoy autonomy and wield relative decision-making power. Thus, in exercising their professional activity, they are able to acquire skills and to maintain their intellectual faculties and their cultural capital.

Although in the social division of labor the higher executives are certainly wage earners, they do not produce surplus values. On the contrary, they contribute to the realization and increase of surplus values for the capitalist class. Ideologically and politically, therefore, they belong to the dominant class. It is this specific position they hold in the process of production that determines the development of the integration policy pursued for their interests by the capitalist class. This policy is revealed in practice by (1) a share in the social product that weighs in their favor—they enjoy high salaries—and (2) the guarantee of career prospects.

The assurance of advancement with age through a succession of hierarchical posts confers on higher executives the ability to antici-pate their future. It must, however, be mentioned that this ability governs the individuals' capacity to control and organize their future and to prepare for their retirement. It will be observed that in this respect higher executives and workers find themselves in contra-dictory situations. While the higher executives are able to adopt an attitude of voluntary planning toward their future, the workers become acquainted throughout their lives with the uncertainty of the morrow and with their own close dependence on the ruling economic situation.

Thus, on account of the position they hold, the higher executives have not only the assurance that their skills and cultural capital will be reproduced, but also the certainty that they will be able to convert their cultural capital into economic capital and into its correlatives—the power to consume and to convert free time into leisure, and so on. At the threshold of retirement, the higher executives enjoy a far greater chance of possessing the resources necessary to remain so-cially inserted and to maintain a network of social exchanges. The retirement practices adopted will represent the exact conversion into activities and social relations of the state of the resources possessed. For agents occupying this position in social relations of production, the cessation of professional activity will simply entail the restructur-ing of social activities, but not social paralysis.

The adoption of an approach aimed at analyzing the structural dynamics of the latter stage of life reveals that old age is dependent as much on the division of labor operating in our society as on the distribution of resources and power. In such a point of view, the emphasis is placed on social structures and on the ways in which these structures determine the contours and characteristics of old age. At the same time, it would seem to open up critical perspectives on the functioning of a system in which those who have held sub-ordinate positions in social relations are regularly condemned to social death on retirement. Finally, it is an approach that would seem capable of furnishing fresh information in the domain of old-age policy. The devising of an old-age policy limited to action on behalf of the aged—such as the policies of most industrialized nations today— can result only in a very partial readjustment of the problem (Guillemard, 1980). In order to change the contours of old age we must also alter the working life and the nonworking life that have shaped these contours.

REFERENCES

Aillaud, Y. *Compte rendu d'activité*. Centre Doria—Fédération des Organismes de Sé-
    curité Sociale de la Région Sud-Est Marseille, 1970.
Balandier, G. *Anthropo-logiques*. Paris: Presses Universitaires de France, 1974.
Bengston, V. L. *The sociology of adult development and aging*. New York: Bobbs-Merrill, 1973.
Chudacoff, H., & Hareven, T. K. From the empty nest to family dissolution: Life
    course transitions into old age. *Journal of Family History*, 1979, **Spring**, 69–83.
Cumming, E., & Henry, W. E. *Growing old: The process of disengagement*. New York: Basic
    Books, 1961.
Desplanques, G. The differential mortality according to social class. *Economie et Statis-
    tiques*, October 1973, **No. 49**.
Friedmann, G. Le loisir et la civilisation technicienne. *Revue Internationale des Sciences So-
    ciales* (Special Issue: "Aspects Sociologiques du Loisir"), 1960, **XII (4)**, 551–563.
Guillemard, A. M. *La retraite: Une mort sociale*. Paris: Mouton, 1972.
Guillemard, A. M. *Retraite et échange social*. Paris: Centre d'Etude des Mouvements So-
    ciaux, 1974.
Guillemard, A. M. *La vieillesse et l'etat*. Paris: Presses Universitaires de France, 1980.
Havighurst, R. J. Flexibility and social roles of the aged. *American Journal of Sociology*,
    1954, **IX (4)**, 309–313.
Havighurst, R. J. Successful aging. In R. H. Williams, C. Tibbitts, & W. Donahue (Eds.),
    Processes of aging (Vol. 1). New York: Atherton Press, 1963.
Lazarsfeld, P. In P. Lazarsfeld & N. Rosenberg (Eds.), *The language of social research*.
    Glencoe, Ill.: The Free Press, 1955.
Litwak, E. Extended kin relations in an industrial democratic society. In E. Shanas &
    G. Streib (Eds.), *Social structure and the family*. Englewood Cliffs, N.J.: Prentice-Hall,
    1965.
Neugarten, B. *Personality in middle and late life*. New York: Atherton Press, 1964.
Neugarten, B. (in collaboration with G. Hagestad). Age and the life course. In R. Bin-
    stock & E. Shanas (Eds.), *Handbook of aging and the social sciences*. New York: Van
    Nostrand, 1976.
Parsons, T. Age and sex in the social structure in the United States. *American Socio-
    logical Review*, 1942, **7**, 604–616.
Pollack, O. *Social adjustment in old age: A research planning*. New York: Social Science Re-
    search Council, 1948.
Poulantzas, N. *Classes in contemporary capitalism*. London: New Left Books, 1975.
Riley, M., & Abeles, R. A life course perspective on the later years of life: Some impli-

cations for research. In *Social Science Research Council Annual Report 1976–1977*. New York: Social Science Research Council, 1977.

Sussman, M. B. Relationships of adult children with their parents in the United States. In E. Shanas & G. Streib (Eds.), *Social structure and the family*. Englewood Cliffs, N.J.: Prentice-Hall, 1965.

Sussman, M. B. (in collaboration with L. Burchinal). Kin family network unheralded structure in current conceptualizations of family functioning. In B. Neugarten (Ed.), *Middle age and aging*. Chicago: University of Chicago Press, 1968.

Townsend, P. *The family life of old people*. London: Penguin Books, 1963.

Wright, E. O. Class boundaries in advanced capitalist societies. *New Left Review*, 1976, **98**, 3–41.

10 Some New Aspects of Aging in Britain[1]

DAVID EVERSLEY

Introduction

The "problem of the elderly" has been on the agenda in the United Kingdom for a long time. The welfare state as we know it began with the provision of old-age pensions during the Lloyd George administration before World War I, following the revelations of the Poor Law Commission (1905–1909). After 1945, a long process began to improve the lot of the elderly: better pensions that may be earnings related within a decade or so, better domiciliary services, gradual elimination of the worst form of geriatric homes (workhouses), occupational therapy in day centers, and so on. There are two rival voluntary organizations that look after the general needs of the old plus a number of specialized groups dealing with the blind, the deaf, the severely handicapped, the mentally sick, and other groups. In successive official and unofficial reports (Hunt, 1978; Townsend, 1962; Wicks, 1978) attention has been drawn to the intensification of some aspects of the problem. The fact that the rising number and proportion of the old and the very old is highlighted by falling fertility and ultimate contraction of the economically active age

1. This revised version of the paper delivered at Luxembourg in June 1979 has been prepared with the help of my colleagues at the Policy Studies Institute whom I thank. Although a number of recent British policy-related publications on the problems of the elderly are cited, these works are not to be taken as representative of the entire literature and are not necessarily the best guide to the problem under discussion. Readers interested in further details are advised to consult the publications lists of bodies such as Age Concern, 60 Pitcairn Road, Mitcham, Surrey, or Help the Aged, 32 Dover Street, London W1, and full bibliographies of the writings of such specialists as Peter Townsend, Valerie Karn, and Mark Abrams. The Policy Studies Institute has also published other writings concerning the elderly. A full list will be supplied on request.

groups has been an incidental observation, scarcely rating more than a few paragraphs in the "official" summary of the structural changes in British society (Central Policy Review Staff, 1977).

The present chapter will not cover this ground again. There is little to add to the findings of local and national studies, that there are more old people, that more of them are dependent on the often erratic payment of supplementary benefit, that many of the domiciliary support services as well as the local authority social services are at breaking point. Too many inquests still speak of neglected old people found after they had been dead for many weeks (Abrams, 1979; MacDonald, 1979; National Council of Social Service, 1979). What we want to examine here are some particular aspects of the relationship of the elderly to the rest of the community, especially to the family unit of which the old were once part (Laslett, 1976). Although many of the phenomena described here can now be quantified, this chapter is essentially concerned with the qualitative aspects of observed changes in trends, and with the possibility that the trends may accelerate, stabilize, or even go into reverse.

Some Basic Relationships Reviewed

We get the impression from the reading of the growing literature on family history that the main debates turn on two related questions:

1. What was the composition of the household at various periods and in different places, and what was the relationship of members of the household to each other? We might call this the nuclear–extended family debate (Laslett, 1965, 1972, 1977).

2. What have been the main influences at work in the last few generations that have tended to break up the "traditional" household–family relative to the locality–social group under discussion? In what way have these influences changed the pattern of obligations–expectations of help within the family (Demos & Boocock, 1978; Rapoport & Rapoport, 1980)? Often this discussion, whatever its precise ideological framework, has tended to suggest that economic forces at work have led to the breakup of existing patterns mainly to satisfy the need of capitalistic forms of production for mobile and adaptable labor and that this is a major factor in destroying established communities, with all its attendant disasters. Typically, such research has centered on events in some easily recognizable categories, namely:

changes in agricultural production, destroying both the rural working class and the small working (tenant) farmer; changes in manufacturing industry, destroying established communities based on the existence of powerful and often paternalistic employers in the locality; and changes in the composition of the labor demand of advanced capitalistic societies, especially through the rise of the large metropolitan administrative and commercial centers (Hammond & Hammond, 1913, 1917; Hobsbawm, 1970; Thompson, 1968; Williams, 1961). Another category can be added that has become fashionable in the last 30 years: the breakup of established local communities by "the planners" who wished to redevelop urban land, usually in order to put it to some more profitable use, such as the construction of offices. Also, developers might put some other type of residential units into the place of traditional working-class dwellings, which either did not take into account the social relationships of the previous community or were designed to serve a different housing class altogether (Harvey, 1973; Rex & Moore, 1967; Simmie, 1974). Whichever category is chosen, and they usually turn up in combination, we may anticipate that social cohesion has been destroyed to further the profits of entrepreneurs and that there are distinct manifestations of dysfunction associated with these changes. The antiurban literature, especially of Anglo–American origin, in the last few years has tended to accentuate this aspect in its most extreme forms. In the reports of the Community Development Projects in the United Kingdom, every manifestation of urban poverty, deprivation, disadvantage, and discrimination has been laid at the door of monopoly capitalism, either by its direct actions or through its control of the corporate state, especially "The Local State" (Cockburn, 1977).

It would, therefore, be easy to discuss any one particular problem in the case of the elderly in terms of a simplistic model of economic development. This, however, would not only be useless in policy terms since this sort of analysis leads to the defeatist view that the problem is the outcome of a more deep-seated social malaise that can only be cured by the destruction of society as we know it, it would also be historically wrong. It is part of the purpose of this chapter to point out that there have been a number of developments in the social and economic structure of advanced industrial countries which, when read together with changes of a more purely demographic kind, provide the starting point for a very different sort of analysis. We advisedly use the expression "when read in conjunction with" because there is very little evidence that *current* changes in important aspects of the social structure can be causally related to the demographic phenomena of the past.

To give one striking example: Our preoccupation with the problems of the elderly begins with the fact that there will be, absolutely and proportionately, more of them. In the United Kingdom, this applies in particular to the very old—75 and over. The fact that there are *relatively* more of them is in part because of the recent fall in fertility. Nevertheless, their greater absolute importance is because of other factors: the sharp fall in infant mortality at the beginning of the 20th century from around 160 ca.1900 to 80 by 1920, the fact that the gaps created by war casualties in today's pensioner population were minimal compared with those experienced by the generation born ca.1880, and that after 1920 there were further important advances in the control of the main endemic killer diseases among adults. These influences have been publicized by McKeown (1976). The spread of sulfonamide therapy after 1935 and antibiotics after 1945 bears the main responsibility for diminished adult mortality. In this connection the historical chronology cannot be stressed too much: The main reductions in mortality occurred *before* the advent of any kind of welfare state or, in the United Kingdom, the National Health Service, in particular. The fall in infant mortality continued unchecked through the depression of the thirties; and, as a contrast, the years of fast growth in per capita real incomes since 1960 have witnessed very little further falls in mortality, especially among the older age groups. The increases in expectation of life now foreseen in the industrialized "rich" countries are relatively small. There is not much scope for further reduction of infant mortality even in a now relatively backward country like the United Kingdom (Office of Population Censuses and Surveys, 1978).

Next, we have to look at the changing occupational structure of the population. Once more we are not dealing with some mythical set of demands for labor imposed by late-capitalistic multinational monopolies but very largely the requirements commonly emanating from the state (corporate, imperialist, socialist—it makes no difference) for a vastly increased number of servants in those areas of activity where, as it happens, women predominate. The rise in female labor force participation rates is again a worldwide phenomenon. And in advanced industrial countries this has not taken the form of increased demand for factory labor but in the three now dominant categories:

1. in general public administration, also known as the rise of the bureaucracy;
2. through the increase in the standard of service provided in education, health, and social services;
3. in the distribution of goods and personal services—associated with rising per capita consumption norms. And this again is common to all kinds of economies, except that in many capitalist countries the number of employees in retail distribution has fallen in relation to turnover through the adoption of new methods. The much-publicized future introduction of microprocessors in industry and administration is not likely to affect the relative position of women (Jenkins & Sherman, 1979).

Thus, insofar as we shall describe one aspect of the growing problem of the care of the elderly in terms of the reduction of married women in the family–neighborhood group who are free to undertake what were once seen as the normal obligations of the system, we shall do so by referring, not to a "breakup," but much more positively to the outcome of changes in the occupational structure. Most people would regard these changes as an advance—first, because they are indications of an increase in the standard of living and in publicly provided essential services and, second, because of the much greater opportunities now open to women to undertake qualified and, in some cases, much more highly paid work outside the home.

We will consider another aspect of social change with repercussions for the family–household unit. The trend of young people leaving home earlier has been described for a long time in terms of a supposed starting situation before the industrial age. They left since they were not required in the family-as-an-economic-unit (Shorter, 1976) and were drafted into domestic service (for girls) or into apprenticed or unskilled child–juvenile labor in industry. Then, during the heyday of the industrial revolution, with the decline of apprenticeship and of domestic service, there was some increase in the tendency of young people to live at home until they married. This is one of the factors that accounts for the relatively large household size ca.1900 as opposed to the fertility effect (Hole, 1965). In the 20th century, young labor became more mobile again, and during the years of economic recession, young people, skilled or unskilled, left home in search of work in other parts of their own country or abroad. To this extent, the fluctuations in household composition can be seen in terms of the exigencies of a fluctuating labor market. But there are now some new factors. First, in all advanced industrial countries, the normal terminal education age is moving up to 18. In many countries anyone leaving full-time education before 18 is counted as a "drop-out" (Central Statistical Office, 1979). More older children stay at home. But at 18, when they launch into higher or further education, their chances of leaving home are now greater, at least in the United Kingdom where students are encouraged to move to a university outside their home areas. This is part of a complex movement involving the habit of sending children away for their tertiary education to other parts of the country or abroad. This practice is in part made possible by the standard of living of the middle classes from which such students are drawn and also by a changing system of grants, loans, and subventions.

Similarly, young people do not now live with their parents when they start work and before they marry to the extent that used to be the case. Norms differ. In Sweden there is the experience of almost total independence at an early age, and this is now spreading to other countries. In West Germany there exists legislation making it obligatory for parents to support children over 18 who are not yet earning, in a separate residence; in other countries (e.g., Ireland) the older customs are still widely observed. Once again we witness a complex system of interactions: more small housing, the subdivision of larger residences, the spread of apartment and house sharing in unrelated groups, relative shifts of family populations within metropolitan areas. We see the outcome, for our purposes, in the rapid disappearance from households of that indispensable, unpaid support of the infirm elderly—the unmarried daughter at home. Not only are the chances of a woman staying unmarried beyond the age of 30 now exceedingly slim in most countries, but the chances that they stay at home are smaller still (Office of Population Censuses and Surveys, 1978).

Last, to end our recital of demographic factors affecting family composition and household structure, we may cite an almost circular argument. There have always been some unmarried, widowed, and divorced brothers and sisters of householders living in the home. We need not believe in an extended family to accept that these people are simply recorded in censuses and surveys as being present, even as late as 1971. In the first instance, they are becoming fewer for the reason, which we cited in the last section that they can now afford separate establishments. But a simple statistical tautology consists of the fact that since the number of children born to each set of parents has declined sharply, the number of siblings from whom such a section of household members could be drawn has declined drastically—from an average of four survivors for the generation that began housekeeping ca.1920 to two survivors in each case including the householder or spouse for those who set up house after 1940 (see Figures 10-1 and 10-2 later in chapter). To sum up, the overall tendency for households to become much smaller conceals a large number of trends that will tend to reduce the presence, in that household, of anyone who is not both working full time and participating in running that household. The precise division of duties will differ and is still changing. But the net effect as shown in the latest United Kingdom surveys, such as the 1978 Dwellings and Housing Survey (Department of Environment, 1976), is one of rapid decline of the economically inactive person of prepensionable age (Office of Population Censuses and Surveys, 1979).

The interaction between that phenomenon and the decline in fertility has been sufficiently commented upon, and sufficient hypotheses as to the nature of the model have been put forward to require no further comment here (Ermisch, 1979). Which of these theories is correct as an explanation for past behavior pattern, let alone which of them has predictive value, will not be discussed here. For our purposes, we need only to ask: Is there anything in these theories that might lead us to believe that there will be a significant reversal of trends, for example, a growth in family size or household size, a reduction of female activity rates, a postponement of marriage combined with a greater tendency of unmarried members of the family to live at home, and so on? The answer must be negative. We have to be cautious at all times. For instance, in the United Kingdom it has been suggested that if unemployment rises sharply, either because of a general recession or because of technological changes in the composition of labor demand, steps should be taken to ensure that economic activity for married women becomes relatively less attractive than it is now. This might be done by such indirectly coercive methods as raising child allowance to such a high level that something approaching compensation level for loss of employment earnings is reached.

Spatial Regrouping

In all countries, household sizes have been falling. Apart from the fertility effect, which alone accounts for more than half the total fall experienced in most countries since the peak early in the century, the main reason for this fall has been the process of household fission, that is, the tendency of members of the household unit not included in the nucleus of adult parents and dependent children to leave the household. This has been described in sufficient detail not to require further elucidation here (Eversley, Ermisch, & Overton, 1980). As before, the discussion as to how widespread was the tendency of unmarried adult relatives to stay at home is now irrelevant. The disappearance of living-in domestic servants does have some significance, but again this was virtually complete by 1940. Between 1945 and 1971, another category disappeared: the boarder or lodger, a person who occupied a separate room in a household to which he or she was not related but who was usually provided with food and services. Domestic servants no doubt played an important part in the care of sick or infirm household members, but this has not been the case for a long time. (For a comparison with the United States, see Modell & Hareven, 1973.)

Thus we are left with the main phenomenon of the separation of generations outside the household or within the residential neighborhood. Here we are still in the middle of a controversy. Writers on social history using quantitative analysis have always pointed out that families were highly mobile (Buckatzsch, 1952). In other words, the young moved and the old were left behind. The industrial revolution, 19th-century voluntary or "forced" emigration, and an increasing desire to give young children a healthy environment have long since driven families apart. Whether this happened because of worsening or of improving economic circumstances, is a matter partially for conjecture, partially for local variations. We do not yet know, however, what distances were involved, and this is crucial. Many surveys pointed out (the Bethnal Green analysis is still the locus classicus for this; see Young & Willmott, 1957) that extended kinship systems persisted in the immediate neighborhood. Mothers-in-law, married or widowed, lived within walking distance of married daughters, and there was a clear system of mutual help in operation. The point of this particular investigation was that the rehousing of the younger generation in a suburban housing scheme 10 miles away deprived these families of much of this support.

We lack sufficient studies to tell us how widespread the Bethnal Green pattern was. Some studies, as summarized in *Samples from English Cultures* (Klein, 1965), indicate the preponderance of such patterns, at least in working-class communities until the 1950s, and some later studies especially in poorer and remote communities (Sunderland and Gosforth in Cumbria: Dennis, 1970, 1972; Williams, 1969) appear to support the idea that this system survived for a long time. Hunt's study of the elderly in Britain in 1976 shows the part still played by close relatives in caring for those needing support but does not tell us how far the process of spatial segregation has gone or exactly what role it played in an age of increased personal mobility (Hunt, 1978).

Even without these details, however, the trend toward greater spatial segregation is clear. We have long since left the pedestrian network behind us. Public transport has become both expensive and unreliable; and now we face the position that even near-universal car ownership at least in the younger generation may not be sufficient to bridge the gap. If we define the "gap" as the distance (real or per-ceived, in time, money, or energy terms) between clients and potential helpers, is this likely to aggravate the problem? We can look at the answer under different headings.

First, the residential settlement pattern presents restrictions. Some observers feel that the ability of older people, on one hand, to choose their preferred retirement location will not increase further and, therefore, the majority will continue to live where they did during their working lives, that is, mostly the accessible urban or suburban areas (Eversley & Bonnerjea, 1980). On the other hand, the out movement of younger, able-bodied families into owner-occupier belts some distance from the traditional metropolitan areas is likely to continue so that those elderly-handicapped groups that are at the moment living in the inner cities, most of them in tenanted properties, will be increasingly isolated (Age Concern, 1977). Various remedies have been proposed (Fox, 1979). New towns and cities such as Telford and Milton Keynes are supposed to make it possible for parents of new workers to obtain suitable accommodation—such as small houses, bungalows, sheltered group housing—nearer to their families (Age Concern, 1972). Whether this can be achieved is a matter of available resources and the priorities of the new community planners (Birley, 1979).

Alternatively, just as it is possible for pensioners to exchange an existing suburban owner-occupied house for another in a retirement location, it is possible for them to move back into a well-serviced urban area, if necessary, to be geographically nearer the younger generation, although if they did they would then be competing in a market where families of working age are also looking for housing. Very little is known so far about the degree of mobility of elderly people (Karn, 1977) or the relative costs and availability of suitable housing. We can only point to the problem and say it is likely to get worse unless there is either a reversal of the overall trends or successive moves are facilitated to enable the elderly to change their life style according to their requirements (Mooney, 1978). The fact that for the younger generation occupational mobility also means spatial mobility will aggravate the situation for the elderly who can only be expected to make a limited number of moves.

Here again a statistical model can point toward a possible deterioration in the circumstances the elderly face. The potential support system of elderly people could be presented as the sum of all first-degree relations available—the higher that figure, the greater the chance that at least one female unmarried/married-not-working/able-bodied retired relation is living within accessible distance. (We say "female" until we have evidence that males are at all likely to perform such a role in significant numbers.) We have already postulated that the generation now nearing the end of its life was born into households of 3+ children; and for most of the period 1920–1965 the average was 2.5 children per couple (with the exception of the early 1930s). There was near-universal marriage by the age of 30 until about 1970, and only a minority of women were economically active until very recently (1965 in the United Kingdom). So for that generation there is, it seems, a relatively ample potential supportive network, although even that is small compared to, say, an Asian immigrant family in Leicester today.

If we go to the other end of the spectrum, the potential retirers of the last decade of the century will have one surviving sibling apiece, if that. They will have had one or two children, and all women in the younger generation will be working. Judging by recent changes in nuptiality patterns, we may even question whether the useful institution of the daughter-in-law will be quite as widespread as she was. Serial monogamy (cohabiting or married, same sex or hetero-sexual) may be regarded without any moralizing as an institution not conducive to close supportive intergenerational relationships. Recent United States and French work on this subject (Glick & Norton, 1977) as well as the statistics provided by successive British surveys of household patterns suggests that there are trends at work that might make the expected support somewhat precarious (Dunnell, 1979).

Lastly, communications are vital to the lives of the elderly. We have, unwittingly no doubt, built up patterns of social integration by universal car and telephone ownership, following the United Kingdom model. If we were to adopt one of the many pessimistic scenarios now put forward as measuring future energy availability, then a settle-ment pattern based on frequent visiting by car over large distances (the public transport network having perhaps been dismantled) would lead to further restrictions on physical contact (cf. the Californian settlement pattern). Telephones have become relatively inexpensive, though not inexpensive enough for all pensioners in the United Kingdom, and in many advanced countries coverage is still patchy. Legislation exists by which social service departments may install and help to maintain telephones for the elderly in danger of isolation. Here again we are dealing with questions of relative income, public policy, and distance. In some of the more fanciful microprocessor scenarios, we see the older generation lovingly monitored on the videoscreen by their distant relatives or even centralized social work-ers. Technically, this is not impossible, but are we preparing to allocate the resources to families or through public social support systems?

For convenience, we have drawn Figures 10-1 and 10-2 repre-senting the family structures of two imaginary cohorts—couples married in 1920 and 1950, respectively. In these figures we show the change in patterns described in the last few pages. The nuptiality and fertility patterns for each cohort correspond to the observed values; the "below-the-line" assumptions of Figure 10-2 are in accord with current official British projections (cf. Foner, 1978).

Our conclusion must be that the danger of isolation is likely to grow. Technical advances and rising real standards of living might help to keep a support system intact. If living standards decline, the degree of geographical mobility may be reduced and thus keep more of the existing network intact. On the other hand, this would restrict

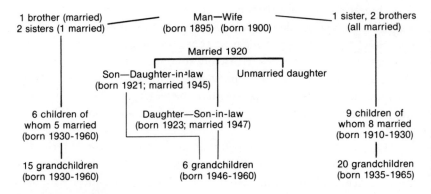

SUMMARY OF POSITION IN 1980

Man and wife aged 85 and 80
Surviving sisters and sisters-in-law (out of 6 in first generation):   4 (none working)
Surviving daughters and daughters-in-law: 3 (2 working)
Surviving nieces and nieces-in-law: 13 (8 working)
Female grandchildren and grandnieces: 22 (18 working or
                                                                        still in education)

Total female relatives alive: 42 (14 not working)

Out of all these only 3 need to be living within reach and not working full time to provide an adequate support system.

Figure 10-1. Cohort family structure—Type I.

our ability to improve the technical aids and increase public expenditures necessary to provide a reasonable standard of service. There is, therefore, no certainty that *any* given rate of growth, technological change, or policy direction could of itself ensure a more acceptable future for the elderly.

Alternative Models

What has been said about the elderly applies, by implication, to other groups in the community. Those most "at risk" are those with (acute and chronic) mental disorders whether of working age or geriatric; both juvenile and adult offenders who increasingly are being "returned to the community" rather than placed in institutions (Central Policy Review Staff, 1978); the physically disabled and chronically sick; one-parent families; large families with low-earning heads; and all the familiar inventory of the disadvantaged and disabled. In every case the problem is the same. If people with one or more of these

handicaps are physically separated from the potential voluntary
helpers, related or not, then there will have to be a considerable
buildup of professional services to cope with their problems (Eversley,
1978). Even if the financial resources for such an increase in the level
of services are available, it is not by any means certain that it will be
possible to recruit professionally qualified people to serve in the
localities where they are needed. In the United Kingdom, the in-
equalities in the manning levels of services required, on one hand, in
"undesirable" inner-city areas, especially outside London and, on the
other hand, in the preferred "shire" counties, are notorious. We
assume other countries have their equivalents. Short of the compulsory allocation of trained personnel to areas of need, there seems
no way of ensuring effective cover. Such obligatory postings have
been usual in certain professions—teaching and social work—but had
little long-term effect. If anything, they were counterproductive

Figure 10-2. Cohort family structure—Type II.

| 1 brother
(married 1954) | Man—Wife
(born 1925) (born 1925) | 1 sister
(married 1955) |

Married 1950

| Son   Daughter

Not married yet | Son
(born 1952; married)
1 child
(born 1975) | Daughter
(born 1955; married)
2 children
(born 1975-1976)
(divorced 1979) | 1 daughter
(born 1957)

1 illegitimate
child |

Projected to the year 2000

| 3 grandchildren | No further
children | 1 child
(married 1995)
1 unmarried child | Lost contact |

SUMMARY OF POSITION IN 2005

Man and wife aged 80
Surviving sisters and sisters-in-law: 2 (both retired)
Surviving daughters and daughters-in-law: 2 (1 working)
Surviving nieces and nieces-in-law: 3 (all working)
Female grandchildren and grandnieces: 4 (in education)

Total female relatives alive: 11 (3 not working)

Therefore, all surviving nonworkers would have to live within reach to provide support
system.

because the most difficult areas tended to be staffed by the least experienced recruits. For this reason a good deal of experimenting has already taken place to see whether the family network, on one hand, and the "official" social services network, on the other, can be supplemented or even replaced by some rearrangement of resources (Eversley, forthcoming).

Many observers, especially in the United States, have commented on the fact that retirement communities are not totally dependent on outside help. By definition, they will always have active entrants at the lower end and increasingly dependent populations at the upper age limit. If there is this constant self-renewal, through a cycle of entry and exit by death and a wide range of ability and willingness among the residents to cope, there is no reason why a system of mutual help among the elderly should not develop. It may require some official underpinning, encouragement, and financial support, and some experiments along these lines are under way in the United Kingdom. We have long had Meals on Wheels and hospital car services, very largely run by other retired or economically inactive people. There are day centers, old people's clubs, shopping services, and so on, all of which run on a voluntary basis. Some local authorities have started a system of paid street wardens even where there is no specially adapted housing with alarm bells, and so on, but simply a person, normally a woman, whose job it is to monitor the well-being of elderly or other disadvantaged residents daily and to call in additional help if required.

Clearly this can be extended, the more so if specially adapted housing is grouped and a professionally qualified warden acts as the resource center for help (Age Concern, 1972). In theory this is a solution that is cost effective, is cheaper than institutional models, preserves the independence of the elderly longer, and does not exclude conventional contact with their families. It is, however, noticeable that this type of development, much encouraged and subsidized by the British government, has not spread very widely. In Britain, voluntary housing is financed by the Housing Corporation that, at any rate, up to the beginning of 1979, had sufficient capital available to increase very considerably the effort to build sheltered housing, but largely for middle-income people. There are many difficulties in increasing the scope of such efforts. Housing for the elderly is almost by definition built at rather low densities and, therefore, planners will seek to move it onto peripheral sites or onto low-value, inaccessible land. A sensible social-planning policy would, however, dictate that such housing be located centrally, in a district affording a pleasant environment and a high degree of amenities near parks, public transport modes, and shopping centers. Unfortunately, that description also fits locations for luxury residential blocks and offices, and the elderly cannot compete for such sites. These speculations about planning arrangements, expenditure levels, legislation, and institutional changes, however, are relatively insignificant when compared with the possibility that some much more fundamental changes in trends may also occur.

The Family: Only One Future?

As has been noticed earlier, much of the literature on the family is written in terms of its progressive breakup. Sometimes this is recorded merely as a fact, but many authors (Cooper, 1970; Leach, 1967) welcome the "death of the family" because the disappearance of the functional unit is seen as affording a chance for the establishment of a more rational system of human relationships. The "family" is seen as perpetuating traditions, restrictions, taboos, superstitions and preventing the full development of "people," especially women (Statham, 1978). On the other hand, movements to "reestablish the family" are usually seen as reactionary, often associated with right-wing Roman Catholicism, fascism, pronatalism, opposition to birth control, rejection of the institutions of the welfare state, and so on (Bethusy-Huc, 1978).

Meanwhile, until quite recently indicators tended to show that whatever our ideological view of the consequences of such movements, there was an increase in the rate of the disappearance of the traditional family and/or household. The more important outward sign of this is usually taken to be the divorce rate and the increase in the proportion of one-parent families, in illegitimacy, in childless cohabitation, in homosexual relationships, and so on. Many writers, commenting on the decrease in fertility, especially at the time of the very rapid falls in the 1930s and since 1964, have described the movement in terms of rising materialism, the desire for the enjoyment of consumer goods, personal freedom, and so on, or in terms of the rejection of the notion of personal responsibility. More frequent changes of partners have been used, alternating with increased employment opportunities for women, as obvious "explanations" for the fall in fertility.

Yet surveys of family-building intentions do not point to any increase in expressed preferences for no children at all, as opposed to a shift from a two-three-child choice to a one-two-child choice. The intention to dissolve the partnership without procreation is not expressed at the time of marriage. Marriage is still, at the time of writing, the normal outcome of heterosexual relationships, as are children within marriage, though marriage takes place later, the first child arrives later and the last child earlier, compared with the pattern of the 1950s and 1960s.

It must not, therefore, be assumed that these trends are irreversible or that a movement toward the reestablishment of more traditional family relationships need necessarily be associated with some kind of neoconservatism, neoromanticism, or even the coercion of the corporate state. We must accept it as inevitable that if fertility falls below a certain critical point, the state of whatever political color will intervene. It may do so for primitive "strategic" reasons as is alleged in relation to recent French and German profamilial measures and as was explained at the time of the 1974 World Population Conference in Bucharest when the less-developed countries would not subscribe to fierce Anglo-American antinatalism. State intervention may rather more subtly result from the gradual realization that if the support of the family is no longer available, as in the case of the elderly outlined in this chapter, the resultant strain on the publicly supported services may become intolerable; and therefore, measures to raise fertility at least to the replacement level and some administrative devices to make it easier for generations to remain physically close to each other will be attempted.[2]

2. We have not raised the question of the *fiscal* burden that may be imposed on the state in the long run if the number of pensioners becomes too large in relation to earners. This omission is because of the United Kingdom origin of the paper: The level of pensions payable in the foreseeable future is so low and the ability to pay even these amounts so much more dependent on economic growth rates than on demographic structure, that it would be nugatory even to raise the question. This is a serious matter, however, in countries where adequate retirement payments are usual and where the ability to pay them is not in question, so that the matter of an equable distribution of resulting burdens is an acute one (Rürup, 1979; Schmidt-Kahler, 1979). It may be added that even in the United Kingdom where welfare payments are very low, the mandatory inflation proofing of noncontributory pensions was virtually abandoned in 1980 (Central Policy Review Staff, 1977; Pitts, 1978).

So apart from these foreseeable pressures to reestablish some of the former patterns, we need to consider whether other pressures, internal to the new social structure as it were, may not arise that may arrest the trends we have observed. In terms of our previous analysis, the main changes in indicators would be these:

1. relatively fewer women (overall and especially during their reproductive age) being engaged in full-time work;
2. return of fertility to long-term replacement family size (2.1 children per marriage, assuming almost total nuptiality);
3. a rise in the average duration of any one union;
4. a slowing down of the propensity to dissolve all complex households into minimum units;
5. a slowing down of the trend in settlement patterns that result in maximum segregation by age.

Most of these changes can come about either because of changes in economic pressures or changes in individual preferences or, more likely, an interaction of the two. To give some examples: Present forecasts of labor demand for the 1980s in the United Kingdom foresee large-scale unemployment. Most of the projections agree that this will come about in part through failure of economic growth, especially in manufacturing industry, combined with the fact that growth, where it does take place, may involve shedding of labor. On the other hand, it is foreseen that the situation for women will be much more favorable since the occupations in which they are now established are not likely to require less labor, even with automation in offices. Only complete economic disaster and consequent cuts in public expenditure, for example, in health and education, might produce a reversal of trends.

Thus we would face a situation of relatively full employment for women, whose contribution to household incomes will then be even more crucial than it is now. To this situation there are various responses. One is role reversal, now the subject of much fanciful speculation, where the unemployed male performs all female tasks short of childbearing and breastfeeding.

Another, perhaps more realistic suggestion is that more men should train to perform tasks now performed by women in shops, offices, hospitals, and schools and compete with them on equal terms. This might lead to a more balanced employment situation—certainly it would reduce the number of economically active women at any one time. This would not be a question of denying women education, training, or a career, but it might lead, say, to a woman spending only half her life between education and retirement at work and the other half in family and household care. And this would not be incompatible with men dividing their lives similarly. There has been little discussion of this, especially because the idea of "work sharing," more people at work with a shorter working day–week–year–life, does not appeal to either employers or unions. This is one direction, however, in which a relatively small change might put the role of the family in a different light.

To take another example: The present trend of "serial monogamy," especially when it takes the cyclical form of marriage–reproduction–divorce–remarriage–reproduction, is setting up intolerable financial strains in the remaining family units that were not foreseen or which seemed irrelevant as long as real earnings were rising at the rate that was prevalent in the 1960s. Before the various reforms in divorce law, it was usually the wife who was left in financial straits with the children. Now that men are being made to assume a larger share of the burden, and this trend has been observed in the United States for some time, we more and more frequently have the case of both former partners facing considerable financial hardship as the result of the dissolution of the marriage. This, to say the least, must take some of the gilt off the gingerbread of easier divorce.

One would not suggest that financial hardship should be used to enforce monogamy, but it has often been claimed that divorce was once the prerogative of the rich and that divorce law reform has now brought the device within the means of the less affluent. If, therefore, the process becomes financially more painful, especially for the male, there may be some reconsideration of the practice. On the other hand, it might equally lead to the indefinite postponement of the commitment to marriage, on traditional Malthusian grounds— prudential restraint but without the restraint.

On the question of housing and settlement patterns, it is at least possible that the very high degree of mobility we have recently experienced may be impaired. As an extreme example, if personal incomes fail to rise in relation to housing costs, or even fall, the process of fission may be arrested. Unused spare rooms may once more be allocated to relatives. Accumulated capital in the form of real estate may be pooled in a larger, but divided, dwelling. In London, the modern ideal of each over-18 adolescent occupying his or her own self-contained flat has always been unattainable, except for a small minority. The cuts in health service budgets announced in 1979 will make the level of provision for the elderly in the public sector so totally inadequate, that short of being able to afford private residential care, families may have to reassume responsibilities they have only recently shed. Conditions in geriatric and mental hospitals and recent changes in attitudes on the part of the so-called "caring" professions toward their clients may lead to some fundamental reassessment of the division of responsibility (Townsend, 1962, 1979).

And, lastly, we really must not assume that the development of the human personality can lead only toward the extremes of "individuation" (Spenser, 1899), total self-reliance, the right to total determination of our life style, the abdication of all traditional obligations. As was pointed out long ago by Nef, industrial society could never have been established but for the emergence of charitable organizations to undertake tasks formerly exclusively performed by the family (Nef, 1958). The succeeding centuries mainly saw the transfer of such functions from private, mainly religious, effort to the organs of the state. But Nef did not claim that this was a limitless process. Besides, much of our literature is now written in terms of the postindustrial society and its numerous variants, known as "alternative societies." It should not be excluded from the range of possibilities in a society that is no longer growing, especially in the industrial sense, and in which the organs of public care are increasingly failing to perform their statutory functions adequately by our present notions, that one day we shall discover the family as if it were some sort of innovation. The family may become a very convenient unit that, by sharing the labor and costs of sheltering and feeding people; by providing entertainment, warmth, companionship, and active help to casualties, may achieve living standards that can no longer be purchased by individuals on their own from cash earnings in the market economy or adequately supplemented by public provision paid for by increasing fiscal imposts. If it is objected on the grounds that this would be like reinventing the wheel, we can only say that there are various ways in which we are having to reinvent the wheel—in the form of wind and water power, bicycles, and other forms of intermediate technology because other kinds of energy and locomotion are failing us. Why should it, therefore, be so fanciful to suppose that Western industrial nations may one day turn back to the institution of the family as the principal support system for society?

REFERENCES

Abrams, M. The future of the elderly. *Futures*, 1979, **11**, 178 ff.
Age Concern. *Role of the warden in grouped housing.* London, 1972.
Age Concern. *Profiles of the elderly* (Vol. 1). London, 1977.
Bethusy-Huc, G. V. Das System der Sozialen Versicherung vor der Bewaehrung. In W. Dettling (Ed.), *Schrumpfende Bevoelkerung und Wachsende Probleme.* Munich: Olzog, 1978.
Birley, M. Old age—To help or to be helped. In *Social work service.* DHSS, No. 20, 1979.
Buckatzsch, E. The constancy of local population and migrations in England before 1800. *Population Studies*, 1951–1952, **5**, 62–69.
Central Policy Review Staff. *Population and social services.* London: HMSO, 1977.
Central Policy Review Staff. *Housing and social policies.* London: HMSO, 1978, p. 41.
Central Statistical Office. *Social trends* (No. 10). London: HMSO, 1979.
Cockburn, C. *The local state: Management of cities and people.* London: Pluto Press, 1977.
Cooper, D. G. *The death of the family.* New York: Pantheon, 1970.
Demos, J., & Boocock, S. S. (Eds.). Turning points: Historical and sociological essays on the family. *American Journal of Sociology*, 1978, **83**, Supplement 1.
Dennis, N. *People and planning.* London: Faber & Faber, 1970.
Dennis, N. *Public participation and planning blight.* London: Faber and Faber, 1972.
Department of Environment. *National dwellings and housing survey 1978.* London: HMSO, 1979.
Dunnell, K. *Family formation 1976.* London: HMSO, 1979.
Ermisch, J. The relevance of the "Easterlin Hypothesis" and the "New Home Economics" to fertility movements in Great Britain. *Population Studies*, 1979, **33** (1), 39.
Eversley, D. Welfare. In Council of Europe (Ed.), *Population decline in Europe.* London: Edward Arnold, 1978.
Eversley, D. Social policy: Implications of change in the demographic situation. In D. Eversley & W. Koellmann (Eds.), *Population change and social planning.* London: Edward Arnold, forthcoming.
Eversley, D., & Bonnerjea, L. *Changes in the size and structure of the resident population of inner areas.* London: SSRC, 1980.
Eversley, D., Ermisch, J., & Overton, E. *Household formation research project* (First Report). London: Policy Studies Institute, 1980.
Foner, A. Age stratification and the changing family. In J. Demos & S. S. Boocock (Eds.), *Turning points: Historical and sociological essays on the family. American Journal of Sociology*, 1978, **83**, Supplement 1.
Fox, D. The housing needs of the elderly. *Housing*, 1979, **March**, 5 ff.
Glick, P. C., & Norton, A. J. Marrying, divorcing and living together in the U.S. today. *Population Bulletin*, 1977, **32** (5).
Hammond, J. L., & Hammond, B. *The village labourer, 1760–1832.* London: Longmans, 1913.
Hammond, J. L., & Hammond, B. *The town labourer, 1760–1832.* London: Longmans, 1917.
Harvey, D. *Social justice and the city.* London: Edward Arnold, 1973.
Hobsbawm, E. J. *Industry and empire from 1750 to the present day* (Pelican Economic History of Britain, Vol. 3). Harmondsworth: Penguin, 1970.
Hole, W. V. Housing standards and social trends. *Urban Studies*, 1965, **2** (2).
Hunt, A. *The elderly at home.* London: HMSO, 1978.
Jenkins, C., & Sherman, B. *The collapse of work.* London: Eyre Methuen, 1979.
Karn, V. *Retiring to the seaside* (Age Concern England Manifesto Series, No. 9). London: R.K.P., 1977.

Klein, J. *Samples from English cultures* (2 vols.). London: Routledge & Kegan Paul, 1965.

Laslett, P. *The world we have lost.* London: Methuen, 1965.

Laslett, P. (Ed.). *Household and family in past time.* Cambridge, England: Cambridge University Press, 1972.

Laslett, P. Societal development and aging. In R. Binstock & E. Shanas (Eds.), *Handbook of aging and the social sciences.* New York: Van Nostrand Reinhold, 1976.

Laslett, P. Characteristics of the western family considered over time. *Journal of Family History,* 1977, **2** (2), 89–95.

Leach, E. *A runaway world.* BBC, Reith Lectures, and London: Oxford University Press, 1968.

MacDonald, J. S. The demography of ageing in Britain and the USA. In V. Carver (Ed.), *An ageing population.* Milton Keynes, England: Open University, 1979.

McKeown, T. *The modern rise of population.* London: Edward Arnold, 1976.

Modell, J., & Hareven, T. Urbanization and the malleable household. In T. K. Hareven (Ed.), *Family and kin in urban communities, 1700–1930.* New York and London: New Viewpoints, 1977.

Mooney, G. H. Planning for balance of care of elderly. *Scottish Journal of Political Economy,* 1978, **25** (2), 149 ff.

National Council of Social Service. *The inner cities programme (2): The elderly.* London: NCSS, 1979.

Nef, J. *Cultural foundations of industrial civilisation.* Cambridge, England: Cambridge University Press, 1958.

Office of Population Censuses and Surveys. *Demographic review 1977.* London: HMSO, 1978.

Office of Population Censuses and Surveys. *General household survey 1978.* London: HMSO, 1979.

Pitts, A. M. Social security and aging populations. In T. S. Espenshade & W. J. Serow (Eds). *The economic consequences of slowing population growth.* New York and London: Academic Press, 1978.

Rapoport, R., & Rapoport, R. *Families in Britain.* London: R.K.P., 1980.

Rex, J., & Moore, R. *Race, community and conflict.* Oxford: Oxford University Press, 1967.

Rürup, B. Zum Problem der langfristig en Alterssicherung. In *Politik und Zeitgeschichte,* Beilage zur Wochenzeitung. *Das Parlament.* B27/79 77/79.

Schmidt-Kahler, T. Wie sicher sind unsere Renten? In *Politik und Zeitgeschichte,* Beilage zur Wochenzeitung. *Das Parlament.* B27/29 77/79.

Shorter, E. *The making of the modern family.* New York: Fontana, 1976.

Simmie, J. *Citizens in conflict. A sociology of town planning.* London: Hutchinson: 1974.

Spenser, H. *System of synthetic philosophy, principles of biology* (Vol. II, Part VI, Chapter XII). London, 1899.

Statham, D. *Radicals in social work.* London: R.K.P., 1978.

Thompson, E. P. *Making of the English working class.* New York: Penguin, 1968.

Townsend, P. *The last refuge.* London: R.K.P., 1962.

Townsend, P. *Poverty in the United Kingdom.* Harmondsworth, England: Penguin, 1979.

Wicks, M. *Old and cold: Hypothermia and social policy.* London: Heinemann, 1978.

Williams, R. *The long revolution.* London: Chatto & Windus, 1961.

Williams, W. M. *The sociology of an English village: Gosforth.* London: R.K.P., 1969.

Young, M., & Willmott, P. *Family and kinship in East London.* London: R.K.P., 1957.

Author Index

Subject Index

Sociology, 4
developmental focus in, 127
and historical methods, 127–129
and life course, 27
and mezzolevel, 189
as *physique sociale*, 148
and praxis, 141, 142
psychosociological factors in, 224, 225
scientific method in, 128, 130
theoretical limitations in, 221
Solar energy and postindustrial society, 195
Stereotypes, 203–205
Stratification, social literature on, 128
Stress (*see also* Hypertension)
and age, 66
and coronary disease, 188, 191
and productivity, 191
situational, 65, 66
Structuralism, 128, 129, 131
interpretation in, 134–137
limitations of, 147–149
structural dynamics analysis, 221–243
and retirement, 225–242
and roles–status, 223–228
Structure–functionalist framework, 128
Subculture theory, 187
Suicide, 204
Sulfonamide therapy, 248
Summer before the Dark, The (Lessing), 111
Superego and social reality, 48
Survey research, 128
Sweden
and integration in society of elderly, 198, 202
socialization of independence in, 250
social welfare system in, 213
Symbolic interactionism, 28, 29, 187
Synchrony and diachrony, 130

Tale of Genji, 118
Technological changes rate as macrotheoretical factor, 189, 190
Temptation of Jack Orkney, The (Lessing), 111
Third-age retirement, 230, 230n., 232
(*see also* Retirement)
Time
and historical approach, 5–17, 21
and intellectual aging, 151–182
conclusion on, 178
contextual models on, 154–163

hierarchical models of, 164–178
universalistic growth–regression models on, 152–154, 157
and roles, 5, 6
and strategic necessities of life, 141
Transitions, 223, 224 (*see also* Life course approach)
and birth of children, 56
cumulative impact of, 9
and death, 56, 109, 110
and economic depression, 8, 9, 31, 75–107
and family, 3
and life cycle, 194
and self-esteem, 59
as strategic points of analysis, 116, 117
Tribes and survival, 34
Troncans, 48

Ulcers and stress, 188
Understanding, illusion of complete, 40, 41
Unemployment, 70, 78, 79, 213
mass, psychological consequences of, 137
self-recrimination for, 104
Unions (*see* Labor structure)
University of Laval Institute for Human Sciences, 45
Urbanization, 186
and family patterns, 197
and industrialization, 195, 197
and isolation of elderly, 198
and kinship patterns, 23
Utakorderingshjon, 198

Values, 135n., 147 (*see also* Attitudes)
and attitudes, 206–211, 215, 216
and biography, 44
conflict in, 186, 187
and family structure alterations, 60
and industrialization, 195
instrumental/terminal, 207, 208
material–sociostructural bases of, 210, 211
origin of, 209–211
personal/social, 207
pluralism in, 28
and postindustrial society, 196
and psychoanalysis, 50
and sociocultural change, 31